DEATH VALLEY '49ERS

The right horizon marks the Mouth of Furnace Creek Wash through which the '49ers entered Death Valley. Just below the left horizon is the famous Furnace Creek Inn. In the foreground appear the Twenty Mule Team Borax wagons and a part of the team.

Photo courtesy Mrs. J. Q. White and now in Bear State Library.

DEATH VALLEY '49ERS

BY
FRANK F. LATTA

BEAR STATE BOOKS
P.O. BOX 96   EXETER   CALIFORNIA   93221

Death Valley'49ers
Frank Forrest Latta

Published by:

Bear State Books
Post Office Box 96
Exeter, California 93221

ISBN: 1-892622-19-X

California History
Copyright © Latta Family Trust, 1979

Printed in the United States of America

First Edition Copyright © 1979, Frank F. Latta
Edition Copyright © 2003, Chris Brewer

Edition Printing, June, 2003

Bear State Books
Post Office Box 96
Exeter, California 93221
(559) 592-6760
(559) 592-5779 fax
k1718@earthlink.net

TABLE OF CONTENTS

TABLE OF CONTENTS

LIST OF ILLUSTRATIONS

LIST OF ILLUSTRATIONS

FOREWORD

Death Valley has had its full share of books and articles, from the publication of W. L. Manly's *Death Valley in '49* to the numerous later works, but with the exception of Manly's book all have dealt largely with the Valley itself. The heroic trek of the '49 parties, the first whites of record to enter the area, has been the subject of a chapter or two, rather than the main theme.

After twenty years of studying the available records of these pioneers it frequently has occurred to me that the importance of this tortuous journey from Salt Lake City to San Fernando Valley lay more in the heroism and bravery of the participants than in the details of the day-by-day stages and camps.

Frank Latta had this in mind in preparing this volume and his research had as its purpose the selection of the human episodes from the numerous available letters and records, most of which previously had been passed over by former writers, and to give credit to the almost neglected heroism and fortitude of Mrs. Brier and others who previously had received so little credit.

For this, if for no other reason, his book should prove of great interest in emphasizing the sturdy fortitude and dogged spirit of those early Americans who overcame seemingly unsurmountable obstacles in their efforts to build a new and great nation.

T. R. Goodwin, Superintendent,
Death Valley National Monument,
April 8, 1949.

PREFACE

Death Valley, the greatest and most forbidding depression in the west, reaching a point almost two hundred and eighty feet below sea level, offers no view like that from the mouth of Furnace Creek Wash. It was there on Christmas Day, more than one hundred and seventy-five years ago, that the first white people visited that place. After having been lost and starved for sixty days, finally weakened from a twenty-hour, forty-six-mile journey afoot and suffering agonizing thirst, they found streams of pure water, glistening in the sun. They looked out across the salt beds of Death Valley and saw opposite them snow-covered mountains higher than they had supposed existed. Faced with the most impossible portion of an eight-hundred-mile desert journey, they simply gritted their teeth, took new courage and began looking for a way out.

As a result of the search during centennial years for interesting material concerning western migrations of American pioneers, the historic trek of the various parties of '49 across the Great American Desert and through Death Valley at last came into its own. December 3, of 1949, Death Valley '49ers were honored by a fitting pageant enacted in Desolation Canyon four miles south of the mouth of Furnace Creek Wash. Sixty thousand motorists jammed roads for many miles in several directions. About twelve thousand saw the pageant.

Many books have been written about Death Valley, omitting almost entirely those people who supplied its very name. Most important book of all is William Lewis Manly's *Death Valley in '49*. But Wm. Chalfant, Carl Glasscock, G. P. Putnam, Bourke Lee and others have added their bit to the geological history and description of the scenic beauty of Death Valley. On the following pages I have attempted to present something of the trials and hardships endured by those eighty-odd men, women and children who, in the winter of 1949-'50, spent more than four death-defying months journeying between Salt Lake and Los Angeles.

My interest dates back to a time more than seventy years ago, when
William Lewis Manly spent the night at our home and discussed with
my father the experiences of those '49ers in crossing the deserts of the
southwest. That interest culminated in this volume. I studied the *Jay
Hawk Papers,* preserved by their historian, John Burt Colton. Those
papers were in the Huntington Library at San Marino, California, and
comprised many scrapbooks and hundreds of letters written by members of that tough, heroic band of '49ers. In 1870 they began holding
reunions. They continued these until 1919 when there were only two
survivors. The last surviving member of the Jay Hawks was L. D.
Stephens, of San Jose, California.

Stephens passed away in 1921, seventy-one years after; a walking
skeleton, he had stumbled to the door of an adobe house on the Santa
Clara River near present Newhall, forty miles north of Los Angeles.

After his book was published in 1895, Manly received word from
many people who had more data about the famous trek across Death
Valley in 1849—word by letter and in person.

About 1902 Manly started to gather the last data he needed for a new
edition of his book. Someone had told him that my father had traveled
to California from Salt Lake with Train Captain Jefferson Hunt in
1849-50.

I remember very well when Mr. Manly came to interview my father.
We were living on Garzas Creek in northwestern Merced County. He
was a shaky old man, driving a shaky old horse, hitched to a shaky old
buggy. There was box of about fifty of his books in the back of the
buggy.

Manly was financing his trip by trading copies of the book for food
and lodgings for himself and his horse. Also, he was selling the books
for two dollars and fifty cents apiece. I remember that my parents could
not spare the price of the book.

It developed that my father did not come to California with Hunt, but
from Arkansas via Fort Smith, Socorro and Los Angeles. He had started
to California after a farewell 18th birthday party on April 8, 1849, but
because of a misunderstanding, his train had left Fort Smith, Arkansas,
two weeks earlier.

Caution about traveling through the Indian Territory alone caused
him and two older brothers to return to Vineyard, Arkansas. They went
to school at Cain Hill College for a year and then left for California with
another train.

xii But the two old men had so many common acquaintances and experiences that they talked until after midnight. I was ten years of age and absorbed the meaning of much of their talk, some of which had to do with "the Briers".

In the meantime, my mother had me unhitch the horse, water it, put it in the barn, unharness and feed it. Mr. Manly had supper with us. He slept in my bed and I slept on a cot on the porch. I hitched his horse to the buggy and he left after breakfast the next day. We did not end up with a copy of the book.

In 1923 when we moved to Porterville, I continued interviewing pioneers. Both William Rice and Frank Creech of Tipton furnished me with the final paragraphs of the final chapter in the life of Mr. Manly. Creech was a relative of Mrs. Manly. Rice was a pioneer mining engineer in Death Valley. Both Rice and Creech interviewed Manly over a period of several days. They told me that when Manly left our ranch he worked his way south to Tipton.

After a few days at Tipton, Manly drove to Porterville to the home of his foster daughter. There he became sick. The daughter accompanied him on the train to his San Jose home. He soon died and is buried at Woodbridge. Creech told me that the horse, buggy and a box of books were left in Porterville.

As soon as I decently could leave Creech, I hurried home to Porterville on the trail of that box of books. I found it.

The foster daughter had left the box in a horse-barn on the alley when she moved away. A new tenant had set the box in the alley under the eaves of the barn. Several years of rainfall had reduced the books to a mass of paper pulp.

Dr. N.B.C. Evans, a Hollywood script writer, was selected to write the script for the Pageant celebrating the Centennial of the passage of the '49ers through Death Valley. Because of my library of data regarding Death Valley and a manuscript, begun in 1923, Dr. Evans asked that I be appointed Historian and Librarian for the entire Centennial Celebration, including the staging of the Pageant.

In order to explore the route thought to have been taken by Manly and Rogers over the Panamint Range, Death Valley Monument Ranger Matt Ryan, Dr. Evans and I were transported by Monument Superintendent T. R. Goodwin by jeep from Monument Headquarters via Stovepipe Wells, Towne Pass, Wild Rose Canyon and South Park Canyon to the summit of the Panamint Range at the head of Six Springs Canyon.

There, at 4:00 a.m., Goodwin unloaded us. Fanning out, we made the trek afoot down Six Springs Canyon, guided in reverse by a copy of Manly's narrative. We arrived at the west edge of the Valley floor at 4:00 a.m. the next morning.

This exploration verified our belief that this was the route taken by Manly and Rogers on their first trip out of Death Valley, also on the their return and on the journey out again while guiding the Ařcan and Bennett families.

Also, I made an airplane trip over the route taken by the Death Valley '49ers from a point east of Ash Meadows and Forty Mile Canyon to Desert Spring. The view out and return over this route did much to make clear to me the several written accounts with which I had to work in preparing the manuscript for this book. Being made after the foot trek of Ranger Ryan, Dr. N.B.C. Evans and myself down Six Spring Canyon, it confirmed me in the decision that the Manly-Rogers-Bennett-Ařcan route out of Death Valley was up the main fork of Six Springs Canyon, across the Summit Valley to the southwest and down Pleasant Canyon. But most of all the air trip impressed on me the tremendous, ghastly desolation conquered by most of the Death Valley '49ers.

During an organization meeting of Death Valley Centennial Committee at Furnace Creek Inn, a name was being sought for the organization. The Publicity Committee included Otto K. Olson (Los Angeles City Postmaster), T. R. Goodwin (Superintendent of Death Valley National Monument), and Dr. N.B.C. Evans. There were others. They were unable to find a suitable name.

I was in another room, meeting with the General Committee headed by Andy Noon (Chairman of Kern County Board of Supervisors). Others were Maury Sorrells (Chairman of Inyo County Supervisors), Lloyd Mitchell (Representing California State Department of Finance), Barney Barnes (of Kern County Superivsors) and others.

Dr. Evans came to me and told me that the Publicity Committee was in a stalemate regarding a name. He knew of the name I was, and still am, using for this book. he asked me if I would be willing to reveal it to the Committee—that they would "go for it".

Evans led me to the room where the Publicity Committee was meeting. I informed them that I had been working for many years on a manuscript built around a title not used in any publication, that I would be willing to tell them about it with the understanding that I still could use it if they decided to adopt it. To this they agreed and I revealed to them my title, *Death Valley '49ers.*

PREFACE

This account has been prepared from all accessible sources. But no account can give more than an impression of the terrible experiences of that band of Argonauts of '49. In 1895 when Manly put his book on the market, he met with protests from many Death Valley '49ers. Those who read it stated that it told all that was possible, that the rest could not be printed, if written.

Frank F. Latta
304 High Street
Santa Cruz, California
April 8, 1977

DEATH VALLEY '49ERS

CHAPTER ONE

INTO THE VALLEY OF DEATH

"I was the only woman in the party. Mr. Brier, our three boys, Columbus, John and Kirk—the oldest being nine, the next six, and Kirk not three—and two young men, Lummis St. John and Patrick, made up our 'mess' as we called it.

"We reached the top of the divide between Ash Meadows and Death Valley, and oh! what a desolate country we looked down upon. The men said they could see what looked like springs down in the [Death] Valley. Mr. Brier was always ahead to explore and to find water; so I was left with our three boys to help bring up the cattle. We expected to reach the springs in a few hours and the men pushed ahead.

"I was sick and weary, and the hope of a good camping place was all that kept me up. Poor little Kirk gave out and I carried him on my back, barely seeing where I was going, until he would say, 'Mother, I can walk now.' Poor little fellow! He would stumble on a little ways over the salty marsh and sink down crying, 'I can't go any farther.' Then I would carry him again and soothe him the best I could.

"Night came down and we lost all track of those ahead. I would get down on my knees and look in the starlight for ox tracks and then we would stumble on. There was not a sound and I didn't know whether we would reach camp or not. About midnight we came around a big rock and there was my husband at a small fire.

" 'Is this camp?' I asked.

" 'No, it is six miles farther on,' he said.

"I was ready to drop, and Kirk was almost unconscious, moaning for a drink. Mr. Brier took him on his back and we hastened to camp to save his little life. It was 3 o'clock Christmas morning when we reached the springs. I only wanted to sleep; but my husband said I must eat and drink or I would never wake up.

Juliette W. Brier, who, afoot, led three small children from Ash Meadows, now in the State of Nevada, to Rancho San Francisquito, near present Newhall Ranch at the junction of Highway #99 and the Ventura Highway, and who lacked only a few weeks of living to celebrate her one hundredth birthday. When she left Salt Lake, Mrs. Brier weighed one hundred and fifteen pounds and, surprisingly, only a little more than one hundred and twelve pounds when she reached Los Angeles. Some Death Valley '49ers lost more than one hundred pounds of weight on that journey.

2 Photo courtesy Huntington Library and now in Bear State Library.

"Good, kind Mr. Masterson gave us each a piece of bread—we were then on rations—and we lay down to obtain the rest we so greatly needed. When we awakened the sun was shining down upon us and a half dozen streams of water of every temperature were glistening in his rays.

"Oh, such a horrible day and night! We found hot and cold springs there and washed and scrubbed and rested. That was a Christmas none could forget.

"Music and singing? We were too far gone for that. No body spoke very much, but I know that we were all thinking of home, back East, and all the cheer and good things there. The men would sit looking into the fire or stand gazing silently away over the mountains; it was easy to read their thoughts. Poor fellows!

"Having no other woman, I felt lonesome at times, but I was glad, too, that no other woman was there to suffer, as I did.

"Distances were so deceiving and we were so thirsty that all just had hurried onward. In those twenty hours of continuous marching, we had come forty-six weary miles.

"The men killed an ox and we had a Christmas dinner of fresh meat, black coffee and very little bread. I had one small biscuit. You see we were on short rations then and didn't know how long we would have to make provisions last. We didn't know we were in California. No one knew what untold misery the morrow might bring; so there was no occasion for cheer.

"Fred Carr said to me that night, 'Don't you think you and the children had better remain here and let us send back for you?'

"I knew what was in his mind. 'No,' I said, 'I have never been a hindrance, I have never kept the company waiting, neither have my children, and every step I take will be toward California.' Give up! I knew what that meant; a shallow grave in the sand.

"Then I was troubled no more. As the men gathered around the blazing campfire they asked Mr. Brier to speak to them—to remind them of home—though they were thinking of home fast enough anyway. So he made them a speech. It was a solemn gathering in a strange place.

3

"So ended, I believe, the first Christmas ever celebrated in Death Valley."

It was the Christmas of 1849 and Mrs. Juliette Brier was describing it, breaking a silence of forty-eight years. This wisp of a lady, weighing only one hundred and fifteen pounds when the start was made from Salt Lake, was one of the first three white women to enter Death Valley. She was accompanying the first party of white people ever to cross the Great American Desert and enter California through Furnace Creek Wash and Death Valley. The Brier and other wagons had been abandoned in Ash Meadows. Afoot, through a heartbreaking rough and waterless country, they had traveled forty miles in twenty hours. Her husband searched ahead for water that did not exist. Mrs. Brier had led and carried her three small children to the mouth of Furnace Creek, to the very brink of the deepest, greatest and most desolate sink-hole in the western hemisphere.

The Briers were not alone. Scattered along Furnace Creek Wash and across Death Valley were about ninety other California-bound stranded, tottering pioneers who had left Salt Lake two months earlier. They had been too late to take the northern trail. Against the advice of such plainsmen as Jim Bridger, Peg Leg Smith, Jim Baker and Kit Carson they had decided to follow the old Spanish pack-trail to San Bernardino and Los Angeles. They had started under the guidance of Jefferson Hunt, who had been a Captain in the Mormon Battalion during the Mexican War. No wagons ever had gone over the trail. Hunt became confused. He halted for three days and searched for a trail over which the wagons could pass. When he returned, as one member of the train stated, "with his tongue hanging out," many lost confidence in him.

At Mountain Meadows, about two hundred miles south of Salt Lake and near the present town of Enterprise, Utah, almost all of the drivers of the train on one hundred and ten wagons decided to desert Captain Hunt and cut directly west across the great interior desert, which John C. Frémont had marked on his map of 1845 "Unexplored."

The first portion of the route followed led to the brink of a deep gorge. For several days no way was found to descend to the valley. Meanwhile, all but about forty wagons returned to the Spanish trail. The rest drove down through a narrow, steep canyon to a branch of the Virgin River, through which now runs the Union Pacific Railroad. At the point where now there is a railroad siding named Carp, they left the canyon and

4

plunged directly into the Great American Desert, which had been pronounced by the most competent American frontiersmen as impassable.

After what they then considered the worst trail they possibly could endure, these desperate men and women, some despairing of all hope, straggled out of Furnace Creek Wash. Theirs was the greatest known example of the extremities to which human endurance can be pushed. When these jaded travelers tumbled down the rocky alluvial fan of Furnace Creek their troubles just had begun. It was five weeks later, after having suffered daily more dreadful privations than up to this time they had imagined possible, that they struggled into a land of plenty.

Along the center of the great sink, which these poor, starved people were to name Death Valley, to the north and south as far as they could see, lay a belt of glistening white from three to ten miles wide. To one who never has seen such a formation, this belt looks like snow. But the eighty desperate men and women had been fooled time and again by the dry salt and alkali lakes of the Utah desert, now the State of Nevada. When they first had seen one of these they had hurried through falling night to camp as close to its shores as it was safe. Feeling certain of a bountiful supply of water in the morning, they had used every drop of their meager store, husbanded for more than forty-eight hours. Morning had come and they had found the bed of this "lake" blowing in a cloud of alkali dust. As they had crowded on to another dry camp their enthusiasm for Utah lakes had dwindled to less than nothing. No, they were not fooled by the salt beds of Death Valley.

Beyond the belt of salt arose the Panamints, the highest range of mountains the '49ers ever had seen. To the southwest of the mouth of Furnace Creek, where they stood gazing with growing apprehension, arose the great snow-capped pinnacle of the entire range. That peak is Telescope, more than eleven thousand feet high.

From the top of this towering, monolithic Panamint range those pitiful, struggling men and women expected to see the Pacific Ocean. They hoped that when this range was crossed they would be in the famed San Joaquin Valley of California and that their trouble would be over. Forty years later Tom Shannon wrote:

> "For some years after I arrived in California, I tried to forget
> the experience of our trip rather than to remember it. I think
> I can say no one of the boys ever under any circumstances

saw Tom Shannon cry. Yet he did cry on one occasion. It was this way. When our party got to where we thought we should be able to see the Pacific Ocean from the top of the highest peaks, Bill Rude, Ale Palmer and myself started from camp about midday determined to ascend the peak in full confidence we should see the Pacific. We climbed the rugged mountain side until dark and had not reached the top. I was given out and prayed to the boys to camp and finish the ascent in the morning. This they declined and went on. I wrapped my blanket around me and lay down among the rocks. I was comfortable and perhaps asleep when some unknown power carried me home to the scenes of my boyhood. I was watching the sheep in the green meadow when I heard the pitiful bleating of a lamb that was lost from the flock. I rose up quickly to look after the lamb and my vision fled. There was nothing real but the bleat of the bighorn or mountain sheep. That is when I cried, if I ever cried. The other two boys reached the summit but saw no ocean."

How well we of today know that those '49ers were separated from the Pacific Ocean by four hundred miles of forbidding deserts and mountains.

Almost directly to the west, and in the direction in which those heartbroken destitutes had been traveling for more than two months, lay Tucki Mountain. On a low shoulder of its slopes was a patch of snow. This would furnish their next supply of pure water for it was perfectly plain that there would be none nearer.

A group known as the Jay Hawks, youngest and strongest of the several groups, started across the valley with their oxen and carts, only to be completely stopped by the alkali bog and salt water of the sink. They skirted the salt pools to the northwest until they were stopped by the sand dunes east of present Stovepipe Wells Hotel, where later we shall find them waiting for us.

Frantic with the sudden realization that still more deserts lay ahead, these eighty-odd destitute Argonauts split into no less than eight separate groups, or parties, and fought desperately to force their way through to the gold mines of California. Deserts and experiences worse than they had come through lay ahead. Their terrific battle against rock and brush, mountain and lack of water constitutes not only the

most determined effort ever made to reach the California El Dorado; it is the most astounding of all migratory epics to be recorded in the history of the settlement of America.

Let us briefly go over the events that led to the situation that existed that Christmas morning in 1849, one hundred and twenty-eight years ago.

Near "Division Spring" in Southwestern Utah late in November, 1849, a party of about eleven men left the wagon train, packed provisions on their backs and started directly west over rocky mountain and alkali dry-lake for Owens Lake at the base of the Sierra Nevada Mountains. Meager accounts state that nine of these men perished and that only two survived, Savage and Pinney. They were guided to water by a Pah-ute Indian and found the Walker and Frémont trail which skirted the eastern slope of the Sierra. Entering the San Joaquin Valley by way of Walker's Pass they proceeded to the placers. The rest are thought either to have been killed by Indians or to have perished of thirst on the desert. It is probably that these men passed north of Death Valley.

A party under a man named Towne and composed of eight men, three of them negro slaves, packed food on their backs and escaped through a pass now named for their leader. They were a portion of a larger party known as the "Mississippi Boys".

The "Georgia Boys", also known as "The Bug Smashers", under Captain James Martin, composed of about fifteen men, abandoned everything. They also "packed out", leaving by way of the north shoulder of Tucki Mountain and passing a short distance north of where the mining town of Skidoo later was located. They killed oxen and dried as much meat as they could carry, gave the remainder of their oxen to the Briers, shouldered their packs and trudged into the black, hanging, rock-canyons of the Panamints.

Their objective in taking this route, as had been that of the Jay Hawks, was to reach the patch of snow and thus to secure their fill of pure water and to fill their canteens for the march westward.

At this snow patch there transpired an event which was to lead party after party to Death Valley and to cause more than two hundred mines to be burrowed into the Panamints. The Georgians were miners. Near the snow they found the Jay Hawks sitting on what the Georgians said was an extremely rich deposit of silver ore. One of them picked up a piece of pure silver. Later, at the Mariposa mines, he had this silver made into a gunsight. This gave rise to the legend of the Gunsight Lead. Another Georgian could get no one to help him carry his load of five thousand dollars in gold coin, so he went to one side, lifted a rock and 7 dumped the gold coin under it. Stories of these two happenings still lead miners and treasure hunters to the slopes of old Tucki Mountain.

Leaving the Jay Hawks on New Years Day, 1850, the Georgians have left almost no trace of their fate. One story is that they proceeded directly west to the Walker Trail and over Walker's Pass to the San Joaquin Valley. This account states that all but two were massacred by the Chauchela Indians while they were crossing the Chowchilla River in present Madera County. Another story is that through desperate starvation they were reduced to cannibalism, casting lots to see who should die and living on the flesh of the condemned until only two remained. This same account states that afterward Savage, one of the survivors, when questioned about their experience, burst into tears and could not talk about it.

At some lost point in Indian Wells Valley one of the Jay Hawks suggested cannibalism and was drummed out of camp for doing so. Years later a member of the Jay Hawks wrote that they never knew what happened to this outcast comrade.

No known statement has been preserved accounting for the safe arrival of the Georgians at the mines. It is depressing to think that these brave pioneers, reduced to walking bags of bones by the hardships of the most terrible trek in history, should enter a paradise of game and water just twenty miles from the Southern Mines, only to be slaughtered before they regained their strength or had panned a grain of gold.

Most desperate of all parties which had passed through Death Valley in the winter of '49 and '50 was that mentioned before and known as the *Jay Hawks*. According to the *Jay Hawk Papers* in the Huntington Library the name later was corrupted to *Jayhawkers*. Most of these were young men. One was just past eighteen years of age when he entered Death Valley. In the desert east of Death Valley they had cut their wagons in half and made carts of them. At Jayhawker Well on the west edge of Death Valley, they cut up the side boards of the carts and made pack saddles for the remaining oxen. Drying the lean, stringy meat of some of their poor, starved brutes over fires fed by wood from their ox-yokes and the remainder of their wagons, they began a frantic drive to reach the coast settlements, which they hoped were only a few days travel ahead. Little did they know that more than five weeks would elapse; five weeks of cruel, heartbreaking struggle against a seemingly endless desert before they finally could reach Rancho del

8

Valle near present Newhall Ranch on Highway 99 north of San Fernando.

After they left Jayhawker Well one group of the Jay Hawks went five days without a drink of water. They crossed the Panamint and Argus Ranges and the Panamint Valley and searched for a day and night in the north end of Searles Lake Valley before water was found. It was on this route that eight men were left to die along the trail and that two of them did die.

During the trip from Burned Wagons to Rancho del Valle, four men were to die of exhaustion, the last starved and wearied to a point where he was unable to crawl the last fifty feet to the campfire. They were to be reduced to virtual walking skeletons, bones with a parchment-like brown skin drawn across them and treadlike muscles and sinews holding the whole together. If the reader considers the above description exaggerated, will he consider the statement of the youngest member of the group, John B. Colton, that he was more than six feet tall and weighed just sixty four pounds when he reached Rancho del Valle, having lost almost one hundred pounds of weight after he left Salt Lake. The fresh bones alone of an adult skeleton weigh more than thirty pounds. Several others lost one hundred pounds in weight. Reverend J. W. Brier, Sr., a man forty-five years of age in 1849, wrote, "I weighed only seventy-five pounds although I am six feet tall." Brier lost an even hundred pounds.

Others lost weight in proportion. The single exception, and this will come as a surprise to all, was the little lady quoted at the beginning of these pages. In a letter written by her husband, the statement is made that she completed that terrible journey with a loss of almost no weight. From Christmas Day until Rancho del Valle was reached, five weeks later, the Jay Hawks had nothing to eat but the stringy, nutritionless meat of their oxen.

At one place John B. Colton became weak from drinking poisoned water, probably from the salt spring at present Valley Wells, north of Searles Lake. He stated that he was through, sat down on the sand of Indian Wells Valley and refused to go any farther. Seeing that drastic measures must be taken, C. B. Mecum, his boyhood chum, came up and began abusing him for being a quitter.

Mecum slapped Colton's face as hard as he could. This angered Colton so that he arose to his feet, promising Mecum that he would kill him at his first opportunity. As soon as Colton was on his feet, Mecum kicked him in the pants and then helped place him on an ox, a little better able to travel than he, and described by his companion as "a steer having two eyes, a little hide and some bones." One of Colton's companions stated that the steer, turned upside down would have made a better harrow than an ox. Colton's back, from which the shirt had been torn, and the back of his neck looked as bad as that of the steer. The ox lay down and they were forced to camp. During the night Colton gained enough strength to take the trail again. Only one nourishing meal was enjoyed by the Jay Hawks between Burned Wagons and Rancho del Valle. In Antelope Valley, near the head of Soledad Canyon, they killed a wild mare and two colts. Wrote L. D. Stevens in 1881 to his brother Jay Hawks:

> "Will recall to your minds one night of feasting on mustangs, after we passed Death Valley and neared the Sierra Nevada Mountains. That was the first game we came to. We killed three, and eating was kept up nearly all night, and in the morning nothing was left of the old mare but the bones and hoofs."

Following these faltering, struggling, water-searching, starved skeletons were the Briers. Diminutive Mrs. Brier revived one after another of the exhausted Jay Hawks, encouraged them by word and example, placed their packs on their tottering oxen when they were too weak to do so and cinched the packs in place. This information was left by the Jay Hawks themselves and amply verified by others of the party. The strength and endurance exhibited by Mrs. Juliette W. Brier is the most astounding and unexplainable of any such instance in western history.

Most significant of all facts concerning the extremity to which the Jay Hawks were forced is the fact that one died and one became crazed and wandered away on the day before Rancho del Valle was reached and, that on the next day, even Mrs. Brier was unable to urge seven of the men to go forward. They were left in Soledad Canyon to die. However, vaqueros from the rancho rode back with water and food and brought them in.

But this is only a portion of the story of the Jay Hawks and other Death Valley '49ers. We will return to them later.

Following the Jay Hawks and the Briers was a group of seven wagons carrying twenty-two people, including three women and five small children. This group has become known as the Bennett-Arcan Party. Following them were wagons belonging to the Wade and Earhart families.

In the pressure of fear from starvation and the difference of opinion as to the best route out of Death Valley, this last group finally split into at least two and possibly three parties. Scout and guide of these people was twenty-nine-year-old William Lewis Manly, from St. Albans, Vermont.

Mr. Manly visited the Jay Hawks at present Jayhawker Well while they were burning their carts and drying meat and learned from them that it was not possible to take the Bennett and Arcan wagons out through the gap now known as Towne Pass. So he guided the Bennett-Arcan Party across Death Valley and to a spring located about one-fourth mile north of the present ruins of the Old Eagle Borax Works on the east slope alluvial fan of the Panamint Mountains. Here Manly struggled up a boulder-cluttered playa,—some of these boulders as big as modern automobiles—climbed a mountain and scanned the territory to the south using a powerful telescope which belonged to Mr. Arcan. The desolate, low-lying range to the south reminded him so of the dry, alkali-encrusted lands he had crossed east of Death Valley that he decided the only safe course lay over the Panamint Range near the south shoulder of Telescope Peak.

A consultation in camp resulted in the decision to follow Manly's advice and to go forward without scouting ahead and to attempt to take the wagons over the Panamints through one of the canyons on the lower portion of the range south of Telescope Peak. This attempt resulted in failure and the party again encamped at the spring. It was then decided that two of the strongest men should go to the Spanish settlements on the coast for help. The lot fell to William Lewis Manly and a gigantic Tennessean named John Haney Rogers. The story of the heroic struggle of these two starved men through the Panamint Range, Panamint Valley, across the Slate and Argus Ranges, across Indian Wells Valley, through Last Chance Canyon, across Antelope Valley and the Coast Range to the north outskirts of Los Angeles—and back—: This was a dangerous, hurried, exhausting journey of twenty-six days and is worthy of one entire chapter in this story.

Waiting a few days after the departure of Manly and Rogers, the Wades and Earharts abandoned their wagons and attempted to pack their oxen over the Panamints, probably up Six Springs Canyon. Finding this impossible they returned to their wagons and the Wades drove out of the south end of Death Valley to Los Angeles. The Earharts' 11 wagon broke down and was left, while the men shouldered packs and followed the Wades.

The story of struggle and privation suffered by these Argonauts of '49 is one of intense interest. To cover it in full we must leave them in this terrible situation and go back to those eastern states where they caught the "California Fever" and where they rolled away from their comfortable homes and well laden tables to experience this most desperate of all migrations known to have been undertaken by any people in the history of the settlement of America.

CHAPTER TWO

THE CALIFORNIA GOLD FEVER

It was early in 1849 that news of the discovery of gold at Sutter's Mill in California swept over the eastern United States, finally reaching that portion of Illinois and Iowa where our Jay Hawks, Shin Pickers, Bug Smashers, Buckskins, Briers, Bennetts, Arcans, Wades and Earharts then were living. Contemporary accounts refer to this wave of excitement as the California Gold Fever. It attacked blacksmith and barber, minister and preacher, farmer and merchant, and even the immigrant fresh from the old countries of the eastern hemisphere. There soon arrived in California a motley crowd, each person in it speaking only his own language and including Chinese laundrymen, Kanaka and Portugese whalers, Germans, Hindus, French, Englishmen, Danes, Norwegians, Swedes, Poles, Finns, Russians, and members of almost every other race and nationality under the sun. A person who could speak two or more languages could make more money clerking in a store than he could working a mining claim.

In January of 1849, this California Gold Fever at last struck the little town of Galesburg, Illinois. Living in Galesburg at that time was a storekeeper, a State of Maine man, by the name of Colton. Clerking in this store and helping operate his nearby farm was his young son, John Burt Colton. Born at Monson, Maine, August 11, 1831, young Colton was, in January of 1849, past seventeen years of age. We might think of John as a mere boy, but he was far from being such. He was more than six feet tall, weighed more than one hundred and fifty pounds and was mature mentally and physically far beyond the average boy of his years. He was destined not only to become the youngest member of the '49ers who crossed the Valley of Death, but to live to celebrate the seventieth anniversary of that event.

John B. caught the California Gold Fever and caught it badly. Nothing would do but he would head the first party to leave that portion of Illinois for the gold diggin's. It is difficult to imagine a father of such a boy encouraging his son to jump off into an uncharted wilderness, infested by wild animals and wilder Indians. While there is no record 13 that Colton, Sr., encouraged young John to start for California, there is also no record that he *dis*couraged him.

The result was that John soon was outfitted with a good wagon, four yoke of oxen and all the supplies thought necessary for a journey of more than two thousand miles overland to the gold fields of California. Additional supplies were shipped by boat to St. Joseph, Missouri (St. Jo, Mizoo, to the boys of '49). There John expected to jump off for California.

It was on the first of April, 1849, that John Burt Colton and his two traveling companions, Sidney P. Edgerton and John Cole, were ready to start. The start was made about noon from in front of the Colton store. Half of the townspeople were present to bid the young adventurers goodbye. As they rolled out for St. Jo, someone rang the bell of the church as a token of farewell. Another, less venturesome than the young departing trio, remarked that All Fools' Day was an appropriate time for their leave-taking.

As the Colton wagon rolled slowly from Galesburg west it was joined by four others, making a total of five from the vicinity of Galesburg. In the second wagon were Alonzo Clay, Charles B. Mecum and Luther A. Richards. In the third were Marshall G. Edgerton and Urban P. Davidson.

In another of these wagons were Harrison B. Franz and John Groscup. With one of the Galesburg groups was Lorenzo Dow Stevens, who later wrote and published a small volume titled *Life Sketches of a Jayhawker of '49*.

The party made their first stop at the home of Alonzo Clay, four miles west of Galesburg. Near there they were joined by Captain Asa Haynes and his party from Knoxville, Illinois. Here the enthusiastic, impatient California-bound Argonauts were held for five solid days by an incessant torrent of rain. It was a delay difficult for them to endure. There was little to be done. They went over their equipment, but harness, wagons and clothing had been repaired. So they sat in their wagons day after day, fussing and fuming and enduring the fun poked at them by the friends who visited their camp.

It was fortunate that in the exhuberance of youth, this delay was not viewed as having any significance concerning the success of their venture. But it was only the beginning of one long delay after another: a detour to St. Joseph, ox stampedes on the Platte and disappointments by the dozen on the deserts of Utah and California and what is now the state of Nevada. The days stretched into weeks and the weeks into months until an entire year had passed before some of them arrived in the diggin's. A few days and a year after (April 12, 1850), the father of this writer left Fort Smith, Arkansas and, traveling with mule teams, arrived in Los Angeles on the 20th of August, a little more than four months on the way.

Two days after leaving the Clay farm John B. Colton wrote to the Galesburg newspaper editor. He had forgotten to have his home town newspaper sent to him while he was in California. Here is reproduced this first letter by young John, "Written on my knees":

"Encampt at Old Man Hutchinsons

"Apr 8th 1849

"Mr. I. B. Patterson
"Sir
"Will you please send a copy of your paper to San Francisco, California—and Father will settle with you for the
same. Please to send 5 back numbers—

"Yours sc
J.B. Colton

"P.S.
"Written on my knees—J.B.C."

The Galesburg wagon train crossed the Mississippi River at Burlington, Iowa.

It was a rainy spring and the little band was badly used up by muddy roads and swollen streams. In 1916, Dow Stevens wrote:

"That spring happened to be a very wet one, and the roads
were almost impassable. The streams were swollen and overflowing their banks, bridges were washed away, and consequently much time had to be spent repairing and building
new ones. On many of the larger streams we constructed
rafts of logs and rafted the wagons over, and the cattle were
made to swim. Through Iowa we found many prairie sloughs,
and they seemed bottomless. Here we had to cut sod and lay
several thicknesses before we could pass over."

At the newly established village of Washington, Iowa, young Colton wrote to his father. The train had now increased its number to eighteen teams and their force was thought to be equal to making the trip 15 through to Salt Lake. Amusing to us modern tourists is the fact that the travel and outdoor life had made them ravenously hungry, ". . . don't think that there is enough (provisions) to last us halfway to California the way we eat," wrote young John. His letter is here reproduced in full:

"Camped near Washington, Iowa
"Sunday Apr 15, 1849
"Dear Father
"As I have a few moments to spare this evening, I thought I would write you a few lines to let you know how we are getting along. Although we are but 40 miles from Burlington after I wrote you the Ferry Boat came over with the Knoxville Teams which we have joined and we are going through with. Capt. Findly would not go to Council Bluffs and St. Joseph was chuck full. We have eighteen teams and we think we are strong enough to go through. When we started from Burlington each wagon put in one dollar per yoke to bear expenses to Council Bluff but our team is going to——on account of food being so high. We think we can get along cheaper to go two teams together. We have been cooking today and we have got about done. We have had very cold weather for 3 or 4 days. If you have not written your letter you may direct it to Council Bluffs instead of St. Jo. If you have sent it, Price has gone ahead to get it. Our teams stand it well enough though it is very muddy. The cows work well. We can yoke them anywhere. I want you to be sure and send me some money if you have not written. Today as we camped here Mr. A. C. Olmey that used to go to school in town he is teaching school in Washington. I don't think he is worth much but I would send his note to some lawyer if I was in your place.
"Give my respect to all the folks. Tell squire Barnes that I shall write to him when I get to Council Bluffs. We are all well and hardy. Sid says he is going to get another lot of provisions as he don't think that there is enough to last us halfway to California the way we eat.
"Yours sc J B"

16 Wrote Dow Stevens about this portion of the westward journey:

Lorenzo Dow Stevens, who accompanied the Jay Hawks to California via Death Valley and who wrote an account of his experiences. He passed away in 1921 at the age of ninety-four years and was the last known survivor of the adult Death Valley '49ers. He lived to celebrate the seventy-first anniversary of his deliverence at Rancho San Francisquito.

For many years Stevens lived in San Jose, California, and was a manufacturer of windmills for pumping water, an appropriate occupation for one who had suffered from thirst for so many months.

Photo courtesy of Huntington Library and now in Bear State Library.   17

"Iowa, at this time, was sparsely settled. Farm houses were twenty miles and more apart, and we found here and there villages of cheap unpainted houses. We found game in plenty, consisting chiefly of deer, wild turkeys, and prairie chickens."

The old California Turnpike over which these California-bound wagons passed led between the house and barn of one Lewis Campbell, near old Tallyrand, twelve miles from Washington. The little hand-hewed cabin which served as a wayside station to west-bound travelers later was incorporated into a larger frame house and still (1950) is standing, as is the hand-hewed frame barn across the road. Many gold rush parties of 1849 and later fed their oxen in that barn. In later years some of the teams, returning from California, were put up in the same barn. In 1857 Lewis Campbell noted in his diary that he had traded one of these returning Argonauts feed for his team in return for a recipe for "California Liniment." Lewis Campbell was the father of Harmonia (Campbell) Latta, mother of this writer.

Another interesting fact in connection with this old town of Washington, Iowa, is that it was founded by Col. Thomas Baker, who also joined the gold seekers in 1849 and came to the California mines. In 1852, aided by Patrick, O. K. Smith, Loomis St. John and others of the very Argonauts with whom this work deals, he founded the County of Tulare and surveyed the city of Visalia, California. In 1872 this same Col. Baker founded the city of Bakersfield, California, where this writer lived for fifteen years.

Across the remainder of the State of Iowa, the Galesburg and Knoxville boys passed with only one delay and no serious trouble. Their supplies had been shipped to Council Bluffs with a steamboat man named Price, probably from Burlington, Iowa. Water was low in the Missouri River and Price was afraid he could not land the supplies at Council Bluffs. So he unloaded them at St. Joseph and sent out an express to inform the Galesburg boys where their supplies could be found. This necessitated a trip of one hundred and twenty miles out of the way in order to touch at St. Joseph.

From Council Bluffs young John Colton again wrote his father, informing him of what had taken place since his last letter. It contains much of interest, particularly an insight into the mature mind of young Colton as evidenced by his concern about his father's ability to collect

18

debts. As it furnishes an on-the-spot view of more than a hundred and twenty-five years ago, it is reproduced in full.

"Council Bluffs, Iowa
"May 22 1849

"Dear Friends

"As this is the jumping off place from civilization into Eternal uncivilization I employ this last opportunity of writing to you as it may be for some time. And although you would naturally think that it being the last place inhabited by civilized people I should have feeling akin to sorrow but this is not the case. I think I have seen quite enough of the inhabitants of Iowa especially, and I am itching for morning to come when we shall cross the river. Since I wrote to you at Washington we have traveled over a great extent of wild country. About a week after we had grass so that with what corn we had we kept our oxen in pretty good spirits. They are now in better order than when we left home. They fatted up right away as soon as they come to have plenty of grass. We have not had out a guard yet but there is considerable many Indians this side. Tomorrow we cross and then we begin. We have a regular organized company consisting of 36 wagons. Asa Haynes of Knoxville is elected Captain. The Canton and part of the Rock Island Company have united with us. We are going through under a military regulation. Since I wrote you last we have enjoyed good health all of us. At any rate we give most wonderful evidence of it from the way the provisions disappear. The season is very cold and backward. The people have not begun to sew their grain here yet in some places. The reason of our not reaching this place any sooner was that we sent Price around with our stuff and as it was low water he was afraid it would not get here so he stopped it at St. Joseph and sent out an express and we went in there about 120 miles out of our way. We got there and found our flour but our bacon, picks, axes, and so forth together with some of Clays things were amongst the missing. Father wrote me by Price that he had insured it, but that did not good. The steamboat had been there and left so we had to content ourselves with paying 13.50 for freight and buying new bacon. I don't remember the name of the firm but there

John Burt Colton just before he left Galesburg, Illinois, April 1, 1849, to come to California. He became the official historian of the Jay Hawks and was the youngest member of that group. He lived to attend the reunion at the 69th anniversary of his arrival at Rancho San Francisquito February 4, 1850. Colton mined at Sonora, California and returned to Galesburg in 1852.

Photo courtesy of Huntington Library and now in Bear State Library.

is only two storehouses in St. Joseph, and if you think that you can collect anything, you can find out by writing to the P.M. It is the largest establishment. The first chap that I fell in with was Peter Manners, Esq. I knew him as quickly as I saw him. He owns a first rate dray and horses. I think you can collect the debt. You can write to the P.M. for a lawyer—the town swarms with them.

"Iowa is full of nothing but Mormons and all going to the Salt Lake. They are perfect shaves. You have to look out for them or they will clean the cash out of you in a hurry. We had a first rate road while we was going on the Bluff road, but when we turned on the St. Joseph road, it was very hard for our cattle's feet. There was some cholera in St. Joseph and there is here. The mail starts from here tomorrow for Salt Lake. At. St. Joseph they was all backing out and the bacon not coming and all, put together, made Sid (Sidney Edgerton) so homesick that he wanted to sell out. He was offered $80 a yoke for our cattle, and could have sold our wagon and so forth, for cost. Sid wanted to go home so bad that I finally told him that he might sell and I would buy a share in Marshall's wagon. As we got out of town, though, he began to feel better. There was about 1,500 wagons to cross when we was there and that looked rather gloomy. Two ferries were at work constantly. Ray left about two weeks before we got there. We stopped one week at Keasangua to recruit our cattle so they got the start of us. This is the last place a man will have the privilege of backing out as he cannot come back after leaving here one hundred miles on account of Indians. By the time this gets there Richards. . . ."

Evidently, sudden preparations to cross the river at Council Bluffs interrupted young Colton's letter writing, as the above letter was neither concluded nor signed. Later, the same day, Colton had a few minutes to spare. He made good use of that time by scribbling a pencil letter to the home folks. Hastily written, weathered and worn from much handling, it has been very difficult to decipher. One name and a phrase still are undeciphered:

"Kanesville, Iowa
"May 22, 1849

"At the Ferry

"Dear Friends

"I have a chance to write back to you from here so I thought I would for the purpose of letting you know that you could send me a letter by Salt Lake every month which I wish you would do. I have paid Mr. Hyde for several copies of his paper which I send you one of others to map. You will find our names and pictures. We are to have an express sent from this place to us with our letters when they come so I shall get your letters which I thought I should have to content myself with doing without. Mr. Babbit starts with the mail today from Council Bluffs to Salt Lake. You probably have heard that he had the contract this year. Next month Mr.   one of the twelve goes through. I was on guard duty all night last night so of course I do not feel very keen. Be sure to write in time to have it get to the Bluffs in time to be mailed. There have been two or three nights that we have had no wood but I tell you our cows

We have had milk every noon while some of the rest have had to drink water. They have nearly all got cows now. Goodbye.

"J. B. Colton"

This letter was the last that is known to have been written by Colton until after he reached San Francisco, so we have from him no on-the-spot details of the remainder of the journey to California. But we do have many letters of reminiscences, written in later years by him and others of the Jay Hawks. So it is from reminiscences that we know much of what transpired during those easy, joyous, fun-filled days on the way to Salt Lake and down to that doubly fateful point, Mountain Meadows, where they departed from the Old Spanish Trail to California and where, eight years later, more than a hundred Arkansas immigrants were murdered.

The party crossed the Missouri at the point where Omaha now stands, the crossing being made on a log raft, which landed just above where Farnum Street touches the river. There then was no Omaha. Nothing was there, save a few squaws sunning themselves on the bank, 22 watching the party with sullen interest.

Dow Stevens preserves details of the Missouri River crossing:

"We had quite an experience crossing the Missouri River. The ferry was a small scow and could carry but one empty wagon at a time. The scow was propelled by two oars, two men at an oar, and the current was very swift. Imagine the time to transport fifty wagons and the loads it took; we had difficulty getting the cattle to swim at first. We didn't realize that the sun shining on the water made such a difference, so the first time the cattle swam round and round for two hours, and we were compelled to let them land again where they started. But next morning before sunrise we started a small boat with a couple of men having a steer in tow, all the rest of the cattle followed without any trouble and made the opposite shore safely."

Then the forty wagons started upon the long stretch of prairie to the mountains, the trail being nearly the same as the route now traversed by the Union Pacific Railroad. Several times the Indians stampeded the oxen. At other times the oxen stampeded from fancied Indians.

Dow Stevens wrote of their first experience with Indians:

"Our first experience with the Indians came with our first camp across the river. Our camp fires were going nicely, supper was started, when we heard gun shots, volley after volley. In a few minutes from over the ridge came two or three hundred Pawnee Indians, riding at full run straight for our camp. It was a few minutes work for us to get our rifles in readiness, but the Indians put up a white flag, and they were allowed to enter camp. It seemed that a party of the Sioux tribe had given them battle, the two being at war, and the Pawnees had rushed to our camp, expecting protection, but we ordered them off, telling them we wished no trouble with the Sioux as we had to travel their country, and wanted no enemies. We took the precaution to organize our body with regular military style with Colonels and Captains. For awhile we were very vigilant. Our picket guards were stationed three hundred yards from camp, and had to lie down to see any approaching object, but firing was strictly prohibited unless you thought an enemy approached.

"We did not want any false alarms, but like many others we grew careless of danger. Many of us went two or three miles from camp, often being away all day hunting and looking over the country. I remember that two of us traveled a long distance on the bank of the river, when, without any warning, an Indian appeared before us. At the same time geese were flying overhead and the Indian said, 'Shoot, shoot'. My companion raised his gun, and I made a quick dash to lower it, and said, 'We had better not waste our shot, for I don't like the looks of things'. We had moved but a few steps when arrows rained down all about us, but not an Indian in sight, except the one we had spoken with. After a short distance more, beyond the range of arrows, we turned and saw over a dozen Indians raising up out of the grass.

"I was carrying a very fine rifle with twenty-seven pieces of silver mounting, and I think this was what they wished. We must have been a little out of range for them to shoot directly at us, but a falling arrow would answer their purpose just as well. It is needless to relate that all possible haste was made for our train, ten miles away. Of course our story was rather doubted by the other boys, and we were joshed about the scalps we didn't take.

"On the Black Hills we came into the Crow Indian country, but we never saw one. They were not friendly to the whites, and when an Indian is not friendly you never see them in their own country. We came to the Show-shu-nees Tribe, or Snake as they were sometimes called, but they disliked the name Snake. They were friendly to us. At one time my chum and I slipped away, and visited their camp and they treated us royally. The chief's wife talked good English, and we were shown all through the camp, there being over five hundred in number. They had many pets, both birds and beasts. We were invited to go with them on a buffalo hunt, and I should have enjoyed it, but all my possessions were with the train, se we remained only the day. But this was long enough to worry the older men of the party, especially the father of my chum, and all.thought we had been murdered by the Indians."

24   The party that crossed Green River was full of fun and horseplay.

Records left by the Jay Hawks, later known as the Jayhawkers, give many details. In a letter written in 1872 for a reunion of the Jay Hawks, Charles B. Mecum wrote:

> "The first of the many little incidents I shall attempt to call to mind all commence after crossing Horn River where we were all barbered and took new names corresponding with those of the place we were in."

This incident probably took place on the Platte River, as the next item relates to the stampedes which kept them chasing lost cattle half of the time. It was this delay, added to the time lost detouring to St. Joseph for their supplies that made them almost two months late at Salt Lake and induced them not to take the northern or Humbolt Sink route to California.

While Mecum's letter was intended only as a reminder to his old Jay Hawk pals who would remember all the implied details, it is of enough interest to us to quote in part. He wrote:

> "The next little incident of note was where we had stopped to lunch at noon and one John A. Fenton persisted that his head had been run over and broke. But fortunately for him there was one horn broke off in that stampede—an old cow's. No other casualties at the time, except the little Deacon [Richards] breaking our table all to bits with one portion of his pants as he started out apparently on his own hook for a new survey of those old Sage boys. Now, were there any [records] preserved stating how those famous old grindstones of '49 were made by which the art might be handed down to future generations. And also how many grindstones did Fenton eat with the ham in one day while being quite indisposed.
>
> "If I could remember all the stampedes our cattle took up the Platte River, they would be too numerous to mention here—.
>
>
> "C. B. Mecum
> "Alias big paddy
> "Alias Crocket"
>

The journey along the Platte River was remembered by all the Jay Hawks. Dow Stevens wrote about it:

"All up the Platte River, and well into the Black Hills, we had many thunder storms; the lightning seemed to strike all around us, and sometimes very near. On one occasion, we came to a team of four yoke of oxen, hitched to a wagon in regular order, and every one dead, having been struck by lightning. This must have been a terrible misfortune to the owners.

"There were all kinds of disagreements and quarrels over trivial matters, and the only way of settling the difficulty would be to make a division of property. The wagon would be cut in two, one party taking the front and the other the hind part, dividing the team and provisions, and each party proceed on the cart of two wheels.

"We were very much over-loaded and in consequence, the cattle grew weaker day by day. So hundreds of pounds of the finest bacon, beans, flour, and sugar were left on the wayside. The bacon was piled like cordwood, and some of the men poured turpentine on the provisions and set fire to them, so the Indians couldn't eat them. Some men seem to be born mean, but to me, such meanness was despicable.

"Coming to the second crossing of the Platte River we found a small ferry that could accomodate but one empty wagon at a time. The ferry was owned by every train that came along, that is a train would buy the ferry, do their crossing, and then sell it to the next train that was in waiting."

Fifty-five years later, John B. Colton dictated to a newspaper reporter an interesting account of this portion of the trip. A portion of it is of interest here:

"Everybody slept on his guns at night and kept them within reach during the day. We picked up a Mormon scout about this time who was familiar with the country. We had passed the Elk Horn River when our first scare came. It was late at night when a roaring sound awoke us. It was the tramping of many feet. They were coming directly toward us.

" 'Indians!' whispered the gold seekers as they prepared their firearms for use.

"A wild herd of buffalo came dashing by. They became

26

common after this. In fact they were a menace. Our oxen would feel the call of the wild and attempt to desert us. Finally they did and a large number followed herds of buffalo and left us in sore distress.

"On further, we met a national character. It was James Bridger, the scout. We came upon his famous old fort, where with his bands of Indians, he ruled that portion of the world and was a thorn in the flesh of Brigham Young, who had established the Mormons in Salt Lake, 100 miles to the west, two years previously.

"We spent several days with Bridger resting up. This was in July, 1849."

After Charles Mecum had returned to Illinois he dictated to his son an account relating several incidents which had occurred while the Jay Hawks were traveling along the Platte River. As the manuscript of *Death Valley '49ers* was being prepared, this son, Rev. E. W. Mecum, of Los Angeles, gave permission to use the account. It follows:

"We had just left Omaha which was a small Indian village in the Spring of 1849 when we learned of a terrible experience. There were ox-teams ahead of, and behind us. In one of them a foolhearted young man boasted he was going to kill the first Indian he saw. He was warned not to do this, but was heedless. When a few days out from Omaha he saw a harmless old squaw and shot her. Soon the Indian braves gathered in savage indignation. They surrounded the ox-team and demanded immediate deliverance of the young man. His friends, in vain, tried to conceal and protect him. Finally when it was made plain that if they did not surrender him up the whole train would be massacred, they bade him good-bye and gave him over to them, and to wreak their vengence on him, and to warn others against killing harmless and defenseless women they skinned him alive. They stripped his skin off in small pieces, so he lived some hours. The news spread like wildfire and thereafter, on the part of the white men, Indian killing was only for self-defense.

"One night our camp was aroused by some unseen object. Evidently it sought our meat and other provisions. At that time we had some mules in our train. They were good to watch, would throw first one and then the other ear forward, then both, and keep anxious watch in a certain direction. We did not know whether it was Indians, or animals spooking around. The next day several of us, all well armed, skirted around a wooded hill, some going around one way and others going the other way. By and by I heard a rifle report and soon found that a member of the other party had killed an immense mountain lion.

"One day I was walking alone when I observed a large bobcat cutting across the course I was taking. I was unarmed. When he reached the path a few rods ahead of me he stopped and sat down. I also stopped. He did not seem the least bit alarmed, and I tried not to. There would have been a terrible fight if we had gotten together, but he didn't care to start anything, and I didn't. After a few moments he continued his journey, for which I was always grateful, and I continued mine.

"At one period of our journey one man from another party died and was buried. I was alone when I observed a large Lynx digging up a man that was buried the day before. I observed this intruder just about the time he saw me and turned up his nose and showed his teeth to me. I had my rifle—a good one—and believe I could have shot him. Had I wounded him he would have put up a terrible fight. I reasoned there was little to gain and much to lose. This man was dead and could not be further injured. I was no coward, but decided not to be foolhardy. So I concluded to attend to my own business and let him attend to his, which was agreeable to both.

"We had just butchered a couple of oxen. As usual, the Indians came and begged for meat, and gladly took what the white men would not eat, even the hides and entrals. Several big buck Indians stood around ready to carry off all we left. Finally one picked up a big paunch [stomach] all loaded, and with the assistance of his friends, he got it balanced on his head; then supported it by his hands. Just as he started off, one of the Jayhawkers slipped up and gave it a rip with his sharp knife. The Indian's head went thru the slit, and the paunch and its contents slipped down over him. He fairly tore the air until this was removed, and then stood speech-

28

less, not knowing whether to fight or not. The whites were convulsed with laughter. The Indians all but this one then saw the joke, and laughed. This Indian never did see the joke, but was rewarded, nevertheless, with a fine piece of meat, which he doubtless deserved.

"We had just finished a long and hard day's travel. We knew we were in the country of hostile Indians. As usual, we made a large circle with our wagons. There we prepared our food and shelter. Urban Davidson and I were designated to watch the camp that night. It was our turn. The night was dark and cold. We bundled ourselves up, armed ourselves, and took our station. Urb grew chilly and insisted on starting a small fire. I warned him against it, telling him it would only show our whereabouts, and beckon on the Indians. Nevertheless, he built the fire. I then told him I would not sit near it, and I went off about ten rods and laid down. Urb's being alone made him a little watchful. He, too, slipped away a short distance from the fire, and watched. In less than an hour, I heard him shout 'Halt!' I went up, and sure enough, he had a big Indian. We disarmed him, and tied his hands, and then sat and watched him all night, not knowing but what there were many a score more ready to rush upon us. However, none came. We could understand some of the Red man's signs and language. In the morning this Indian begged to be set free and by signs said he had a sick wife and two papooses and they were without food, etc. We did not dare to turn him loose then and there, lest he might immediately summon a band of braves and pursue us, some took him with us and made another long day's march. Toward sun down we gave him some extra food and released him, feeling he was too far away to molest us from his home base. He was exceedingly grateful, and made a bee-line for the territory from whence he had come.

"One day we camped in the country of hostile Indians. We did it not from choice, but from necessity. We had no blazed trail, or well-beaten path to follow, and we had to be our own pathfinders. We learned that the Indians had murdered two white people within a half mile of our camp a couple of days before. We were in a country of hills and woods and we desired, as soon as possible, to find a good way out, and to move on.

"I was one of several sent out in different directions to spy out the country. I was walking along nearly a mile from camp, and had nearly reached the brow of a hill, when suddenly, like magic, fourteen Indians seemed to rise from the ground. They came from behind bushes and trees, and were slowly surrounding me. I backed up against a large tree, and watched every move. They were armed with bows and arrows. I had a fine revolver and a bowie-knife. My hair stood on end, and every fibre of my being was tense. I was sure they intended to kill me, as they had killed two others two days before, and I expected they would accomplish it, but not without sacrificing several of their own number. This they evidently wished to avoid, if possible.

"They slowly approached me and made signs, trying to show they were friendly Indians. I watched to see that none drew his bow and arrow, and I beckoned them to stand off, However, they kept jabbering and edging a little nearer. They asked to see my revolver and my knife, but I refused. Finally one grabbed for the knife in my belt. As quick as a flash, and with God-given strength, I warded off his blow and sent him sprawling nearly twenty feet away. Then I took my revolver in one hand and the bowie-knife in the other and made plain I would kill the first one that raised a bow, or that made an effort to come near me. They jabbered to themselves some more. I really believe I would have gotten a half dozen of them before they got me, and probably they feared this, for I was six feet tall, weighed 185 pounds, and was active as a cat.

"Soon the circle widened a little. They began to gradually scatter and to pick up nuts. When they were several rods away, I did likewise, and left the tree, but never took my eyes from them. Gradually they disappeared over the hill, and when I was assured of it, I turned my toes in the opposite direction and a prairie wolf couldn't have overtaken me before I arrived in camp a mile away. That was the closest I ever came to being scalped.

"We had considerable experience, and no little trouble, with buffaloes on our trip. We saw herds in which there were many thousand. On different occasions we had either to stop or to divide our ox-train to let them through on their line of march. They would not attack us purposely, but seemingly nothing would stop their line of march, especially if they were stampeded.

"One day I, with several others, took a notion we would kill a buffalo apiece. It was my first real experience and I had not, of course, learned their vulnerable points. I picked out a big bull and shot at him and hit him several times, but could not stop him. I concluded he could carry off a peck of bullets. I learned later it was almost useless to shoot at their head for their skull is exceedingly thick and is generally further protected by sand packed in the thick hair of their forehead. Body wounds would not stop them unless in a vital place. I learned later that if they were shot in the small of the back, they would drop; if shot just back of the left fore-leg it seemed vital. Or if you shot and broke one fore-leg, the buffalo would charge and break the other. Perhaps all this is true, but it was not my good fortune to get one.

"On another occasion, I and a companion started out to hunt buffaloes. After we had gone a couple of miles we came to a rise of ground, in fact there was a Basin nearly a quarter of a mile across which was surrounded by a small ridge. Cautiously we looked over this ridge and beheld nearly four hundred buffaloes. Most of them were lying down quietly and resting, with the exception of a few sentinels. We decided one of us would go quietly and unobservedly around to the other side. Each would choose out a young buffalo and, at a given signal, we would shoot, but not before giving the signal.

"I remained where I was, and the companion went to the other side. I saw no signal, but soon heard a shot. The herd sprang to their feet. Almost quicker than it can be told they formed, as if marshalled by a General. The calves were in the center, then the yearlings or young buffaloes, then the cows and on the outside the large bulls. It was a wonderful sight to see them form and I watched them with eager interest. When they had formed they started at full speed in the opposite direction from the shot, but directly toward me. I looked for the shortest way out, knowing I could not block their progress. With all my might I ran toward one side of their line of march. They were rapidly gaining on me. Finally, I threw my gun, yelled, and threw myself forward. They swerved just a little, enough to pass me, and I knew that by a very small margin I had escaped being tramped to death by them. It would have made a great moving picture but there would have been no one left to tell the story!"

And so ends the recollections of Charles Mecum.

From other letters and news accounts we know that the barbering and taking on of new names after crossing Elk Horn River made a hilarious affair, which ended little short of mayhem. In discouragement to the scalp-taking Indians, their heads were shaved and they were obligated to allow their beards to grow. On one head was left a scalp lock, the party being named Big Chief Pawnee. If anyone called another by his former name he forfeited the rest of his meals for the day.

This fun-devoted party was later initiated as Jay Hawks, a ceremony which was performed at Salt Lake and about which we will later know more. But the party of shaved heads, with their outlandish names and continual horseplay must have been long remembered by everyone who came in contact with them. The reader already has learned that this youthful exhuberance was badly used up or bottled for future use somewhere between Ash Meadows and Indian Wells, probably on Christmas Day at the mouth of Furnace Creek. But it was the youthful exhuberance of this joyful, voluntary, oath-bound organization that brought the Death Valley '49ers through the hardest trek of all time and reduced the loss of life to only four known members out of about ninety.

CHAPTER THREE

MANLY AND ROGERS

As long as human beings are interested in Death Valley—a length to be measured in figures of geological time—the most simple, all-encompassing dramatic stark story of those white people who first entered and named that great salt sink will be that of a man from Vermont, William Lewis Manly, author of the book, *Death Valley in '49*. Traveling the entire distance afoot and mostly alone, he climbed almost every high peak within miles of the trail and scanned the surrounding country with a telescope, looking for signs of water. In addition he made a twenty-six day journey afoot from Death Valley to the Los Angeles area and return, bringing help for the stranded families that were camped near Mesquite Well. On this last trip he was accompanied by John Haney Rogers who was working his way to California by driving an ox-team for Asabel Bennett.

William Lewis Manly was born at St. Albans, Vermont, near the east shore of Lake Champlain, April 6, 1820, and so was twenty-nine years of age when he started from Salt Lake in 1849. He died at College Park, a suburb at San Jose, California, February 5, 1903 and is buried at Woodbridge, San Joaquin County, California. His father's people were English and had lived near Hartford, Connecticut, later moving to Vermont. His mother was Phoebe Calkins, born near St. Albans of Welch parents.

In his book, *Death Valley in '49*, Manly tells much about his early life. It is a simple story of a simple people, as were the stories of all westward-bound pioneers of 128 years ago. As it furnishes a much needed first-hand background of understanding concerning the Death Valley parties of 1849 the following is extracted from Manly's first chapter:

"Grandfather and his boys, four in all, fairly carved a farm out of the big forest that covered the cold rocky hills. Giant work it was for them in such heavy timber—pine, hemlock, maple, beech and birch—the clearing of a single acre being a

William Lewis Manly, co-hero with John Haney Rogers in the Death Valley rescue of the starving Bennett and Arcan families and author of the book, *Death Valley in '49*. Mr. and Mrs. Manly both are buried at Woodbridge, California.

Photo coutesy of Frank Creech and now in Bear State Library.

man's work for a year. The place where the maples were thickest was reserved for a sugar grove, and from it was made all of the sweet material then needed, and some besides. Economy of the very strictest kind had to be used in every direction. Main strength and muscle were the only things dispensed in plenty. The crops raised consisted of a small flint corn, rye, oats, potatoes, and turnips. Three cows, ten or twelve sheep, a few pigs, and a yoke of strong oxen comprised the live stock—horses, they had none for many years. A great ox-cart was the only wheeled vehicle on the place, and this, in winter, gave place to a heavy sled, the runners cut from a tree having a natural crook, and roughly, but strongly, made.

"In summer, there were plenty of strawberries, raspberries, whortleberries and blackberries growing wild, but all the cultivated fruit was apples. As these ripened, many were peeled by hand, cut in quarters, strung on long strings of twine and dried before the kitchen fire for winter use. They had a way of burying up some of the best keepers in the ground, and opening the apple hole was quite an event of early spring.

"The children were taught to work as soon as large enough. I remember they furnished me with a little wooden fork to spread the heavy swatch of grass my father cut with easy swings of the scythe, and when it was dry and being loaded on the great ox-cart, I followed closely with a rake gathering every scattering spear. The barn was built so that every animal was housed comfortable in winter, and the house was such as all settlers built, not considered handsome, but capable of being made very warm in winter and the great piles of hard wood in the yard enough to last as fuel for a year, not only helped to clear the land but kept us comfortable. Mother and the girls washed, carded, spun, and wove the wool from our own sheep into good strong cloth. Flax was also raised, and I remember how they pulled it, rotted it by spreading on the green meadow, then broke and dressed it, and then the women made linen cloth of various degrees of fineness, quality, and beauty. Thus, by the labor of both men and women, we were clothed. If an extra fine Sunday dress was desired, part of the yarn was colored and

35

from this they managed to get up a very nice plaid goods for the purpose.

"In clearing the land, the hemlock bark was peeled and traded off at the tannery for leather, or used to pay for tanning and dressing the hide of an ox or cow which they managed to fat and kill about every year. Shoes for the family were either made by a neighboring shoemaker, or by a traveling one who went from house to house, making up a supply for the family—whipping the cat, they called it then. They paid him in something or other produced upon the farm, and no money was asked or expected.

"Wood was one thing plenty, and the fireplace was made large enough to take in sticks four feet long or more, for the more they could burn, the better-to get it out of the way. In an outhouse, also provided with a fireplace and chimney, they made shingles during the long winter evenings; the shavings making plenty of fire and light by which to work. The shingles sold for about a dollar a thousand. Just beside the fireplace in the house was a large brick oven where Mother baked great loaves of bread, big pots of pork and beans, mince pies and loaf cake, a big turkey or a young pig on grand occasions. Many of the dishes used were of tin or pewter; the milk pans were of earthenware, but most things about the house in the line of furniture were of domestic manufacture.

"The store bills were very light. A little tea for father and mother, a few spices and odd luxuries were about all, and they were paid for with surplus eggs. My father and his uncle had a sawmill, and in winter they hauled logs to it, and could sell timber for $8 per thousand feet.

"The school was taught in winter by a man named Bowen, who managed forty scholars and considered sixteen dollars a month, boarding himself, was pretty fair pay. In summer some smart girl would teach the small scholars and board round among the families.

"When the proper time came, the property holder would send off to the collector an itemized list of all his property, and at another the taxes fell due. A farmer who would value his property at two thousand or three thousand dollars would find he had to pay about six or seven dollars. All the money in use then seemed to be silver, and not very much of that. The whole plan seemed to be to have every family and farm self-supporting as far as possible. I have heard of a note being given payable in a good cow to be delivered at a certain time, say October 1, and on that day it would pass from house to house in payment of a debt, and at night only the last man in the list would have a cow more than his neighbor. Yet those were the days of real independence, after all. Every man worked hard from early youth to a good old age. There were no millionaires, no tramps, and the poorhouse had only a few inmates.

"I have very pleasant recollections of the neighborhood cider mill. There were two rollers formed of logs carefully rounded and four or five feet long, set closely together in an upright position in a rough frame, a long crooked sweep coming from one of them to which a horse was hitched and pulled it round and round. One roller had mortices in it, and projecting wooden teeth on the other fitted into these, so that, as they both slowly turned together, the apples were crushed. A huge box of coarse slats, notched and locked together at the corners, held a vast pile of the crushed apples while clean rye straw was added to strain the flowing juice and keep the cheese from spreading too much; then the ponderous screw and streams of delicious cider. Sucking cider through a long rye straw inserted in the bung-hole of a barrel was just the best of fun, and cider taken that way, 'awful' good while it was new and sweet.

"The winter ashes, made from burning so much fuel and gathered from the brush-heaps and log heaps, were carefully saved and traded with the potash men for potash or sold for a small price. Nearly everyone went barefoot in summer and in winter wore heavy leather mocassins made by the Canadian French who lived near by."

Such had been the life of almost all individuals who made up the great crowd of immigrants waiting at Salt Lake during the summer of '49 to jump off for California. Their life in a land of plenty, especially plenty of game, wood, grass and water, the four essentials for overland travel, had entirely unfitted them for the desolate, barren deserts which they were to cross. In later years, Manly commented that where 37 he was raised he climbed a mountain to get wood and went down to the valley to dig for water. On the desert, all the water in the valley was alkaline. The only good water existed either in springs on the mountains or as snow. The mountains were solid rock, absolutely barren of vegetation of any kind. The only wood was dead brush, buried in sand dunes on the lowlands. So, when he left Salt Lake, Manly had to learn to climb for water and dig for wood.

In 1828, the Western Fever struck St. Albans and a year later young Lewis accompanied an uncle in a covered wagon to a farm about twenty miles from Cleveland, Ohio. A year later, they migrated to Detroit, Michigan Territory, part way by boat, and then to Ypsilanti, where they found the parents of Manly, who also had migrated from Vermont and had outstripped their son in the journey.

The Manlys' located on "Government Land" and began clearing a new home on the American Frontier. Young Lewis soon became the hunter for both families. In this he became better than any grown man in the locality. As the years went by, he hewed ties for the Michigan Central Railroad. Three younger brothers were soon able to carry on the work on the Manly Farm, so Lewis, working with a young man named Orrin Henry, built a boat and a provision chest, and with guns, ammunition and all needed supplies they floated down Grand River to a point below Jackson. There they hunted and fished and finally drifted down to Lake Michigan near Grand Haven.

Displaying the restlessness characteristic of all pioneers, Manly worked at one thing and then another. He hunted and fished, cut cordwood to stoke a lead smelter, always working westward and ending up in Wisconsin Territory, isolated from all relatives, friends or acquaintances. Tiring of this he walked back to Lake Michigan where he had left his provision chest. There he found it had been stolen. Going on afoot, market hunting for a living, he visited Mineral Point and finally reached Milwaukee.

United again with Orrin Henry, Manly went to Mackinaw, crossed Lake Huron and visited Detroit on his way to his father's home. He was able to remain at home less than a year. He returned to Wisconsin and to the frontier home of Asabel Bennett, a hunter with whom he was to be associated until after the arrival of the '49ers in Los Angeles.

At this time Bennett had a wife and two children. They were later to all owe their lives to Lewis Manly and John Rogers, who went from Death Valley to Los Angeles and returned with supplies to relieve them 38 and other '49ers stranded on a sun-baked playa of the Panamints.

Manly hunted with Bennett and a man named Edwin Buck over an extensive portion of Wisconsin, killing many deer and bear and continuing their work until they lost all track of days, weeks and even months. Coming from this hunt, Manly found he had one hundred dollars in cash, the most money he had ever possessed. This he invested in eighty acres of government land.

Then he lead mined and hunted and trapped, bidding fair to end up a confirmed frontiersman and was thinking of migrating to Oregon. But just at this time, the winter of 1848-49, the California Fever set in about him in its most contagious form. Bennett sold his farm and began making plans for the trip overland. Manly gave up his dream of Oregon and decided to go to California with Bennett.

Manly started for Prairie du Chein to buy an Indian pony to ride to California, planning to meet Bennett at Council Bluffs. He tanned some buckskins and made for himself a good outfit of clothes from them. Soon he received a letter from Bennett stating that the grass was backward and he was having to delay starting, and that it would be better for Manly to return and travel to Council Bluffs with him and his family. Swimming swollen rivers and hurrying through rain and over muddy trails, Manly reached Bennett's farm to find that Bennett had left two weeks earlier without forwarding any word of his change in plans. He did not see Bennett again until he reached Salt Lake. This was not the last time that Manly was to be disappointed by Bennett.

Manly traveled to Dubuque and crossed the river there. Traveling alone across Iowa, at the Missouri River he met some California-bound wagons. There he could learn nothing of Bennett, who was supposed to be bringing Manly's chest with all of his clothing and supplies. Concerning this predicament Manly wrote:

> "I waded across the low bottom to a strip of dry land next to the river where there was a post office, store, and a few cabins. I looked first for a letter, but there was none. Then I began to look over the cards in the trading places and saloons, and read the names written on the logs of the houses, and everywhere I thought there might be a trace of the friends I sought. No one had seen or knew them. After looking half a day I waded back again to the pony—pretty blue. I thought first I would go back and wait another year, but there was a small train near where I left the pony, and it was not considered very safe to go beyond there except with a

pretty good train. I sat down in camp and turned the matter over in my mind, and talked with Chas. Dallas of Lynn, Iowa, who owned the train. Bennett had my outfit and gun, while I had has light gun, a small light tent, a frying pan, a tin cup, one woolen shirt and the clothes on my back. Having no money to get another outfit, I about concluded to turn back when Dallas said that if I would drive one of his teams through, he would board me, and I could turn my pony in with his loose horses; I thought it over, and finally put my things in the wagon and took the ox whip to go on. Dallas intended to get provisions here, but could not, so we went down to St. Jo, following the river near the bluff. We camped near town and walked in, finding a small train on the main emigrant road to the west. My team was one yoke of oxen and one yoke of cows. I knew how to drive, but had a little trouble with the strange animals till they found I was kind to them, and then they were all right."

From St. Jo they crossed the Missouri and headed for the Platte bottom. Of the crossing of South Platte, Manly wrote the following:

"Reaching the South Platte, it took us all day to ford the sandy stream, as we had the first to sound out a good crossing by wading through ourselves, and when we started our teams across we dare not stop a moment for fear the wagons would sink deep into the quicksands. We had no mishaps in crossing, and when well camped on the other side a solitary buffalo made his appearance about 200 yards away and all hands started after him, some on foot. The horsemen soon got ahead of him, but he did not seem inclined to get out of their way, so they opened fire on him. He still kept his feet and they went nearer.

"Mr. Rogers being on a horse with a blind bridle, getting nearer, fired his Colt's revolver at him, when he turned, and the horse, being unable to see the animal quick enough to get out of the way, suffered the force of a sudden attack of the old fellow's horns, and came out with a gash in his thigh six inches long, while Rogers went on a flying expedition over the horse's head, and did some lively scrambling when he reached the ground. The rest then worried him along for about half a mile, and finally, after about forty shots he lay down but held his head up defiantly, receiving shot after shot with an angry shake, until a side shot laid him out.

"This game gave us plenty of meat, which though tough, was a pleasant change from bacon. I took no part in this battle except as an observer. On examination it was found that the balls had been many of them stopped by the matted hair about the old fellow's head and none of them had reached the skull."

Here appears for the first time the name of John Haney Rogers, the giant Tennessee boy, who was a butcher by trade and was co-hero with Manly in the rescue of the starving Death Valley party. From St. Jo to Benecia, California, Manly and Rogers traveled together. There, on separate steamboats, in 1854, they waved goodbye, not to meet again for more than forty-five years.

The Dallas Train passed Court House Rock and met a party of Mormons. The Mormons impressed Manly very much. Here is what he wrote about them:

"One prominent land mark along the route was what they called Court House Rock, standing to the south from the trail and much resembled an immense square building, standing high above surrounding country. The farther we went on, the more plentiful became the large game, and also wolves and prairie dogs, the first of which seemed to follow the buffaloes closely.

"About this time we met an odd-looking train going east, consisting of five or six Mormons from Salt Lake, all mounted on small Spanish mules. They were dressed in buckskin and mocassins, with long spurs jingling at their heels, the rowels fully four inches long, and each one carried a gun, a pistol and a big knife. They were rough-looking fellows with long, matted hair, long beards, old slouch hats and a generally back woods get-up air in every way. They had an extra pack mule, but the baggage and provisions were very light. I had heard much about the Mormons, both at Nauvoo and Salt Lake, and some way or other I could not separate the idea of horse thieves from this party, and I am sure I would not like to meet them if I had a desirable mule

Asabel Bennett, who was an associate of William Lewis Manly in Wisconsin and who was guided by Manly from Division Spring to Los Angeles.
Photo courtesy of T. R. Goodwin and now in Bear State Library.

that they wanted, or any money, or a good-looking wife. We talked with them half an hour or so and then moved on.

"We occasionally passed by a grave along the road and often a small head board would state that the poor unfortunate had died of cholera. Many of these had been torn open by wolves and the blanket encircling the corpse partly pulled away. Our route led a few miles north of Chimney Rock, standing on an elevated point like a tall column, so perfect and regular on all sides, that from our point it looked as if it might be the work of the stone cutters. Some of the party went to see it and reported there was no way to ascend it, and that as far as a man could reach, the rocks were inscribed with the names of visitors and travelers who passed that way.

"At Scott's Bluffs, the bluffs came close to the river, so there was considerable hill climbing to get along, the road in other places finding ample room in the bottom. Here we found a large camp of the Sioux Indians on the bank of a ravine, on both sides of which there were some large cottonwood trees. Away up in the large limbs platforms had been made of poles, on which were laid the bodies of their dead, wrapped in blankets and fastened down to the platform by a sort of a network of smaller poles tightly lashed so that they could not be dragged away or disturbed by wild animals. This seemed a strange sort of cemetery, but when we saw the desecrated earth-made graves we felt that perhaps this was the best way, even if it was a savage custom.

"These Indians were fair-sized men, and pretty good-looking for red men. Some of our men went over to their camp, and some of their youths came down to ours, and when we started on they seemed quite proud that they had learned a little of the English language, but the extent of their knowledge seemed to be a little learned of the ox-drivers, for they would swing their hands at the cattle and cry out, 'Whoa! haw, g—d d—m.' Whether they knew what was meant, I have my doubts. They seemed pretty well provided for and begged very little, as they are apt to do when they are hard pressed.

"We saw also some bands of Pawnee Indians on the move across the prairies. They would hitch a long, light pole on

43

each side of a pony, with the ends dragging behind on the ground, and on a little platform at the hind end the children sat and were dragged along.

"As we passed on beyond Scott's Bluff the game began to be preceptibly scarcer, and what we did find was back from the traveled road, from which it had apparently been driven by the passing hunters.

"In time, we reached Ft. Laramie, a trading post, where there were some Indian lodges, and we noticed that some of the occupants had lighter complexions than any of the other Indians we had seen. They had cords of dried buffalo meat, and we purchased some. It was very fat, but was so perfectly cured that the clear tallow tasted as sweet as a nut. I thought it was the best dried meat I had ever tasted, but perhaps a good appetite had something to do with it.

"As we passed Ft. Laramie we fell in company with some U.S. soldiers who were going to Ft. Hall and thence to Oregon. We considered them pretty safe to travel with and kept with them for some time, though their rate of travel was less than ours. Among them were some Mormons, employed as teamsters, and in other ways, and they told us there were some Missourians on the road who would never live to see California. There had been some contests between the Missourians and the Mormons, and I felt rather glad that none of us hailed from Pike Country."

Soon after this, word was passed about that it was too late to go to California; that the Sierra would be covered with snow and that Mr. Dallas would discharge all of his drivers in Salt Lake. Dallas confirmed this. So Manly and the rest were on the lookout for other means of transportation. When they reached the Big and Little Sandy, tributaries of Green River, Manly wrote the following:

"It was a remarkable clear and rapid stream and was now low enough to ford. One of the Government teams set out to make the crossing at a point where it looked shallow enough, but before the lead mules reached the opposite shore, they lost their footing and were forced to swim. Of course the wagon stopped and the team swung around and tangled up in a bad shape. They were unhitched and the wagon pulled back, the load was somewhat dampened for the water came into the wagon box about a foot. We camped here and laid by one day, having thus quite a little chance to look around.

"When we came to the first water that flowed toward the Pacific Coast as Pacific Springs we drivers had quite a little talk about a new scheme. We put a great many 'ifs' together and they amounted to about this:—If this stream were large enough; if we had a boat; if we knew the way; if there were no falls or bad places; if we had plenty of provisions; if we were bold enough to set out on such a trip, etc., we might come out at some point or other on the Pacific Ocean. And now when we came to the first of the 'ifs' a stream large enough to float a small boat; we began to think more strongly about the other 'ifs.'

"In the course of our rambles we actually did run across the second 'if' in the shape of a small ferry boat filled up with sand upon a bar, and it did not take very long to dig it out and put it into shape to use, for it was just large enough to hold one wagon at a time. Our military escort intended to leave us at this point, as their route now bore off to the north of ours. I had a long talk with the surgeon who seemed well informed about the country, and asked him about the prospects. He did not give the Mormons a very good name. He said to me:—'If you go to Salt Lake City, do not let them know you are from Missouri, for I tell you that many of those from that State will never see California. You know they were driven from Missouri, and will get revenge if they can.' Both the surgeon and the captain said the stream came out on the Pacific Coast and that we had no obstacles except cataracts, which they had heard were pretty bad. I then went to Dallas and told him what we proposed doing and to our surprise he did not offer any objections, and offered me $60 for my pony. He said he would sell us some flour and bacon for provisions also.

"We helped them in crossing the river which was somewhat difficult, being swift, with boulders in the bottom but we got all safely over and then made the trade we had spoken of. Dallas paid me for my pony and we took what flour and bacon he would let go. He gave us some ropes for head and stern lines to our boat and a couple of axes, and we laid these and our provisions in a pile by the roadside. Six of us then gave up our whips. Mr. S. McMahon, a driver, hesitated for some time, but being pressed by Dallas for a decision, at last threw down his whip and said:—'I will go with the boys.' This left Dallas with only one driver, but he took a whip, himself and with the aid of the children and his wife who drove the two-horse wagon, they got along very well. I paid for such provisions as we had taken, as the rest of the fellows had almost no money.

"So we parted company, the little train slowly moving on its way westward. Our military captain, the soldier boys, and the gay young lady taking the route to Oregon, and we sitting on the bank of the river whose waters flowed to the great Pacific. Each company wished the other good luck, we took a few long breaths and then set to work in earnest to carry out our plans."

This writer feels that Dallas, for whom Manly and Rogers drove ox teams to Green River, has been rather roughly treated in Manly's account, most of which is not being quoted here. Dallas settled on the Tuolumne River in Stanislaus County, fourteen miles from where Modesto is now, and became a substantial and influential citizen of that locality. Descendants still live in Stanislaus County. The old Dallas home on the Tuolumne was a haven for all needy who entered that district. Readers will be interested to know more about Dallas and his journey to California.

Charles Dallas was born in Aberdeenshire, Scotland, in 1814. In 1829 he came with his parents to Saratoga County, New York. When he was twenty years of age he married Elizabeth Surroc and moved to Grange County, Indiana. After living there two years he sold and, in 1836, removed to Iowa.

In 1849 Charles Dallas, with his family of six children, left Iowa and joined the mass migration to California. He came by way of Salt Lake. At Salt Lake Dallas and the leaders of several other outfits decided that Captain Hunt's charge of ten dollars a wagon was too much for guidance to Los Angeles over the Old Spanish Trail. So Dallas and some others with him started on ahead of Hunt. Among the others were the Givens brothers, Eleazer and Robert, who sold their ox teams and wagons, and bought Spanish mules with pack outfits. For some distance they traveled with Dallas, but soon decided to travel farther south and crossed the Colorado River into what is now the state of Arizona. After wandering over much of the desert portion of Arizona and recrossing the Colorado near present Needles, the Givens brothers and a man named Wright arrived in a starving condition at the Rubidoux Ranch near Cucamonga with one pack mule. They worked for Rubidoux, cutting willow fence poles on contract, teaching and making shoes for Rubidoux's children until they had recovered physically and financially. Then they went to the Mariposa Mines. In 1853 the Givens brothers settled on Mariposa Creek, a few miles south of the present city of Merced, not far from the Tuolumne River home of Charles Dallas. Two sons of Eleazer Givens, in 1949, still lived on the old homestead. They furnished the above data.

Dallas started from Salt Lake with seven of his own teams. Six of the Dallas ox-teams were loaded with provisions. This was undoubtedly the only well provided outfit on the Old Spanish Trail that season. There were forty other teams with Dallas.

Far out on the trail Dallas was overtaken by twenty-five men who were in a destitute condition. They had left Hunt and had gone afoot to get provisions for their starving families. Dallas gave each man twenty-five pounds of flour. Beside the trail he left two men with a tent and provisions and instructed them to see that each family with Hunt had their share of the provisions, whether they had money to pay or not. In 1881 Dallas stated that he had never received one dollar for any of the provisions furnished.

The Dallas Train arrived in Los Angeles with no difficulty and crossed the Sierra into the San Joaquin Valley sometime in the spring of 1850. In the Sierra a child was born to them. She was named Sierra Nevada Dallas. It is of interest to know that Sierra Dallas lived for many years near another young lady who had entered this world under similar conditions. Her name was Sierra Nevada Summit Collier who died in Turlock, California, aged almost one hundred years.

Of the trip down Green River Manly left a detailed account, but much of it is not of interest in connection with our Death Valley '49ers. We will cover briefly their trip down the river and from the village of the old Indian Chief, Walker, overland to Salt Lake.

The party was composed of Manly, Rogers, M. S. McMahon, Charles and Joseph Hazelbrig, Richard Field and Alfred Walton. Wrote Manly:

"At the mouth of Ham's Ford we passed a camp of Indians, but we kept close to the opposite shore to avoid being boarded by them. They beckoned very urgently for us to come ashore, but I acted as if I did not understand them, and gave them the go-by.

"As we were floating down the rapid stream it became more and more a rapid, roaring river, and the bed contained many dangerous rocks that were difficult to shun. Each of us had a setting-pole, and we ranged ourselves along the sides of the boat and tried to keep ourselves clear from the rocks and dangers. The water was not very deep and made such a dashing noise as the current rushed among the rocks that one had to talk pretty loud to be heard. As we were gliding along quite swiftly, I set my pole on the bottom and gave the boat a sudden push to avoid a boulder, when the pole stuck in the crevice between two rocks, and instead of losing the pole by the sudden jerk I gave, I was the one who was very suddenly yanked from the boat by the spring of the pole, and landed in the middle of the river. I struck pretty squarely on my back, and so got thoroughly wet, but swam for shore amid the shouts of the boys, who waved their hats and harrahed for the captain when they saw he was not hurt. I told them that was nothing, as we were on our way to California by water anyway, and such things must be expected."

They killed antelope and elk, floated about thirty miles a day and were congratulating themselves on the great improvement they had made in travel to California when they entered a narrow, perpendicular-walled canyon which they estimated as two thousand feet deep. They avoided two wrecks on large rocks, either of which would have been fatal to all of the crew, when the current turned the boat up edgewise and pinned it against the third rock. They could no more move it than they could the rock itself. This was at the site where was written the name, "Ashley, 1824."

Spying two large pine trees, Manly proposed making canoes. They worked day and night until the canoes were finished. They were fifteen feet long and two feet wide and were lashed together to make them more stable. They proved too small so a third larger one was made, thirty feet long.

Another start was made and they went into deeper and narrower canyons through a beautiful valley and then into more dangerous 48 water. They were rapidly approaching the Grand Canyon of the Colorado, which, until recent years, claimed the lives of almost everyone who tried to go through it.

The canoes were swamped and the occupants narrowly escaped drowning, Rogers coming out with nothing more than a pair of overalls, a shirt and three half dollars. The guns were gone except for Manly's rifle and McMahon's shotgun. A new start was made but soon they were stopped by an Indian who stood close by the edge of the river with a rifle lying in the hollow of his arm. They landed and found that they were in an Indian village.

By means of limited English and some sign language, they learned that the Indians were friendly to the Mormons. So they all immediately precipitated themselves into the Mormon church. The master of the head lodge was introduced as Chief Walker. He immediately began to dissuade the party from any thought of continuing down the river. He informed them that it was an easy trip overland to "Mormonee" and that it was certain death to continue down the river, that the water was rapid and rough and the river banks narrow and as high as the sky. We know that Walker was attempting no exaggeration.

The Manly party split. McMahon and Fields decided to go on down the river and the rest to go overland to Salt Lake. Walker was going on a big hunt and agreed to pilot the Salt Lake party well on their way. The river men traded some clothing for two horses and the party started across the plains, leaving Field and McMahon to continue down the river. Years later Manly learned that they, too, had finally to leave the river and had almost perished before falling in with Indian traders and reaching Fort Bridger.

On the way to Salt Lake, Manly and his companions crossed the Santa Fe Trail to Los Angeles, but did not know where it led. They had no map and were not familiar with the country so did not follow it.

Concerning Chief Walker and his people, Manly wrote the following grateful tribute:

"The Indians here have the reputation of being blood-thirsty savages who took delight in murder and torture, but here in the very midst of this wild and desolate country we found a Chief and his tribe, Walker and his followers, who were as humane and kind to white people as could be expected by anyone. I have often wondered at the knowledge of this man respecting the country, of which he was able to make us a good map in the sand, point out to us the impassable canyon, locate the hostile Indians, and many points which were not accurately known by our own explorers for many years afterward. He undoubtedly saved our little band from a watery grave, for without his advice we had gone on and on, far into the great Colorado canyon, from which escape would have been impossible and securing food another impossibility, while destruction by hostile Indians was among the strong probabilities of the case. So in a threefold way I have for these more forty years credited the lives of myself and comrades to the thoughtful interest and humane consideration of Old Chief Walker."

John Haney Rogers was born in Tennessee in 1825 and so was twenty-four years of age when the trip to California was made. He was five years younger than William Lewis Manly. From his voters registration record for 1896 in the office of the Merced County Clerk I have learned that he was six feet, two and one-half inches in height—and of dark complexion with brown eyes and grey hair. He then was living in the Lone Tree District, about fourteen miles southwest of Merced. No record of his death has been found. More will appear on these pages concerning him.

At the Mormon Fort on Cobble Creek near Salt Lake, Manly and Rogers fell in with a party of immigrants. Manly looked among the wagons for someone who could give him information. As he was passing the last wagon, a woman came to the front of the wagon and looked out. It was Mrs. Bennett, wife of Manly's old hunting companion, whom he had been following from Wisconsin. Soon Bennett came into camp and arrangements were made for Manly and Rogers to accompany the Bennetts to California, Manly as scout and hunter and Rogers as an ox driver.

And so there began assembling at and near Salt Lake the great group of wagons that soon was to start on its way over the Old Santa Fe Trail into San Bernardino and so to Los Angeles.

CHAPTER FOUR

THE RENDEZVOUS AT SALT LAKE

When the Jay Hawks and other parties traveling with them arrived at Salt Lake, it was too late to take the Northern or Humbolt Sink route to California. At that time word was being passed about concerning the gruesome sufferings of the Donners, a party of almost ninety, more than one-third of whom had perished while they were snowed in at Donner Lake on the summit of the Sierra. Some of those stricken people were forced to resort to eating the bodies of those who had died. Stories about the Donner Party so shocked the delayed parties of '49 that they lay over in Salt Lake, many expecting to start on the Humbolt route the following spring.

While waiting, some of them obtained work with the Mormons. John B. Colton worked for Elder Parley Pratt. He became well acquainted with several leaders in the Mormon church and never tired of relating his experiences at Salt Lake. He was, of course, particularly impressed with Brigham Young. He also was impressed with the old frontiersman, Jim Bridger. In September, 1914, he dictated the following to a newspaper reporter:

> "On December 4, 1904, I held the skull of Bridger in my hands.
>
> "But I had seen Bridger in the meantime in flesh and blood and heard him heap a tirade upon Brigham Young that I shall never forget. It was shortly after we had left him in his mountain rendezvous and our arrival in Salt Lake that he visited that place. He made our camp his headquarters. Just before he got ready to return to his home he decided to call on Brigham Young about some grievance.
>
> "Through boyish curiosity I went along. We rode straight to the tithing house and the Mormon leader came to the door. Bridger was loud and abusive, but Brigham Young was diplomatic. He showed his temper in his expression, but not in his speech.

"Bridger had been threatened by the Mormons. But he had complete control of the Utes, Shoshones, Flatheads, Blackfeet and Sioux, into whose tribes he had married. While Brigham Young stood pale and silent Jim Bridger raved:

" 'If I ever catch sight of one of your Danites in my territory, otherwise than on a peaceful mission, I'll swarm up every Indian within 100 miles and come and reduce your place to ashes!'

"Bridger died in 1881. Major-General G. M. Dodge decided in 1904 to erect a statute to his memory. He [Bridger] had aided the United States Army, helped to survey the Union Pacific Railroad right of way and through his knowledge of the country had saved the company a large sum of money. Gen. Dodge sought my services to secure the remains of Bridger.

"I found his grave through his granddaughter by one of his Indian wives and the body was exhumed from a small cemetery about twenty-five miles from Kansas City and the remains were placed in Mount Washington Cemetery with the monument telling of his many deeds at the head of the new grave. When I held his skull in my hands I thought of my first meeting with him back in '49, and the quarrel with Brigham Young."

Most interesting of all accounts concerning the arrival at Salt Lake and the delay there is the following, left by Dow Stevens:

"At this juncture we were approaching Salt Lake City, so three of us decided to forge ahead of the train. When we reached the first bench or table land we saw spread out before us the city itself, and in the greater distance the Great Lake. When we reached the first little farm our attention was attracted to the garden, full of vegetables of all kinds. How our mouths watered at this welcome sight. We approached the house, asked for accomodations. They made excuses about sleeping quarters, but that didn't trouble us, as we could sleep anywhere out of doors, if one could just have a meal or so. We kept our eyes on the garden, and were willing and glad to help in the preparation of the vegetables.

No one knows how willing we were to pod the peas. We had green corn, peas and other vegetables, something we had longed and starved for four months. Never before or since have I tasted anything that was so good, and we ate and ate until we could eat no more, and only felt sorry that our capacity was so limited.

"We were up bright and early getting peas ready for breakfast. This was a regular bonanza for us, and our bill was fifty cents each. It was well worth five dollars to us if worth a cent.

"Four miles distant lay the city, and a smart walk soon brought us in, where we inquired for a good camping place for a train which had not yet arrived. We soon found a suitable place, convenient to water and grass, the two most essential features for a camping place. We camped between the city and Jordan River, as all emigrants had to camp on that side of the city.

"Our train arrived the same day and we were soon surrounded by the Mormons, principally women enquiring for tea, and if we had any to sell. They seemed to be as much starved for tea as we were for vegetables. Tea was three dollars a pound, and we could get vegetables for a week, for a pound of tea. Some of the women said they had not tasted tea for two years past. They were also short of groceries and wearing apparel. Many women were entirely barefooted, and many scantily dressed. All the clothes had been practically worn out, as there had been no supplies bought for two years, consequently many of them were greatly in need of the luxuries of life. They had seeds and plenty of cattle with them, so they were all well provided with the substantials, all having good gardens, beef milk and butter.

"They raised wheat and ground their own flour, but had no way to bolt it, so had to live on unbolted flour. The women were doing men's work in the fields, pulling up the wheat and thrashing it with flails, they having no harvesting implements, as they were yet very scarce. We saw other women with their three or four yoke of oxen and team going into the canyon, a distance of twelve miles, and bringing down loads of wood. There were no men on the load, and perhaps there would be two or three women to handle the team. After

53

seeing the scheme of things I didn't wonder so much they advocated the plurality of wives, the advantages were so great.

"I became tired of camp life in a few days and decided a change was good for me, so found board with a family named Smithson. There was a large family of children, some of the girls almost grown. The old gentleman was well up in the seventies, and concluded he wanted another wife. His wife was much opposed naturally, and I heard her tell him she would leave if he brought another wife home. The old fellow justified himself by declaring that 'more wives meant more stars in his crown of glory.' This was a heavy argument, but his wife couldn't see the force of the argument. No doubt she felt it better for him to do with a fewer stars in his crown, than for her to suffer the presence of another woman. Years afterwards I heard he never had a chance to add stars to his crown, probably he was too old.

"I stayed with these people a week, then boarded with one of the elders of the church who already had two wives, and had his eyes on a third, a young grass widow, but she said she wouldn't be number three to the best man living. I boarded with the elder's family during the remainder of my stay in Salt Lake.

"The Mormons were all fond of dancing, and fortunately I was invited to several of the parties. Brigham Young always led off with the fairest in the assemblage, and it was always considered an honor to be chosen by Brother Brigham, as he was styled. In build Brigham Young was very much like Theo. Roosevelt. He was a very good speaker, but no orator, but he shone as a leader. His people would do anything he proposed, and his control seemed to reign over them. I have been often asked how many wives he had, and all I have to judge by was the sleeping apartments. In walking past his place of residence I saw about seven or eight wagon bodies with covers on, all in a row, ranged in his back yard, and was told these were occupied by his wives. Across the square from where I boarded were two more, and these I knew quite well.

"The warm springs were there at that time, in an open plain and we all thoroughly enjoyed the bathing. One day there was a dozen of us enjoying our bath when along came a wagon, drove up to almost thirty paces of us and the driver asked if we didn't know this was the ladies bath day. We told him we were entirely ignorant, and would immediately get into our clothes and give them full possession. Which we did.

"Many Mormons had been to California and returned with gold from the mines, and had it coined at Salt Lake into five dollar gold pieces. On one side was printed the All Seeing Eye, and on the other side the Bee Hive. But most of the currency consisted of shin plasters written on paper and signed by Brigham, and circulated only amongst themselves, for all things bought from emigrants had to be paid for in gold coin. The gold was soft, no alloy being used, so lasted but a short time."

Most of the parties which formed the wagon train that started to California stayed in Salt Lake two months or more. Younger men enjoyed they stay by joining in all of the entertainment possible, particularly the dancing.

Supplies of all kinds were purchased, especially a large quantity of coffee which lasted some until they reached Los Angeles. Wagons and other equipment were repaired and strengthened and everything possible was done to make ready for the long overland journey from Salt Lake to the California placers.

By the first of October one hundred and ten wagons had assembled, all impatient to start. The Mormons wanted a road opened to San Bernardino. They had taken pack trains south to a point near Little Salt Lake, where they took the Old Santa Fe Trail into California. They saw an opportunity to have a wagon road opened and to be paid for it as well.

Jefferson Hunt, a Captain in the Mormon Battalion during the Mexican War, had been over the Old Spanish, or Mormon Trail. He thought that wagons could be taken into San Bernardino over that old trail. So the owners of one hundred and ten wagons paid Captain Hunt ten dollars apiece to guide them to San Bernardino. There were about two hundred people with the wagons.

A Captain Baxter of Michigan was elected captain of the train, and a Doctor McCormack of Iowa City, Iowa, was elected Lieutenant. These officers were replaced after a few days. The train was well organized. Each wagon with a leader was organized into a mess.

Concerning this organization Lewis Manly wrote the following: 55

"The scattering members of the train began to congregate, and Capt. Hunt said it was necessary to have some sort of system about the move, and that before they moved they must organize and adopt rules and laws which must be obeyed. He said they must move like an army, and that he was to be a dictator in all things except that in case of necessity, a majority of the train could rule otherwise. It was thought best to get together and try a march out one day, then go in camp and organize.

"This they did, and at the camp there was gathered one hundred and seven wagons, a big drove of horses and cattle, perhaps five hundred in all. The train was divided into seven divisions and each division was to elect its own captain. Division No. 1 should lead the march the first day, and their men should take charge of the stock and deliver them to the wagons in the morning, and then. No. 1 should take the rear, with No. 2 in the lead to break the road. The rear division would not turn a wheel before 10 o'clock the next day, and it would be about that time at night before they were in camp and unyoked. The number of animals cleaned out the feed for a mile or two each side of the camp and a general meeting was called for the organization of the whole. Mr. L. Granger got up so he could look over the audience and proceeded to explain the plan and to read a preamble and resolutions which had been prepared as the basis for government."

This company organization was known as the *San Joaquin Company*. They were headed for the southern mines, which bordered the San Joaquin Valley of California. But the name was never understood by the members of the company. It was new to them and from a strange language. They undoubtedly misunderstood it entirely. They had no occasion to remember it for several weeks. Then, after they had plunged off into the Great American Desert, they referred to it sarcastically as the *Sand Walking Company*. None of them knew it as anything else.

The Jay Hawks completed their organization. An initiation was held. Each member was carried three times around camp at the head of a procession. He was carried face down by four of his party holding his legs and arms. When each circuit to the camp fires had been made, the initiate was stood on his feet and his pants legs were rolled above his knees. He was made to swear that he would abide by all of the orders and rules laid down by the train officials. Then a pinch of hair was pulled from his leg. (Some writers have stated that a piece of skin was pinched from his leg.) If he did not flinch, he was considered to be duly initiated into the Jay Hawks. Each mess was named. There were the Shin Picker's mess, the Wolverines, the Buckskins, the Hawkeyes and others. This hilarious group carried on their work far into the night.

Other groups entered into this fun. From the lips of the Iowa and Illinois boys came the verses of a song then being sung on every hand:

> Then Ho! boys Ho! and to
>   California go;
> There's plenty of gold in the
>   world untold,
> On the banks of the Sacramento.

There has been much confusion about the name of Jay Hawks, or Jayhawkers, as applied to this little band of '49ers. Many have supposed that they took their name from the Kansas Jayhawkers who became famous about 1857 because of their raids into Missouri. But the Kansas Jayhawkers came into existence several years after the Jay Hawks had disbanded. We are fortunate that the Jay Hawks themselves left several statements as to the origin of their name. Answering a query about the name, Urban P. Davidson, of the Jay Hawks of '49 wrote in 1903:

> "In answer I will state that our company was made up from school boys at Galesburg, Illinois. We formed an order of our own. One of our party suggested the name of Jayhawk, so that was adopted. Our company has gone by that name ever since."

It will be noticed that Davidson used the name of Jayhawk and not Jayhawker. Many of the '49ers never adopted the term Jayhawker, made common after the Kansas boys became famous. Almost always they wrote the two words separately, *Jay Hawk*.

Ed Doty also told William Lewis Manly his own version of the origin of the name, Jay Hawk. It resembles other stories but probably is the account of how the name was first applied to the Illinois boys, except that Doty used the later form of the name.

Edward Doty who, on the desert near Indian Wells, succeeded Asa Haynes as Captain of the Jay Hawks. He was a large, active man and had much to do with the survival of many of the Jay Hawks. He was born on the same day as was William Lewis Manly, April 6, 1820. Doty settled at Goleta near Santa Barbara and passed away there about 1894. Descendants of Doty still live in the vicinity of his old Santa Barbara home.

Photo courtesy of Huntington Library and now in Bear State Library.

Here is what Manly wrote about it:

"One day when Doty was engaged in the duty of cooking flap-jacks, another frolicsome fellow came up and took off the cook's hat and commenced going through the motions of a barber giving his customer a vigorous shampoo, saying:—'I am going to make a Jayhawker out of you, old boy.' Now it happened that Ed Doty was chosen captain, and no sooner was the choice declared than the boys took the newly elected captain around on their shoulders and carried him around the camp introducing him as the King Bird of the Jayhawkers. So their division was afterwards known as the Jayhawkers."

Taking part in a friendly controversy concerning the origin and meaning of the name, John B. Colton, official historian of the Jay Hawks, wrote in 1903:

"I will say that it was coined on the Platte River, not far west of the Missouri River, in 1849, long before the word Kansas was known or heard of. I cannot tell why, but I was there. Some kind of hawks as they sail up in the air, reconnoitering for mice and other small prey, look and act as though they were the whole thing; then the audience of jays and other small but jealous and vicious birds sail in and jab him until he gets tired of show life and slides out of trouble in the lower earth. Now perhaps this is what happened among fellows on the trail, jaybirds and hawks enact the same role, pro and con, out of pure devilment and to pass the hours of a long march. At any rate ours was the crowd that created the word Jayhawker, at the date and locality above stated. Another thing, in the mountains and mines of California, in those early days, words were coined or born, climatic surroundings materially contributing, the words were short, like the latter day tenderfoot, short hand meant a line, a sentence, and perhaps a whole page. I have heard a word spoken that meant a whole life time to the other fellow."

Regardless of the finer meanings of the word it was used very broadly by the Galesburg boys, who almost all used the original form of *Jay Hawks.*

59

It was at this point in the proceedings at Salt Lake that Jim Bridger, Kit Carson and Pegleg Smith all advised against attempting to take wagons over the Spanish Trail. They had been over it on horseback and stated that it was not safe to attempt the trip with wagons, especially when accompanied by women and children.

This route was first explored in the winter of 1829-'30 by a band of Santa Fe trappers led by William Wolfskill. Wolfskill settled in Los Angeles and has descendants living there now. The Spanish traders and horse runners from Santa Fe had used the old trail since the time of its discovery. It was a difficult old trace and was lined with the bones of mules and horses that had died of thirst while traveling along it. This was the Old Spanish Trail over which Captain Jefferson Hunt proposed to guide the '49ers to Los Angeles.

Concerning the Great American Desert itself, Carson is stated to have said that he had been west with Frémont, who with all of the resources of the United States government, could not cross it. But we find this little band of Argonauts unwilling to be delayed in their journey to California. By way of Los Angeles, the road from Salt Lake to the mines bordering the San Joaquin Valley was about twelve hundred miles in length. Across the Great American Desert the distance appeared to be about six hundred miles. Six hundred extra miles by ox team was not to be undertaken if it could be avoided. They had not decided, but they were thinking hard.

CHAPTER FIVE

DIVISION SPRING

Many of the '49ers had delayed at Salt Lake more than two months. Some had been able to find work and thus support themselves. But many had eaten a large portion of their supplies and were eager to be on the road. When the time came to leave, few were interested in writing down any of the details of their leave-taking. William Lewis Manly, hero of the Death Valley tragedy, has left the best account of many happenings on the cutoff between Division Spring, near present Enterprise, Utah, and the Southern Mines. Concerning this leave-taking at Salt Lake, Manly wrote:

"We moved off in good style from this camp. After a day or two and before we reached what is called Little Salt Lake, an attempt was made to make a short cut, to save distance. The train only went on this cutoff a day or two when Captain Hunt came back from the front and said they had better turn back to the old trail again, which all did. This was a bad move, the train much broken and not easy to get them into regular working order again. We were now approaching what they called the Rim of the Basin. Within the basin the water all ran to the north or toward Great Salt Lake, but when we crossed the rim, all was toward the Colorado River, through which it reached the Pacific Ocean. About this time, we were overtaken by another train commanded by Capt. Smith. They had a map with them by one Williams of Salt Lake, a mountaineer who was represented to know all the routes through all the mountains of Utah, and this map showed a way to divide off from the Southern route not far from the divide which separated the waters of the basin from those which flowed toward the Colorado, and pass over the mountains, coming out in what they called the Tulare Valley, much nearer than by Los Angeles."

This was the beginning of all trouble for a great many of the Hunt train. The above Captain Smith was O. K. Smith, traveling with several other Mormons. Smith was in possession of a copy of the map which accompanied Frémont's report of his travels in the Far West. It was in the center of this map that there appeared the large blank space, known as the Great American Desert and marked "Unexplored."

Across this map one Barney Ward had traced a trail showing plenty of water and camp sites all the way to the Sierra Nevada mountains in California. The trail ended near Big Pine, north of Owen's Lake, which was described as a beautiful body of water, surrounded by woods and abundant game and fed by numerous clear, running streams; in fact, excepting the clear waters of Owen's River, this alluring body of water as shown had almost everything that Owen's Lake never did have.

Not shown on Smith's map, but passing along the east foothills of the Sierra there actually was a trail known as the Walker's Pass or Frémont Trail. It led south by way of Big Pine, Lone Pine, Indian Wells, Coyote Holes, Desert Springs and Willow Springs to connect with the Old Spanish or Santa Fe Trail, which wandered across the desert to cross Green River at the site of the present village of Green River, Utah and the Colorado River north of the Grand Canyon at the present village of Moab, Utah, on U.S. Highway 160.

Crossing the Old Spanish Trail on the Mojave Desert, the old Indian trail continued southwest. Soon it branched, one branch entering the head of Soledad Canyon and the other leading to Elizabeth Lake. Both of these trails led to Rancho San Francisquito (now Newhall Ranch), San Fernando Mission and Los Angeles. Continuing south, the main trail led to San Diego and across the desert to Yuma and Old Mexico. This was an old trail, one over which many of the Spanish pioneers came from Sonora, Mexico, to establish the first white settlements in California. Other '49ers came from Fort Smith, Arkansas, by way of Santa Fe and Socorro, New Mexico, to join this old trail from Mexico east of the Colorado River. They made a great sweep to the south in order to avoid the Grand Canyon of the Colorado.

About fifty miles south of Owen's Lake there was shown on Smith's map a trail branching from the one which paralleled the Sierra on the east, leading to the west over Walker's Pass and entering the San Joaquin Valley only a short distance south of the Southern or Mariposa mines, the destination of these '49ers. By way of San Bernardino and Los Angeles it was more than twelve hundred miles to the mines. O. K. Smith claimed that his route, which had been laid out by Barney Ward,

62

would save more than six hundred miles of travel. From the first this new route was a terrible temptation to the impatient gold seekers. The map was constantly exhibited and its merits were discussed by many who knew nothing at all about the route or the conditions that were to be encountered on the way. But the map showed every camp on the short trail and that there was water and grass at every place where it would be needed.

Mr. William R. Palmer of Cedar City, Utah, made a close study of the route taken by the Death Valley '49ers after they reached the Old Spanish Trail, which they had struck just north of Little Salt Lake. According to Palmer, the group left the Old Spanish Trail near present Enterprise, Utah. From there they traveled through Enterprise Canyon to Mount Misery. They then dropped down a steep canyon into Meadow Valley Wash. There they entered the bounds of the present state of Nevada.

Traveling northwest along Meadow Valley past present Acoma, Panaca and Pioche, Nevada, they detoured southward and then plunged blindly westward into the Great American Desert.

Captain Hunt was consulted about the advisability of taking the short cut and thus saving about sixty days of travel. His reply follows:

> "You all know I was hired to go by way of Los Angeles, but if you all wish to go and follow Smith I will go also. But if even one wagon decides to go the original route, I shall feel bound to go with that wagon."

Hunt also stated that he was doubtful if any white man had ever been over the short cut and that he did not consider it safe for those who had wives and children in that company. "But," said Hunt, "if you decide to follow Smith, I will go with you even if the road leads to Hell."

When O. K. Smith and his party reached the point on the Old Spanish Trail where the cutoff branched to the west, he and his companions immediately turned west and soon were lost to sight of the members of Hunt's party. It is proper to record here that Smith soon turned east and took the Old Spanish Trail, beating the Hunt party into San Bernardino, and was soon in the mines. This O. K. Smith lived in Tulare County for many years. He participated in the election when Tulare County was formed, July 10, 1852. In the election of September 11, 1853, Smith was elected Sheriff of Tulare County. In 1853 he erected and operated a saw mill near Visalia, cutting the local oak timber for 63 constructing the first buildings in that new County Seat. In 1853 Smith became an Associate Justice of Tulare County.

In 1870 O. K. Smith had either located at Santa Barbara or had gone there on a visit. While traveling along the ocean front at Rincon, east and south of Santa Barbara, he disappeared. A wheel from his buggy was thrown upon the beach by the waves. It was thought that he had been accidentally drowned when the tide caught him in the Rincon. Later a body was washed upon the beach near Carpenteria and identified as that of Smith. His team was finally located in Inyo County where it had been taken and sold. It was then decided that he had been murdered and robbed. (The first portion of the above is from the *History of Tulare County* by Katherine Edwards Small, page 71. That referring to the death of Smith was obtained from Cesario Latiallade of Santa Barbara.)

It was thought by many of the Death Valley '49ers that Smith had been purposely sent out by the Mormons to lead them into the desert and thus dispose of them for all time.

On the trail south the Hunt train passed in sight of Sevier Lake and close to Little Salt Lake, which was almost entirely dry and was surrounded by a beach of salt as white as snow.

About the division of the train at the cutoff, Lewis Manly has left us the following description:

"It was really a serious moment when the front of the train reached the Smith trail. Team after team turned to the right while now and then one would keep straight ahead as was at first intended. Capt. Hunt came over to the larger party after the division was made, and wished them all a hearty farewell and a pleasant happy journey. My friend Bennett, whose fortune I shared, was among the seceeders who followed the Smith Party.

"This point, when our paths diverged was very near the place afterward made notorious as Mountain Meadows, where the famous massacre took place under the direction of the Mormon generals. Our route from here up to the mountain was a very pleasant one, steadily up grade, over rolling hills, with wood, water and grass in plenty. We came at last to what seemed the summit of a great mountain, about three days journey on the new trail. Juniper trees grew about in

64

bunches, and my experience with this timber taught me that we were on elevated ground.

"Immediately in front of us was a cañon, impassible for wagons, and down this the trail descended. Men could go, horses and mules, perhaps, but wagons could no longer follow that trail, and we proposed to camp while explorers were sent out to search a pass across this steep and rocky cañon. Wood and bunch grass were plenty, but water was a long way down the trail and had to be packed up to the camp. Two days passed, and the parties sent out began to come in, all reporting no way to go farther with wagons. Some said the trail on the west side of the cañon could be ascended on foot by both men and mules, but that it would take years to make it fit for wheels.

"The enthusiasm about the Smith cutoff had begun to die and now the talk began of going back to follow Hunt. On the third morning a lone traveler with a small wagon and one yoke of oxen died. He seemed to be on this journey to seek to regain his health. He was from Kentucky, but I have forgotten his name. Some were very active about his wagon and, some thought too much attention was paid to a stranger. He was decently buried by the men of the company.

"This very morning a Mr. Rynierson called the attention of the crowd and made some remarks upon the situation. He said, 'My family is near and dear to me. I can see by the growth of the timber that we are in a very elevated place. This is now the seventh of November, it being the fourth at the time of our turning off on this trail. We are evidently in a country where snow is liable to fall at any time in the winter season, and if we were to remain here and be caught in a severe storm, we should all probably perish. I, for one, feel in duty bound to seek a safer place than this. I shall hitch up my oxen and return at once to the old trail. Boys (to his teamsters) get the cattle and we'll return.' This was decisive, and Mr. Rynierson would tarry no longer. Many others now proceeded to get ready and follow, and as Mr. Rynierson drove out of camp quite a respectable train fell in behind him. As fast as the hunters came in and reported no road available, they also yoked up their oxen and rolled out. Some waited for companions yet in the field and all were ready to move, when a party came in with news that the pass was found and no trouble could be seen ahead. About twenty-seven wagons remained when this news came, and as their proprietors had brought good news they agreed to travel on westward and not go back to the old trail."

Many scouts had been out looking for a way down from the elevation which some of them called Poverty Point, but which the Jay Hawks referred to as Mount Misery. Not only Manly climbed a mountain to look for a way, but Rev. J. W. Brier climbed the tallest tree on top of the tallest mountain and located what he thought was a way out. But the most detailed account of the Jay Hawks' discovery of a narrow canyon which could be made passable by cutting down some trees was that left by John Groscup. In 1885 he wrote the following concerning the discovery of this route, the most unfortunate discovery made on the entire journey to California:

"I never shall forget the place where the counsel was held which way we should go, to the north or to the south and then a reconnoiter party was sent out which is [was] as follows: Thomas Shannon, William Rude, Elic Palmer and myself. We took the large spy glass that the company had and we started early in the morning and got back very late in the evening. We went up a very hih mountain and with the aid of the spy glass, we could see a great distance and a great deal of the country and that it was rough south and plenty of snow peaks there and that it was open and barren north and we thought that we ought to go that way, but there was one man in the company who you all know. He could lay off all the mountains and call them by name whether they hit or not. He made the start and we all followed down into the Great American Desert."

There has been some difference of opinion concerning who was responsible for the actual start on the new route. John Groscup has indicated above that one man led the way. That man was the Rev. James W. Brier, husband of Mrs. Juliette W. Brier, quoted in our first chapter. Years later, Rev. Brier dictated the following for publication in a newspaper:

66

"About fifty miles south of Little Salt Lake we camped at a large spring, where the old Spanish Trail (to Santa Fe) turned to the left and Walker's Cutoff to the right. Here we held a consultation as to which road we should take. I favored the cutoff. Hunt replied laconically, 'If you take it you'll go to hell.' The great majority of us, however, chose the cutoff. So next morning 100 wagons of us started down the cutoff, while five wagons followed Hunt along the Spanish trail. We had no trail on the cutoff, and simply trusted to fortune to reach Los Angeles, which was about 800 miles from that point.

"After traveling a day and a half we reached the 1,000 foot gorge of the Santa Clara, a tributary of the Rio Virgin. As we had to bring our water up that fearful slope we named the place 'Deep Diggings.' We were there two days trying to get away but our progress was blocked by high mountains and terrible gorges, and we finally decided to turn back. After some prospecting, however, I found open country to the west. My company—I was with a lot of great hearted, Mississippi boys—voted to go that way, and we started, with Jayhawkers following. My wife was the only woman in the outfit; and my three boys—aged four, seven and nine years, respectively—the only children. We spent Sunday at the very spot which was, in later years, the scene of the Mountain Meadows massacre, and I preached there."

According to some of the Jay Hawks, Rev. Brier's text at this fateful spot, oddly enough, was *There Shall Be No More Death*.

Three days were spent at the place called "Deep Diggings" by Rev. Brier. It was more than one thousand feet down the steep bluff to water. A little Frenchman carried up many bucketsful of water, charging one dollar a bucket. This furnished little more than enough water for the people. The stock had almost no water during this time. Here all got their first taste of what was to come.

When the Jay Hawks' scouts returned and reported that there was a wagon way down one of the gulches, they elected Jim Martin captain of their organization and decided to make the plunge into the canyon which was to lead them into the most dreadful trails ever trod by an expedition anywhere. They were willing to make the journey or leave their bones bleaching on the Great American Desert, which at least four did. But they were not willing to have parties with women and children following their lead. In an open meeting they rejected the Rev. J. W. Brier and his family; J. B. Arcan, his wife and two year old son, Charles; and Asabel Bennett, wife with three small children, George, Melissa and Martha.

The Wades were not mentioned by the Jay Hawks because they stayed a day's travel behind all others. Also, Mr. Wade and his fourteen-year-old son, Harry George, had worked the Wade family west from Pennsylvania by freighting through almost trackless frontier territory. Mr. Wade was the only one of these desert-bound travelers who carried more than fifty gallons of water in cans for both animals and family.

It is well to note here that the Jay Hawks warned these people not to follow and that they could not be responsible for women and children. Many persons have accused the Jay Hawks of abandoning these women and children in the middle of the desert. Such was not the case.

There have been preserved many lists of that little band of Jay Hawks in '49. From these the following has been prepared. It is perhaps as complete as any ever will be. It should constantly be consulted as we will come across the names many times in the pages that are to follow. Let us take them up alphabetically:

George Allen was from Knoxville, Illinois. He was born September 6, 1831, and died in San Francisco, September 11, 1877.

Edward F. Bartholomew was from Farmington, Illinois. He was born about 1828 and died in Pueblo, Colorado, February 13, 1891.

Brian Byram was from Knoxville, Illinois. He died in the U.S. Military Hospital, Keokuk, Iowa, April 11, 1865.

Carter was from Wisconsin. Nothing is known of what happened to him after the party reached Rancho del Valle, February 4, 1850.

Charles Clark was from Henderson Grove, Illinois. He died there September 9, 1865.

Alonzo Cardell Clay was from Galesburg, Illinois. He died there September 9, 1865.

John Cole was from Knoxville, Illinois. He mined at Sonora, California, and died there in 1852.

John Burt Colton, who was born at Monson, Maine, August 11, 1831, was from Galesburg, Illinois. He died at Grand Island, Nebraska, October 23, 1919. He was the historian of the Jay Hawks and attended the

68

sixty-ninth anniversary of their arrival at Rancho del Valle, February 4, 1850.

Urban P. Davidson died near Thermopolis, Wyoming, December 18, 1903.

Edward Doty was from Knoxville, Illinois. He was born in New York State, April 6, 1820, and died near Santa Barbara, California, June 14, 1891.

Marshall G. Edgerton was from Galesburg, Illinois. He died in Montana about 1865.

Sidney P. Edgerton was from Galesburg, Illinois. He died at Blair, Nebraska, January 31, 1880.

Fish was from Lima, Indiana. He perished of thirst on the Argus Range, west of Panamint Valley, January 13, 1850.

Harrison B. Franz was from Henderson Grove, Illinois. He died at Rye Valley, Oregon, January 16, 1902, after having mined for fifty-two years.

Unnamed Frenchman. There has been much speculation concerning the identity of this lost Frenchman, the little man who carried so many buckets of water up the high bluff at Mount Misery at one dollar a bucket. In 1903 Jerome Bonaparte Alrich passed away in the San Bernardino County Hospital, aged 94 years. It was claimed that Alrich left Cobble Creek, Utah, in November, 1849, with the Jay Hawks and accompanied them almost into Los Angeles, but then turned back and became lost. Alrich may have been the Frenchman who turned back to chase the ox which was carrying his belongings and was stampeded by the Indians in Antelope Valley, south of Willow Springs.

Gould was from Oskaloose, Iowa. He is thought to have mined and then gone to Pen Yan, New York, where he died about 1860.

Frederick Gretzinger was from Joliet, Illinois. He died at Portland, Missouri, October 1, 1875.

John Groscup was from Henderson Grove, Illinois. He was born September 29, 1829, and died near Laytonville, California, February 24, 1916.

Asa Haynes was from Knoxville, Illinois. He was born in Duchess County, New York, February 9, 1804, and died at De Long, Illinois, March 29, 1889.

William Isham was from Rochester, New York, He died of exhaustion on the desert north of Searles Lake, California, January 13, 1850.

Aaron Larkin was from Knoxville, Illinois, and died at Humbolt, California, in 1853.

Asa Haynes, who was Captain of the Jay Hawks from Division Spring to Indian Wells Valley, where he almost died of thirst and starvation. He was the oldest member of the Jay Hawk party.

Photo courtesy of Huntington Library and now in Bear State Library.

Thomas McGrew was from Knoxville, Illinois, and died at Boise, Idaho, in 1864.

Charles Bert Mecum was from Galesburg, Illinois. He was born at West Suffield, Connecticut, August 25, 1822 and died at Mt. Vernon, Iowa, February 20, 1905.

Alexander S. Palmer was from Knoxville, Illinois. He died at Chandlerville, California, March 27, 1854.

John W. Plummer was from Knoxville, Illinois. He died at Toulon, Illinois, June 22, 1892.

Luther A. Richards was from Galesburg, Illinois. He was born at Westminster, Vermont, April 12, 1818 and died at Beaver City, Nebraska. June 15, 1899.

William Robinson was from Knoxville or Magoon, Illinois. He died of thirst and starvation at the head of Soledad Canyon, California, January 28, 1850, the last of the '49ers known to have perished on the journey to California.

William Rood was from Knoxville, Illinois. He was drowned in the Colorado River at Rancho La Paz, Arizona, April 29, 1871. His surname has often been spelled Rude, and sometimes Roods, but letters written by Rood himself and others written by his sister use the spelling Rood. In signing his name, Rood made a practice of ending it with a flourish which ended by underlining the name. This made it appear as though he intended to end the name with an s.

Thomas Shannon was from Knoxville, Illinois. He was born in Ohio, January 25, 1825, and died near Los Gatos, California, November 15, 1903. Before starting to California Tom Shannon had served in the United States Army during the Mexican War. After his trek to California he served with the Union Army in the Civil War.

Lorenzo Dow Stevens was born at Hackettstown, New Jersey, December 21, 1827, and died in Oakland, California. February 10, 1921. He lived to celebrate the seventy-first anniversary of his arrival at Rancho del Valle and was the last survivor of these Jay Hawk '49ers.

Wolfgang Tauber was from Joliet, Illinois. He died at sea enroute home from California, November 15, 1850.

John Lewis West was from Knoxville, Illinois. He was born about 1818 and died at Sacramento, California, January 12, 1898.

Leander Woolsey was from Knoxville, Illinois. He was born at Ashtabula, Ohio, June 28, 1826, and died at Oakland, California, October 7, 1881.

Sheldon Young was from Joliet, Illinois. He was born in Connecticut, 71

C. B. Mecum, a prominent Jay Hawk, who wrote a number of interesting letters about the journey to California. He returned to Galesburg, Illinois, and was host to the Jay Hawks during several of their reunions.
Photo courtesy of Huntington Library and now in Bear State Library.

July 23, 1815, and died at Moberly, Missouri, October 18, 1892. He was a sailor and kept a "log" of his voyage across the Great American Desert. We will find good use for his record in tracing the '49ers across Death Valley and into Rancho del Valle, for he was very accurate in his brief statement of the direction and distance traveled each day.

In a short time Rev. Brier abandoned his private route and fell in with the Mississippi boys behind the Jay Hawks, traveling with them until they reached a point in Panamint Valley near present Ballarat. Manly and Rogers traveled with the Bennett family, Rogers as a teamster and Manly as a guide. Bennett also had two other drivers, Silas Helmer and S. S. Abbott. Behind all of these was a family named Wade, and two "Earhart" or "De Hart" or "Ahart" brothers, one with a grown son. This "Earhart" family was from Iowa City, Iowa. Since the time of their leaving Death Valley, nothing is known of them.

WADE FAMILY HISTORY

The Wades are deserving of a thorough introduction to readers, especially readers who are familiar with the trackless, barren desert country over which this western trek was made. *Harry Wade* was born in Rochester, England, March 16, 1800. He died in Alviso, California, October 13, 1883. At the time of his marriage, Harry Wade was coachman to the King of England. At that time serving in the Royal Service was *Mary Reynolds Leach*. She was a governess to the children of the French Ambassador to the Court of Great Britain.

The hand of Mary Leach was being sought by a young man who was acceptable, both to Mary and, what was more important in English society, to her parents as well. But Mary became more and more interested in the coachman. He was a tall, straight, fine-looking fellow in his well-tailored livery. When Mary's French charges wanted to go driving, Mary found it easy to secure Harry Wade and his carriage. Finally matters came to a head when both suitors approached Mary's parents and asked for her hand in marriage. The first-mentioned young man wanted to marry Mary and bring her to America. Harry Wade wanted to marry Mary and continue with his job as coachman to the King.

Father and Mother Leach would not listen to any plan that involved the transportation of young Mary to faraway America. Much as they regretted that Mary's other suitor was a mere coachman, they at last consented to his marriage to Mary.

73

Thomas Shannon, who served in the U.S. Army during the Mexican War, accompanied the Jay Hawks through Death Valley to the gold mines of California and afterward served in the U.S. Army during the Civil War. For many years Tom Shannon lived at San Jose. Before he passed away, he became almost totally blind.

Photo courtesy of Huntington Library and now in Bear State Library.

And how did this arrangement work out? Did Harry and Mary marry and live happily, in old London town, ever after? Hardly. Two weeks after the first born, *Harry George Wade*, arrived upon the scene, December 18, 1835, Harry Wade came into the house, placed his top hat carefully upsidedown on the center table, placed his gloves carefully inside of it and said, "Mary, get everything packed to leave in a week. I have tickets for New York."

Anyone who knew Harry Wade knows that all parental protests fell on deaf ears. Mary and Harry came to New York. They were accompanied by George Wade, brother of Harry, and by two-weeks-old Harry George Wade.

For a time Harry Wade freighted from New York into Pennsylvania. Then he moved to Tioga County, Pennsylvania, where three more children were born: *Charles Elliott*, August 12, 1883; *Almira*, June 21, 1840; and *Pristina* in 1842. Pristina died in 1847.

From Pennsylvania Harry Wade freighted into Illinois and finally moved his family to Will County in that state. There one more child was born to Harry and Mary: *Richard Angus,* October 19, 1844.

About 1847 the Wades traded their farm near Joliet, Illinois, for an ox team and traveled into Missouri where they lived about a year.

It was this family of four children and their parents that left Missouri on April 1, 1849, for the gold fields of California. They were destined to be the only immigrants to bring a wagon and ox team across the Great American Desert and through Death Valley to Los Angeles. This wagon and team was used to freight from San Pedro to Los Angeles until enough money was accumulated to carry the family to the mines.

Soon after leaving Salt Lake it became necessary for Harry Wade to scout ahead for water, stockfeed and a route passable for his wagon. The teaming then was taken over by 14-year-old Harry George who followed that vocation until he died at the age of seventy-six years. In scouting, Harry Wade rode the family saddle mare, named Pet. All of the rest of the time she was led behind the wagon and carried an English riding saddle.

There has been some misunderstanding as to why Harry Wade did not travel and camp with the other parties. There were two reasons. The first was that Harry was a man of very fixed opinions and handled his team as he would have handled a coach and four for the King. Therefore, he was very unpopular with others in the train. They were not friendly to him. The second reason was that Wade was a mature man with fourteen years of experience in freighting over the frontier 75

Sheldon Young, the Jay Hawk ex-sailor who kept a "log" of his journey from Salt Lake to Rancho San Francisquito.
Photo courtesy of Huntington Library and now in Bear State Library.

trails of America. Most of the Jay Hawks, who broke most of the trail across what now is Utah, Nevada and Death Valley were "school boys" and had all to learn.

Harry Wade rode ahead on Pet and benefited by the scouting and developing of water. Then he rode back and, making many cutoffs, guided Harry George to the spring, filled with clean water. In addition to all of this, the Wades carried 50 gallons of water in large cans. All of this efficiency and preparedness made the Wades much disliked by most of the other Death Valley '49ers. The result was that the Wades always camped at springs of clean, fresh water. This, also, failed to make them popular with those who scouted ahead.

Traveling over what later was to become a well-established road into the San Joaquin Valley, Harry Wade brought his family by way of Newhall, San Francisquito Canyon, Elizabeth Lake, Antelope Valley and Grapevine Canyon to Fine Gold Gulch on the Tuolumne River. Mining there for a few months and having all of his possessions stolen by the Chauchela Indians during the Indian War of 1850-'51, Harry Wade decided to quit mining and settle down on a good farm.

So the oxen were yoked, Rosie, the milch cow, and Pet, the saddle mare, were tied behind the wagon and the last journey was begun. Over Altamont Pass, down Niles Canyon to Mission San Jose and to Saratoga, the trail led. Camp was made under a large oak tree, but not for long. The place was alive with fleas. Late in the night camp was moved to another oak tree. That night, January 2, 1851, a covered wagon baby, *Mary Ann,* was born to Harry and Mary Wade.

This sketch of the Wade family has been presented in such detail because their story is remarkable in many respects: to travel by ox team across the continent; to enter the Valley of Death with twenty other wagons, which all were abandoned; to forge on to the mines over a road opened to wheeled vehicles only a few months; and then to land at Saratoga with a covered wagon baby just about exhausts the possibilities of experiences for California Argonauts. The oak tree is said still to be standing. The Wades settled in February of 1851 at Alviso, where Harry began a freighting business which was continued by his eldest son long after Harry died at the age of 83. The Wades still (1960) own property at Alviso and many descendants still live nearby. Much more history of the Wades will be presented farther along on these pages.

As our little train of forty wagons has rolled out from Cobble Creek, near Salt Lake, has crossed the transverse foothill ridges of the Wasatch

Harry Wade, one of the most remarkable men of all the Death Valley parties. He was born in Rochester, England, married in London, and brought his wife and oldest child, Harry George Wade, to America by sailing vessel. He, his wife and Harry George came by ox team from New York City to Saratoga, California, by way of Pennsylvania, Illinois, Iowa, Missouri, Utah, Death Valley, Los Angeles, Grapevine Pass, San Joaquin Valley, Mariposa mines, Altamont Pass and San Jose, having a child born at Saratoga before they moved out of the wagon. Three children were born in Pennsylvania.

Photo courtesy of Mrs. J. Q. White, daughter of Almira Wade and now in Bear State Library.

Range, has passed Lake Sevier and has dropped down the canyon from Mount Misery into the canyon of Beaver Dam Wash, it is best that we introduce more of those Argonauts, some of whom were to leave their bones bleaching on the desert and mountains around Death Valley.

Reverend James Welsh Brier was born near Dayton, Ohio, September 11, 1814. He died at Lodi, California, November 2, 1898. The Briers left Iowa City, Iowa, on their journey to California.

Juliette W. Brier was born at Bennington, Vermont, in September of 1813. She died at Lodi, California, May 26, 1913, aged almost one hundred years, after having spanned the entire continent by ox team. She stood the terrible trip across the Nevada and California Deserts and through Death Valley better than any other person. Weighing one hundred and fifteen pounds at the beginning of the journey, she lost almost no weight, while some men lost more than one hundred pounds.

Christopher Columbus Brier was born September 11, 1841, in Indiana. He died in Oakland, California, December 7, 1907. Afoot, Columbus drove the loose oxen belonging to the Briers across much of the Nevada and California Deserts.

John Welsh Brier was born May 28, 1843, in Michigan. He became a prominent California clergyman. He died at Lodi, California, February 14, 1914.

Kirk White Brier was born May 5, 1845, and died at Sacramento, California, in January of 1883. It was thought by some of the Brier family that Kirk's early death was due to the hardships endured in crossing the Great American Desert.

Asabel Bennett was from Mineral Point, Wisconsin. He was born about 1807 and died April 22, 1891, at Idaho Falls, Idaho.

Sarah Dilley Bennett died in 1857 near Moss Landing, California, undoubtedly from the effects of her terrible struggle through Panamint, Argus, Slate and San Gabriel mountain ranges and across the Panamint, Searles, Indian Wells and Antelope valleys to reach Rancho San Francisquito near present Newhall. She is buried in an unmarked grave in the old Moss Landing Cemetery.

George Bennett was born in June, 1841, so was eight years of age when the journey to California was begun. Instead of being younger than Melissa, as generally has been though, he was older. About 1862 he accompanied his father to Salt Lake. About 1880 he returned to California. When he passed on March 10, 1884, he was living in Wilmington with his sister, Martha (Bennett) Johnson.

Melissa Bennett was above five years of age when she was brought 79

Mrs. Harry Wade, Mary Reynolds Leach, at one time governess to the children of the French Ambassador to England, and who accompanied her husband by covered wagon from New York City to Alviso, California. Mary experienced everything a pioneer mother could experience. When the Sioux Indians stole her favorite cast iron kettle, she went into their camp at midnight, crawled under the side of a tepee and stole it back. Before they settled at Alviso, her last child was born in a covered wagon under an oak tree near present Saratoga.

80   Photo courtesy of Mrs. J. Q. White and now in Bear State Library.

through Death Valley and over the Panamint and Argus ranges of mountains. She retained only two remembrances of that dreadful journey. As she rode by on the ox, Old Crump, she could remember having seen the body of Mr. Fish where it lay among the rocks, unburied. She could also remember that when they were out of all food except dry ox meat, stringy and hard as a stick of wood, her mother gave her and her little sister, Martha, tallow candles to chew on. She married Judge Rolfe of San Bernardino, died when she was twenty-four years of age and left an infant girl, later Mrs. Agnes Lindner of San Bernardino.

Martha Bennett was about one year of age when her parents started to California. She married William Johnson. She is buried in Wilmington, California.

Jean Baptiste Arcan was of French Basque descent. He was born April 14, 1813, and died at Santa Cruz, California, September 15, 1869. He is buried in the beautiful tree and shrub-covered Evergreen Cemetery at Santa Cruz. According to descendants the name is correctly spelled and accented, Arcan.

Abigail Harriett (Ericsen) Arcan was of Danish parentage. She died at Santa Cruz, California, February 24, 1891, and is buried beside her husband. Mrs. Arcan's ancestry spoils one good Death Valley story. It was not her French love for finery which caused Mrs. Arcan to load herself with such when she left the Bennett Long Camp. It was her Danish sense of economy. She stated that she wasn't going to leave silks and satins out there for those "Piute" Indians to carry away.

Charles E. Arcan was born in Illinois in 1846. He became a famous swimming instructor and life guard at Neptune Baths in Santa Cruz. He is buried beside his parents.

"Captain" Culverwell was thought to have been a seafaring man. Shortly before he started to California he was employed in a government office in Washington, D.C. He died about eight miles south of the Tule Spring Camp in Death Valley in January, 1850.

William Lewis Manly was born at St. Albans, Vermont, April 6, 1820, and died at San Jose, California, February 5, 1903. He was the author of *Death Valley in '49*, the most detailed account ever published about the Death Valley immigrant parties of '49.

John Haney Rogers, or "Giant John" as he sometimes was called by the '49ers, was from Tennessee. He was a butcher by trade and accompanied William Lewis Manly from the Missouri River to Death Valley. He was on Manly's noted journey from Death Valley to Los Angeles after supplies for the Bennett and Arcan families. He has been the 81

Harry George Wade, born in London, England, December 18, 1835. He was fourteen years of age when he drove the Wade ox teams from Division Spring to Los Angeles via Death Valley, the only '49er to take a wagon through that desolate sink. He freighted and operated a stage from Alviso to Guadalupe, Gilroy, Almaden, San Jose and other stations in the Santa Clara Valley. He was the father of Mrs. Margaret (Wade) Higgins of San Jose. The stage that he operated now is in the historical collection of Wells Fargo Bank in San Francisco.

Photo courtesy of Mrs. J. Q. White and now in Bear State Library.

forgotten man of the Death Valley '49ers. All trace of him was lost from 1854 until 1895 when Manly found him living with a life-long friend near Merced, California, an almost blind cripple, stumping about with the aid of two canes. He had inhaled mercury fumes while retorting amalgam in the gold mines and had lost both of his feet at the instep. He died soon after Manly visited him and is buried at Merced.

Silas Helmer and *S. S. Abbott* were ox drivers for Bennett. They left Bennett before they reached Death Valley and proceeded toward the California mines afoot. Nothing was heard of them afterward.

Of the Mississippi boys, to whom Rev. Brier had attached himself, little is known. Two of them, *Crumpton* and *Masterson*, were traveling with the Brier mess when they camped at the Indian village in the mesquite thicket in Panamint Valley. They were dissatisfied that Mrs. Brier was rationing supplies and demanded that they be given all they wanted to eat. Mrs. Brier gave them what flour they had left. This they cooked into hard, unleavened cakes and tramped alone out across the Panamint Valley. Later Mrs. Brier saw them in the most agonizing stages of starvation, one of them, she later wrote, "with tears streaming down his cheeks, begging for the entrails of a crow."

Besides Masterson and Crumpton there were two *Turner brothers,* three negro slaves, *Tom, Joe* and *Little West*; and *"Captain" Towne*. It was for this last party that Towne Pass was named.

A group of Georgians, also known as the Bug Smashers, is mentioned many times by the Jay Hawks and other writers. They are stated to be miners and to have located the famous Gunsight Lead in the Panamint Range. Their captain, *James Martin*, is the only member whose name has been preserved. L. Dow Stevens wrote that they numbered about twenty men. The mystery of what happened to the unnamed members of this party has given rise to many stories of perished '49ers.

About 1890 William Lewis Manly located in Fresno, California, one *Edward Croker,* who gave him a list of persons who accompanied him when he traveled through Death Valley with the '49ers. It consisted of *"Captain" Nat Ward, James Woods, John D. Martin, Fred Carr* and *"Old French"* or *"Frenchy"*. These are all the names not already listed that Croker could remember of twenty-one who, he claimed, traveled in his party over Walker's Pass to the mines.

The most mysterious of all parties of Death Valley '49ers is an almost legendary one known as the *Savage-Pinney* party from the fact that those two named were the only ones known to survive of the ten or eleven who tramped out of the Nevada desert into California. The 83 names of the missing are listed as follows: *John Adams, Wiley Webster, Charles McDermet* and others named *Allen, Lemoore, Baker* and two of the name *Ware*. In the mines Savage reported to a Jay Hawk that they ran out of food and cast lots to see who would be shot and eaten until only he and Pinney were left and that they were guided to Owens, or probably to Owens Little Lake and over Walker's Pass, by friendly Indians.

The mystery surrounding what actually happened to these missing '49ers also has given rise to many tales of perished groups of men. Most common of these is that nine dried-up bodies were found in Death Valley by Governor Blasdel of Nevada about 1860. Wm. Rice in 1898 found in Death Valley a man who claimed he helped bury them on the north side of the gulch at Hot Springs, below Gold Hill in Death Valley, and that, when found, their canteens still had some water in them. This is the only account that this writer has heard of the findings of a perished group of '49ers that bears any possibility of verification.

In addition to the above, mention has been made of other persons who at one time or another were in contact with the parties already listed. Most definite of these are *Loomis St. John* and a man named *Patrick*, who had served in the Mexican War. They traveled with the Briers and aided with their cattle westward from a point in Indian Wells Valley. According to Wm. Rice, who was born near Visalia, California, in the 1860's and who was a pioneer mining engineer in Death Valley, both of these last named settled near Visalia, St. John's branch of the Kaweah River having been named for Loomis St. John. Loomis St. John participated in the election held on July 10, 1852 when Tulare County was formed. He was elected Justice of the Peace in Tulare County in 1852 and soon after became an Associate Justice of the Court of Sessions. He was wounded by an Indian arrow on Tule River in the Indian War of 1856. No trace of St. John has been found following this last date.

Others named are *William Nesbit, John Morse, John Goller, David Funk, Alexander Ewing* and his son *John C. Ewing, Deacon D. Arms, Harry Vance, Robert Price, Norman Taylor* and *Alexander Benson*.

It has also been stated that in Indian Wells Valley one unnamed man was run out of camp by the Jay Hawks because he suggested cannibalism.

The Panamint Indians have consistently reported that soon after the Jay Hawks crossed north of the Panamints they found the dead body of a white man with a broken leg and a bullet hole through the skull.

84   John B. Colton also wrote of *"four Dutchmen"*. Allowing that

Wolfgang Tauber and John Goller may account for two of these, there are still two unaccounted for.

The above list is almost certain to contain no duplicate names but, on the contrary, it is almost as certain to be incomplete. From it we know that probably more than ninety and possibly as many as one hundred and thirteen Argonauts of '49 left the Hunt party at Division Spring in present southwest Utah and plunged blindly into the trackless waste of the Great American Desert, certainly four and possibly thirteen of them, to leave their bones bleaching on the arid plains and mountains in and surrounding Death Valley.

CHAPTER SIX

THE GREAT AMERICAN DESERT

At last the start was made down the steep canyon to a point near where the town of Acoma, Nevada, now is located. There teams were doubled and the wagons were hauled to the rim of the great desert plateau; then all parties struck out in a northwesterly direction. They followed O. K. Smith on the route of the trail which had been sketched on the Frémont map.

O. K. Smith soon was out of sight. One account states that he and the small party of Mormons who accompanied him continued on their northwest route only a few days and then cut east, struck the Old Spanish Trail, and traveled to the mines ahead of the party under Jefferson Hunt. Another account states that Smith fell in behind Hunt, became confused, missed the trail and, in a starved condition, arrived in Los Angeles months after the Hunt party reached San Bernardino.

William Rice, who gathered much data concerning the Death Valley parties of '49, and who had his information from pioneers who had known O. K. Smith, stated that the party had no serious trouble, crossed Walker's Pass into the San Joaquin Valley and arrived at the mines in Mariposa in good condition.

Regardless of the experiences of the party led by Smith, those who started to follow Smith had trouble enough to satisfy the most hardy '49ers. In a few days their die was cast. The road back was impassable and there was nothing left for them to do but to continue across the rocky mountain ranges and drylake-studded deserts of southwestern Utah, now the state of Nevada, hoping that nature would be kind enough to provide them a way through. Today in reading of their heroic struggle, one is impressed with the hopelessness of their situation.

Regarding the improvidence of these '49ers William Rice had the following to say:

> "They had no containers in which to carry more than drinking water for the women and children: Manly made himself a canteen by tying and sewing together two small

powder cans. They had provided no facilities of any kind for carrying water for their stock. More than this, we have no information that they were at any time resourceful enough to carry water in the stomachs of their perished oxen."

In addition, their improvidence regarding the use and conservation of drinking water soon becomes apparent to one who reads about Death Valley '49ers. They made no intelligent use of the Indians who occupied almost every portion of the great desert across which they were traveling. A few presents of coffee, sugar or beads would have caused the Indians to lead them to water or to the trail of the Hunt party which was, during most of the time, only a few days' travel south of them. News of such treatment would have traveled days ahead of them and would have paved the way for their safe and speedy passage to California.

Instead of cultivating the acquaintance and friendship of the Indians, they stole corn, squashes and other foodstuffs from them and gave them every reason to keep out of sight. Indians were following the party at all times.

"Once the Jay Hawks," wrote Sheldon Young, "caught two Pi Ute Indians [who led them to water] . . . let one of them go and kept the other for a while. Caught another in the evening." After having been scared almost to death the last of these "Pi Utes" escaped.

The Indians actually were trying to help them. At the head of Searles Lake Valley a small group of Indians presented themselves to Jay Hawk Deacon Richards, led him to the water which the '49ers called Providence Spring and unquestionably saved the lives of some forty struggling, famished persons.

In January of 1898 Harrison B. Franz wrote to his brother Jay Hawk, Alonzo C. Clay:

"I have just received your kind letter remembering me of the Reunion of the Jay Hawks' trials and tribulations of '49.—I remember very distinctley that I was one of them. I have been Jayhawking ever since '49.—My health is good. I work hard, have not an ache or pain in my body, and just begin to realize that I am an olde man for the simple reason that I cant run a hundred yards in 11 sec any more if I was on the Desert now and those Indians that run I and Clark 14 miles was after me I think I would have to thro in the spung."

In 1900 Franz still could remember running from the Indians. He wrote to John B. Colton:

> "Well, John, I'm still mining, as I have been for the last fifty years and still manage to keep the wolf from the door. I cannot run as fast as I could when the Piutes were after me. I have 3 good rifles and 3 good gray-hounds and am still raaring and taring up and down Barriver."

This brush with the "Piutes" was remembered by many of the Death Valley '49ers; but for records of it, as well as for all definite details of the trip from Meadow Valley to Death Valley, we are indebted to William Lewis Manly, who left the following concerning the start across the Great American Desert:

> "At the organization [for the journey across the desert] Jim Martin was chosen captain. Those who were rejected were Rev. J. W. Brier and his family, J. B. Arcane and family, and Mr. A. Bennett and family; Mr. Brier would not stay put out, but forced himself in, and said he was going with the rest, and so he did. But the other families remained behind. [Manly had forgotten the Wades.] I attended the meeting and heard what was said, but Mr. Bennett was my friend and had been faithful to me and my property when he knew not where I was, and so I decided to stand by him and his wife at all hazards.
>
> "As I had no team to drive, I took every opportunity to climb the mountains along the route, reaching the highest elevations even if they were several miles from the trail. I sometimes remained out all night. I took Mr. Arcane's field glass with me and was thus able to see all there was of the country. I soon became satisfied that going north was not taking us in the direction we ought to go. I frequently told them so, but they still persisted in following on. I went to the leaders and told them we were going back toward Salt Lake again, not making any headway toward California. They insisted they were following the directions of Williams, the mountaineer; and they had not got as far north as he indicated. I told them, and Mr. Bennett and others that we must either turn west, or retrace our steps and get back into the

regular Los Angeles road again. In the morning we held another consultation and decided to turn west here, and leave the track we had been following.

"Off we turned at nearly right angles to our former course, to the west now, over a piece of table land that gave us little trouble in breaking our own road. When we camped, the oxen seemed very fond of a white weed that was very plenty, and some borrowed a good deal of trouble thinking that perhaps it might be poison. I learned afterwards that this plant was the nutritious white sage, which cattle eat freely, with good results. We now crossed a low range and a small creek running south, and here were also some springs. Some corn had been grown here by the Indians. Pillars of sand stone, fifteen feet high and very slim were round about in several places and looked strange enough. The next piece of table land sloped to the east, and among the sage grew also a bunch of grass a foot high, which had seeds. The Indians had gathered the grass and made it in piles of one hundred pounds or so, and used it for food as I found by examining their camps.

"One day I climbed a high mountain where some pine grew, in order to get a view of the country. As I neared its base I came to a flat rock, perhaps fifty feet square. I heard some pounding noise as I came near, but whatever it was, it ceased on my approach. There were many signs of the rock being used as a camp, such as pine burrs, bones of various kinds of animals, and other remains of food which lay everywhere about and on the rock. Near the center was a small oblong stone fitted into a hole. I took it out and found it covered with a fine well of water about three feet deep and was thus protected against any small animal being drowned in it. I went on up the mountain and from the top I saw that the land west of us looked more and more barren.

"The second night the brave Jayhawkers who had been so firm in going north hove in sight in our rear. They had at last concluded to accept my advice and had come over our road quite rapidly. We all camped together that night, and next morning they took the lead again. After crossing a small range they came to a basin which seemed to have no outlet, and was very barren. Some of the boys in advance of the teams passed over this elevation and were going quite rapidly over the almost level plain which sloped into the basin, when they saw among the bunches of sage brush behind them a small party of Indians following their road, not very far off, but still out of bow and arrow range. The boys were suddenly able to take much longer steps than usual and a little more rapidly too, and swinging round toward the teams as soon as possible, for they already had some fears that an arrow might be sticking in their backs in an unpleasantly short space of time, for the Indians were good travelers. When they came in sight of the wagons, the Indians vanished as quickly as if they had gone into a hole, with no sig remaining, except a small dog which greatly resembled a prairie wolf, and kept a safe distance away. No one could imagine where the fellows went so suddenly.

"We drove to the west side of this basin and camped near the foot of a low mountain. The cattle were driven down into the basin where there was some grass, but at camp we had only water in our kegs.

"Some of the boys climbed the mountain on the north but found no springs; coming down a cañon they found some rain water in a basin in the rocks and all took a good drink. Lew West lay down and swallowed all he could and then told the boys to kill him for he never would feel so good again. They finished the pool, it was so small, before they left. In going down the cañon they saw an Indian dodge behind some big rocks, and searching, they found him in a cave as still as a dead man. They pulled him out and made him go with them, and tried every way to find out from him where they were and where Owen's Lake was, as they had been told the lake was on their route.

"But he proved to be no wiser than a man of mud, and they led him along to camp, put a red flannel shirt on him to cover his nakedness, and made him sleep between two white men so he could not get away easily. In the morning they were more successful, and he showed us a small ravine four miles away which had water in it, enough for our use, and we moved up and camped there, while boys and the Indian started over a barren, rocky mountain, and when over on the western slope they were led to a water hole on a steep rocky

91

cliff where no one but an Indian would ever think of looking for water. They took out their cups and had a good drink all around, then offered the Indian some, but he disdained the civilized way, and laying down his bow and arrows took a long drink directly out of the pool.

"He was so long in getting a good supply that the boys almost forgot him as they were gazing over the distant mountain and discussing the prospects, till attracted by a slight noise they looked and saw Mr. Indian going down over the cliffs after the fashion of a mountain sheep, and in a few bounds he was out of sight. They could not have killed him if they had tried, the move was so sudden and unlooked for. They had expected the fellow to show them the way to Owen's Lake, but now their guide was gone, and left nothing to remember him by except his bow and arrows. So they returned to their wagons not much wiser than before.

"All kinds of game was now very scarce, and so seldom seen that the men got tired of carrying their guns, and grew fearless of enemies. A heavy rifle was indeed burdensome over so long a road when there was no frequent use for it. The party kept rolling along as fast as possible but the mountains and valleys grew more barren and water more scarce all the time. When found, the water would be in holes at the outlet of some cañon, or in little pools which had filled up with the rain that had fallen on the higher ground.

"Not a drop of rain had fallen on us since we started on this cut-off, and every night was clear and warm. The elevated parts of the country seemed to be isolated buttes, with no running streams between them but instead, dry lakes with a smooth clay bed, very light in color and so hard that the track of an ox could not be seen in its glittering surface. At that distance those clay beds looked like water shining in the sun and were generally about three times as far as anyone would judge, the air was so clear. This mirage, or resemblance to water was so perfect as often to deceive us, and almost to our ruin on one or two occasions."

The dry lakes and mirages still deceive travelers who for the first time drive over the deserts of southwestern Nevada. After making several dry camps the Jay Hawks once late in the afternoon came in

92

sight of a large lake which they found contained no water. After several such disappointments, mirages and dry lakes fooled them no more. They were to find that three out of five of the water holes they did discover between Meadow Valley and Rancho San Francisquito were salt or alkaline and that some actually were poison. In this early portion of the journey through what then was southwestern Utah, the Jay Hawks several times went for three days and once for *nine* days between water holes. Following a few days behind and profiting by the experience and explanations of the Jay Hawks, the other parties were more fortunate. But most of their good forune was due to the explorations and advice of William Lewis Manly. Let us read what he wrote about this early portion of their desert wanderings:

"I took Arcane's field glass and took pains to ascend all the high buttes within a day's walk of the road, all this enabled me to get a good survey of the country north and west. I would sometimes be gone two or three days with no luggage but my canteen and gun. I was very cautious in regard to Indians, and tried to keep on the safe side of surprises. I would build a fire about dark and then travel on till I came to a small washed place and lie down and stay till morning, so if Mr. Indian did come to my fire he would not find anyone to kill.

"One day I was going up a wide ravine leading to the summit, and before I reached the highest part, I saw a smoke curl up before me. I took a side ravine and went cautiously, bowed down pretty low so no one could see me, and when near the top of the ridge and about one hundred yards of the fire I ventured to raise slowly up and take a look to see how many there were in camp; I could see but two and as I looked across the ravine an Indian woman seemed looking at me also, but I was so low she could only see the top of my head, and I sank down again out of sight.

"I crawled further up so as to get a better view, and when I straightened up again she got a full view of me. She instantly caught her infant off its little pallet made of a small piece of thin wood covered with rabbit skin, and putting the baby under her arm, and giving a smart jerk to a small girl that was crying to the top of her voice, she bounded off and

93

fairly flew up the gentle slope toward the summit, the girl following very close.

"The woman's long black hair stood out as she rushed along, looking over her shoulder every instant as if she expected to be slain. The mother flying with her children, untrammeled with any of the arts of fashion was the best natural picture I ever looked upon, and wild in the extreme. No living artist could do justice to the scene as the lady of the desert, her little daughter and her babe, passed over the summit out of sight. I followed, but when I reached the highest summit, no living person could be seen.

"I looked the country over with my glass. The region to the north was black, rocky, and very mountainous. I looked some time and then concluded I had better not go any further that way, for I might be waylaid and filled with arrows at some unexpected moment. We saw Indian signs almost every day, but as none of them ever came to our camp, it was safe to say they were not friendly. I now turned back and examined the Indian woman's camp. She had only fire enough to make a smoke. Her conical shaped basket left behind, contained a few poor arrows and some cactus leaves, from which the spines had been burned, and there lay the little pallet where the baby was sleeping. It was bare looking kitchen for hungry folks.

"I now went to the top of a high butte and scanned the country very carefully, especially to the west and north, and found it very barren. There were no trees, no fertile valleys nor anything green. Away to the west some mountains stood out clear and plain, their summits covered with snow. This I decided was our objective point: Very little snow could be seen elsewhere, and between me and the snowy mountains lay a low, black rocky range, and a wide level plain, that had no signs of water, as I had learned them in our trip thus far across the country. The black range seemed to run nearly north and south, and to the north and northwest the country looked volcanic, black and desolate.

"As I looked and thought, I believed that we were much farther from a fertile region than most of our party had any idea of. Such of them as had read Fremont's travels, and most of them going to California had fortified themselves before starting by reading Fremont, said that the mountains were near California and were fertile from their summits down to the sea, but that to the east of the mountains it was a desert region for hundreds of miles. As I explained it to them, and so they soon saw for themselves, they believed that the snowy range ahead of us was the last range to cross before we entered the long-sought California, and it seemed not far off, and prospect quite encouraging.

"Our road had been winding around among the buttes which looked like the Indian baskets turned upside down on the great barren plain. What water we found was in small pools in the wash-out places near the foothills at the edge of the valley, probably running down the ravines after some storm. There were dry lake beds scattered around over the plain, but it did not seem as if there had ever been volume of water enough lately to force itself out so far into the plain as these lakes were.

"All the lakes appeared about the same, the bed white and glistening in the sun, which made it very hard for the eyes, and so that a man in passing over it made no visible track. It looked as if it one time might have been a smooth bed of plastic mortar, and had hardened in the sun. It looked as if there must have been water there sometime, but we had not seen a drop, or a single cloud; every day was clear and sunny, and very warm, and at night no stars forgot to shine.

"Our oxen began to look bad, for they had poor food. Grass had been very scarce, and now when we unyoked them and turned them out they did not care to look around much for something to eat. They moved slowly and cropped disdainfully the dry scattering shrubs and bunches of grass from six inches to a foot high. Spending many nights and days on such dry food and without water they suffered fearfully, and though fat and sleek when we started from Salt Lake, they now looked gaunt and poor, and dragged themselves slowly along, poor faithful servants of mankind. No one knew how long before we might have to kill some of them to get food to save our own lives.

"We now traveled several days down the bed of a broad ravine, which led to a southwest direction. There seemed to be a continuous range of mountains on the south, but to the

95

north was a level plain with scattered buttes, and what we had all along called dry lakes, for up to this time we had seen no water in any of them. I had carried my rifle with me every day since we took this route, and though I was an experienced hunter, a professional one if there be such a thing, I had killed only one rabbit, and where no game lived I got as hungry as other folks.

"Our line soon brought us in sight of a high butte which stood apparently about 20 miles south of our route, and I determined to visit and climb it to get a better view of things ahead. I walked steadily all day and reached the summit about dusk. I wandered around among the big rocks, and found a projecting cliff where I would be protected from enemies, wind or storm, and here I made my camp. While the light lasted I gathered a small stock of fuel, which consisted of a stunted growth of sage and other small shrubs, dry, but not dead, and with this I built a little fire, Indian fashion, and sat down close to it.

"Here was a good chance for undisturbed meditation and some way I could not get around doing a little meditating as I added a new bit of fuel now and then' to the small fire burning at my side. I thought it looked dark and troublesome before us. I took a stone for a pillow with my hand on it for a cushion, and lying down close under the sheltering rock I went to sleep, for I was very tired. I woke soon from being cold, for the butte was pretty high, and so I busied myself the remainder of the night in adding little sticks to the fire, which gave me some warmth, and thus in solitude I spent the night. I was glad enough to see the day break over the eastern mountains, and light up the vast barren country I could see on every hand around me. When the sun was fairly up I took a good survey of the situation, and it seemed to me as if pretty near all creation was in sight.

"North and west was a level plain, fully one hundred miles wide it seemed, and from anything I could see it would not afford a traveler a single drink in the whole distance or give a poor ox many mouthfuls of grass. On the western edge it was bounded by a low, black and rocky range extending nearly north and south for a long distance [Funeral Range] and no pass through it which I could see, and beyond this range still another one [Telescope Peak], and lowest place was on the north side, which we had named Martin's Pass [Towne Pass] and had been trying so long to reach. This high peak, covered with snow, glistened to the morning sun, and as the air was clear from clouds or fog, and no dust or haze to obscure the view, it seemed very near."

Here Manly brings the now alarmed parties to a point which we probably can identify as Oak Spring Butte. This is the only point from which Manly could have looked northwest across lava-covered Crater Flat and also have seen Charleston Peak, Emigrant Valley and Timpahute Dry Lake; this last was the point towards which the wagon train was traveling as he watched it through Arcan's telescope. (It is proper to explain that Mr. Manly spelled the name *Arcan* as it was then pronounced by members of the Arcan family, to rhyme with *cane*, although they never placed a final *e* on it. They now pronounce the name to rhyme with *pan.)*

The entire train camped together that night beside Timpahute Dry Lake, the last time that all parties were together on their westward trek.

Manly's view from the summit of Oak Spring Butte made him sick with despair. He continued in his written account:

"Prospects now seemed to me so hopeless, that I heartily wished I was not in duty bound to stand by the women and small children who could never reach the land of bread without our assistance. If I was in the position that some of them were who had only themselves to look after, I could pick up my knapsack and gun and go off, feeling I had no dependent ones to leave behind. But as it was, I felt I should be morally guilty of murder if I should forsake Mr. Bennett's wife and children, and the family of Mr. Arcane with whom I had been thus far associated. It was a dark line of thought but I always felt better when I got around to the determination, as I always did, to stand by my friends, their wives and children let come what might.

"I could see with my glass the train of wagons moving slowly over the plain toward what looked to me like a large lake. I made a guess of the point they would reach by night, and then took a straight course for it all day long in steady

97

travel. It was some time after dark, and I was still a quarter mile from the camp fires, where in the bed of a cañon I stepped into some mud, which was a sign of water. I poked around in the dark for a while and soon found a little pool of it, and having been without a drop of it for two days, I lay down and took a hasty drink. It did not seem to be very clean, but it was certainly wet, which was the main thing just then.

"The next morning I went to the pond of water, and found the oxen had been watered there. They stirred up the mud a good deal and had drunk off about all the clean part, which seemed to refresh them very much. I found the people in the camp on the edge of the lake I had seen from the mountain, and fortunately it contained about a quarter of an inch of water. They had dug some holes here, which filled up, and they were using this water in the camp.

"The ambitious mountain-climbers of our party had by this time, abandoned that sort of work, and I was left alone to look about and try to ascertain the character of the road they were to follow. It was a great deal to do to look out for food for the oxen and for water for the camp, and besides all this, it was plain there were Indians about, even if we did not see them. There were many signs, and I had to be always on the lookout to out-general them.

"When the people found I was in camp this night, they came around to our wagons to know what I had seen and found, and what the prospects were ahead. Above all they wanted to know how far it was, in my opinion to the end of our journey. I listened to all their inquiries and told them plainly what I had seen, and what I thought of the prospect. I did not like to tell them the whole truth about it for fear it might dampen their spirits, but being pressed for an opinion I told them in plain words that it would at least be another month before their journey would be ended. They seemed to think I ought to be pretty good authority, and if I was not mistaken, the oxen would get very poor and provisions very scarce before we could pull through so long. I was up at day break and found Mr. Bennett sitting by the fire. About the first thing he said:—'Lewis, if you please, I don't want you hereafter to express your views so openly and emphatically as you did last night about our prospects.

" 'Last night when I went to bed, I found Sarah [Bennett's wife] crying and when pressed for the cause, she said she had heard your remarks on the situation, and that if Lewis said so, it must be correct, for he knows more about it than all of you. She felt that she and the children must starve.' "

It was in this valley that despair fell on many of the band. Some of the travelers decided to leave their wagons and strike directly west across the rough, rocky mountains to Owen's Lake and Walker's Pass. Although there had been much confusion about where this and the subsequent breakups occurred, it seems probable that the Savage-Pinney party left their wagons near Timpahute Dry Lake and struck afoot westward to the head of Fortymile Canyon which appeared to the west as an open way in the direction they wanted to travel.

At least one authority has separated the Savage-Pinney party from the rest shortly after the entire group followed O. K. Smith and his Mormons into the Desert. William Rice, who will be quoted a number of times on these pages and who had much of his information from Indians of the Nevada desert, stated that the parties all traveled the same route as far as Timpahute Dry Lake. Perhaps the Savage-Pinney party was ahead of the rest and left their wagons before the rest reached that point.

John Rogers, in the *Merced Star* newspaper article of April 26, 1894, gives some interesting details of the early travel on this Utah desert. Note that he places sixty wagons with the cutoff parties:

"There was one man in our party who claimed to have a 'way-bill' through the mountains to California in two weeks."

Rogers also stated that ninety wagons followed the man with the "way-bill" but that a portion later returned to Hunt, leaving sixty wagons on the desert cut-off.

According to Rogers, the party left Salt Lake on October 1, and on December 1 came the first split-up of the desert party:

"The company being dissatisfied sixteen wagons were piled up and burned. [If they were traveling with the Jay Hawks, the log of Sheldon Young would place them somewhere in Emigrant Valley north of Timpahute Dry Lake.] Next morning the owners of the wagons packed their traps on their cattle and drove off."

Ten days later a second split-up occurred and there remained of the party Rogers was with only three wagons, those of "Ahart, Arcane, and Bennett."

The first of these splits probably occurred when the Martin party left afoot. The Jay Hawks had left the train before the second split-up occurred. Probably this last was when the Briers left their wagons and started afoot into the head of Furnace Creek Wash.

Jim Martin had pointed out a supposed pass in the towering range a hundred miles or more to the west. It lay north of a great snow-capped peak which we know today as Telescope Peak. By common usage this gap at the north end of the Panamint Range became known among the '49ers as Martin's Pass. Today it is named Towne Pass.

Traveling faster afoot, the Savage-Pinney party was not seen again by any of the others. In fact, only Savage and Pinney have been reported by any of the '49ers.

Wagons, probably Martin's, also were abandoned at Kane Springs, southwest of Timpahute Dry Lake. In 1893 W. S. Barton and a party of miners went in search of the Lost Gunsight Lead. They found the camp site, which they identified as Martin's, just as it had been left forty-three years before. The rocks were in place where they had placed their kettle to cook. Barton found a picket pin and a blackened silver dollar lost by members of the Martin party. Barton also wrote that when the settlement of Pioche, Nevada, was established, the Piutes burned these wagons and carried the iron parts to Pioche. The Piute squaws rolled the tires from Martin's wagon wheels to that place and sold them. Iron was so scarce in that district that they brought a big price and well they might after the Indian women had rolled them more than seventy-five miles.

In 1891, Dr. T. S. Palmer, while a member of a surveying party in Death Valley, was shown some pieces of old wagons which he was told were from Kane Springs and were parts of the Jay Hawks' wagons, abandoned more than forty years before.

The camp at Timpahute Dry Lake was one of frantic desperation. What remained of the train split at least three ways. In the morning, after the cattle had drunk their fill of the shallow, muddy water, the
Jay Hawks started south-westward down Emigrant Valley and cut

across westward into the head of Fortymile Canyon. Young and still the most optimistic of all the Death Valley '49ers, the Jay Hawks were determined to head straight for Martin's Pass and Owen's Lake. In this grinding struggle to gain time they were to encounter the first serious test of their endurance. They were nine days and nights without finding a waterhole and were saved only by snow storms, when they melted snow for both their cattle and themselves.

It was in this portion of Nevada that the Jay Hawks found the trail too rough for their wagons so they cut them in half and made carts of them. Some writers have stated that the Jay Hawks cut their wagons in half in or near Ash Meadows. The reason for cutting their wagons was that the carts could be taken over much rougher country than could four-wheeled vehicles. Fortymile Canyon and the pass leading into it comprised the most difficult territory the Jay Hawks attempted with four-wheeled vehicles and there they probably found the greatest need to make carts. Margaret (Wade) Higgins told this author that her father, Harry George Wade, fourteen-year-old driver of the Wade ox team while his father scouted horseback for shortcuts, on several occasions stated that the Wades by-passed the area where the Jay Hawks cut their wagons into carts and where the Briers abandoned their wagons and walked out. As the Bennetts, Arcans, Earharts and Wades ended up together at Tule Springs in Death Valley, it is probable that they took the same bypass of Fortymile Canyon and Ash Meadows.

Leaving a dry camp, probably in Pahroc Valley, the Jay Hawks traveled an estimated sixteen miles southwest. In this locality they made their first mistake in their contact with the Indians. It was here that they seized three Indians who were foolish enough to come within reach. One of these they held captive but he later escaped. If they had made the Indians a few presents there would have been in the Jay Hawk camp a dozen or more willing guides. This would have ended the serious troubles of all the desert parties.

The above information is from the "log" of sailor Jay Hawk, Sheldon Young, who kept a brief account of each day's travel, the existence or non-existence of wood, water, and the distance and direction traveled. Where his locations are definitely known, the distances he gives are generally too great—an understandable fault in one who was traveling under such trying conditions.

On the third of December Young wrote, "Had one ox driven off by the Piutes last night. Had bad roads, gravely roads. Southwest. Sixteen miles. This day had harsh, gravely roads, not much grass. Plenty of   101 water. Had a dry camp." This brought them to the north end of Emigrant Valley. Note that this was the second consecutive dry camp.

On December 5 the Jay Hawks traveled fourteen miles south. If we have them accurately located, they were traveling through Emigrant Valley—"No water."

On December 6 Young wrote, "Went five miles. Moved on, dry diggings. Grass plenty. No water. South course. Snowed." Note again that this was the fourth successive dry camp and that they were saved by snow which we know from other accounts was melted in order to obtain water for both men and oxen. Note too the stark effectiveness of Young's entry: not a word wasted. They are now at the northeast end of the Shoshone Range of mountains.

On December 7 they went twelve miles, "Had hard rocks, gravely roads. Grass very scarce. No water. A damned hard looking country." Has the reader ever seen that country? Yes? Then he knows what Young meant. This writer has flown over it and could not pick out a spot where he would be willing to be grounded. This day's travel brings the Jay Hawks into the head of Fortymile Canyon.

On December 8, according to Sheldon Young's log, the party bore southwest an estimated twelve miles.—"No grass or water. Had a dry camp." Note again, the sixth dry camp. What would have happened to this entire party during a summer month with the mercury at 120°? They were now at about the base of Timber Mountain.

On December 9 it snowed again—"No water." Dry camp number seven. Four miles west. They are now going slowly, weak from thirst, and hunger too, for, without water, they could not swallow the food they chewed. Here is where young John B. Colton left some of the one hundred pounds of weight he lost between Meadow Valley and Rancho San Francisquito, then often called Rancho del Valle.

On December 10: "Hard roads [no roads at all, not even a cow trail]. Plenty of Snow. No grass or water. West southwest course. Went ten miles and had a dry camp." Have you counted this last dry camp? Where would they now have been without that "plenty of snow"? They were now out of the mountains and about where Lathrop's Well now is located. But there then was no well. They started from a dry camp, and "Crossed a desert twelve miles, found wood, grass and water just in time to save our cattle. [None of these cattle would have been saved if they had not been traveling *down-hill* in Fortymile Canyon.] A number of our cattle gave out before getting them to water. Southwest."

They are now unmistakenly at Ash Meadows on the Amargosa River.

Sheldon Young's next entry proves our location, for he wrote on December 12, "Went three miles down stream, found better grass and laid in camp." And they rightly "laid in camp" for six days, eating the very last of their provisions, drinking water, feeding, watering and shoeing their oxen. They also killed two oxen and dried their meat.

The site of this camp is identified as Fairbanks Springs, about sixteen miles northeast of present Death Valley Junction. When Dad Fairbanks first went to that location, about 1895, there was a large pile of worn-out ox shoes near the spring.

Carter and Mecum explored and returned on the evening of December 18. They named this Amargosa Valley, Relief Valley. The reader does not need to be told why.

On December 19 they "rolled out of camp" and went eight miles south. They traveled twelve miles west on the twentieth, "This day left Relief Valley", and camped without water or feed.

December 21 the Jay Hawks went west six miles over bad roads down Furnace Creek Wash and with a dismal desert ahead, "No grass or water", and on December 22 we find them at Travertine Springs a half mile above the site of the present palacial Furnace Creek Inn. "Plenty of grass and springs of water." The next day they lay in camp, shoeing oxen and drying the meat of two oxen they had killed, looking out of a large canyon into an alkali valley—*Death Valley,* it soon was to become to them.

We leave the '49ers scattering over a large portion of what now is the southwestern portion of the state of Nevada, but which then was in the state of Utah, worrying and struggling harder than they had thought possible. They now had been on the trail from Salt Lake about thirty days, but they had only begun to struggle and to suffer. Their condition was to become worse and worse and it was to take twice as long again before they were to reach the Spanish settlements in California.

CHAPTER SEVEN

INTO CALIFORNIA

One of the interesting facts about the arrival of the Death Valley '49ers is that until they reached Rancho San Francisquito near present Newhall they were never certain that they were in California. They were passing through an entirely unsettled, uncharted country. A survey of the eastern boundary of California was not attempted until 1861. Even with the use of three camels, the U.S. Government survey party found itself in a serious condition and had to leave the region before the survey was completed.

Concerning the terrible hardships of the remaining groups in reaching the open country at the southwest end of Indian Springs Valley, the description left by William Lewis Manly is not only the best, but is almost the only one extant. Following is what he wrote in his book, *Death Valley in '49:*

"In the morning the Jayhawkers, and others of the train that were not considered strictly of our own party, yoked up and started due west across the level plain which I had predicted as having no water, and I really thought they would never live to get across the western border. Mr. Culverwell and Mr. Fish stayed with us, making another wagon in our train. We talked about the matter carefully. I did not think it possible to get across the plain in less than four or six days, and I did not believe there was a drop of water on the route. To the south of us was a mountain that now had considerable snow upon its summit, and some small pine trees. Doubtless we could find plenty of water at the base, but being due south, it was quite off our course. The prospects for reaching water were so much better in that way that we finally decided to go there rather than follow the Jayhawkers on their desolate tramp over the dry plain.

"So we turned up a cañon leading toward the mountain and had a pretty heavy up grade and a rough bed for a road.

Part way up we came to a high cliff and in its face were niches or cavities as large as a barrel or larger, and in some of them was balls of a glistening substance looking something like pieces of varigated candy stuck together. The balls were as large as small pumpkins. It was evidently food of some sort, and we found it sweet but sickish, and those who were so hungry as to break up one of the balls and divide it among the others, making a good meal of it, were a little troubled with nausea afterwards. I considered it bad policy to rob the Indians of any of their food, for they must be pretty smart people to live in this desolate country and find enough to keep them alive, and I was pretty sure we might count them as hostiles as they never came near our camp. Like other Indians they were probably revengeful, and might seek to have revenge on us for the injury. We considered it prudent to keep careful watch for them, so they might not surprise us with a volley of arrows.

"The second night we camped near the head of the cañon we had been following, but thus far there had been no water, and only some stunted sage brush for the oxen, which they did not like, and only ate it when near the point of starvation. They stood around the camp looking as sorry as oxen can. During the night a stray and crazy looking cloud passed over us and left its moisture on the mountain to the shape of a coat of snow several inches deep. When daylight came the oxen crowded around the wagons, shivering with cold, and licking up the snow to quench their thirst. We took pattern after them and melted snow to get water for ourselves.

"By the looks of our cattle it did not seem as if they could pull much, and light loads were advisable on this up grade. Mr. Bennett was a carpenter and had brought along some good tools in his wagon. These he reluctantly unloaded, and almost everything else except bedding and provisions, leaving them upon the ground, we rolled up the hills slowly, with loads as light as possible.

"Rogers and I went ahead with our guns to look out the way and find a good camping place. After a few miles we got out of the snow and out upon an incline, and in the bright clear morning air the foot of the snowy part of the mountain seemed near by and we were sure we could reach it before night. From here no guide was needed and Rogers and I, with our guns and canteens hurried on as fast as possible, when a camp was found we were to raise a signal smoke to tell them where it was. We were here, as before, badly deceived as to the distance, and we marched steadily and swiftly till nearly night before we reached the foot of the mountain.

"Here was a flat place in a table land and on it a low brush hut, with a small smoke near by, which we could plainly see as we were in the shade of the mountain, and that place lighted up by the nearly setting sun [now Indian Springs Ranch]. We looked carefully and satisfied ourselves there was but one hut, and consequently but few people could be expected. We approached carefully and cautiously, making a circuit around so as to get between the hut and the hill in case that the occupants should retreat in that direction.

"It was a long time before we could see any entrance to the wickiup, but we found it at last and approached directly in front, very cautiously indeed: We could see no one, and thought perhaps they were in ambush for us, but hardly probable, as we had kept closely out of sight. We consulted a moment and concluded to make an advance and if possible capture some one who could tell us about the country, as we felt we were completely lost. When within thirty yards a man poked out his head out of a doorway and drew it back again as quick as a flash.

"We kept out our guns at full cock and ready for use, and told Rogers to look out for arrows, for they would come now if ever. But they did not pull a bow on us, and the redman, almost naked came out and beckoned for us to come in which we did.

"We tried to talk with the fellow in the sign language but he could understand about as much as an oyster. I made a little basin in the ground and filled it with water from our canteens to represent a lake, then pointed in an inquiring way west and north, made signs of ducks and geese flying and squawking, but I did not seem to be able to get an idea into his head of what we wanted. I got thoroughly provoked at him and may have shown some signs of anger.

"During all this time a child or two in the hut squalled terribly, fearing I suppose they would all be murdered. We

107

might have lost our scalps under some circumstances, but we appeared to be fully the strangest party, and had no fear, for the Indian had no weapon about him and we had both guns and knives. The poor fellow was shivering with cold, and with signs of friendship, we fired off one of the guns which waked him up a little and he pointed to the gun and said 'Walker,' probably meaning the same good Chief Walker who had so fortunately stopped us in our journey down Green River. I understood from the Indian that he was not friendly to Walker, but to show that he was all right with us he went into the hut and brought out a handful of corn for us to eat. By the aid of a warm spring near by they had raised some corn here, and the dry stalks were standing around.

"As we were about to leave I told him we would come back next day and bring them some clothes if we could find any to spare, and then we shouldered our guns and went back toward the wagons, looking over our shoulders occasionally to see if we were followed. We walked fast down the hill and reached the camp about dark to find it a most unhappy one indeed.

"Mrs. Bennett and Mrs. Arcane were in heartrending distress. The four children were crying for water but there was not a drop to give them, and none could be reached before some time next day. The mothers were nearly crazy, for they expected the children would choke with thirst and die in their arms, and would rather perish themselves than suffer the agony of seeing their little ones gasp and slowly die. They reproached themselves as being the cause of all this trouble. For the love of gold they had left homes where hunger had never come, and often in sleep dreamed of the bounteous tables of their old homes only to be woefully disappointed in the morning. There was great gladness when John Rogers and I appeared in the camp and gave the mothers full canteens of water for themselves and little ones, and there was tears of joy and thankfulness upon their cheeks as they blessed us over and over again.

"The oxen fared very hard. The ground was made up of broken stone, and all that grew around there was a dry and stunted brush not more than six inches high, of which the poor animals took an occasional dainty bite, and seemed hardly able to drag along.

"It was only seven or eight miles to the warm spring and all felt better to know for a certainty that we would soon be safe again. We started early, even the women walked, so as to favor the poor oxen all we could. When within two miles of the water some of the oxen lay down and refused to rise again, so we had to leave them and a wagon, while the rest pushed on and reached the spring soon after noon. We took water and went back to the oxen left behind, and gave them some to drink. They were somewhat rested and got up, and we tried to drive them in without the wagons, but they were not inclined to travel without the yoke, so we put it on them and hitched to the wagon again. The yoke and the wagon seemed to brace them up a good deal, and they went along thus much better than when alone and scattered about, with nothing to lean upon.

"The warm spring [Indian Springs] was quite large and ran a hundred yards or more before the water sank down into the dry and thirsty desert. The dry cornstalks of last years crop, some small willows, sage brush, weeds and grass suited our animals very well, and they ate better than for a long time, and we thought it best to remain two or three days to give them a chance to get rest. [John Rogers stated that they rested eight days at this Indian Rancheria.] The Indian we left here the evening before had gone and left nothing but a chunk of crystalized rock salt. He seemed to be afraid of his friends.

"The range we had been traveling nearly paralell with seemed to come to an end here where this snow peak stood, and immediately north and south of this peak there seemed to be a lower pass. The continuous range north was too low to hold snow. In the morning I concluded to go to the summit of that pass and with my glass have an extensive view. Two other boys started with me, and as we moved along the snow line we saw tracks of our runaway Indian in the snow, passing over a low ridge.

"As we went on up hill our boys began to fall behind, and long before night I could see nothing of them. The ground was quite soft, and I saw many tracks of Indians which put me on my guard. I reached the summit and as the shade of its mountain began to make it a little dark, I built a fire of sage brush, ate my grub, and when it was fairly dark, renewed the fire and passed on a mile, where in a small ravine with banks two feet high I lay down sheltered from the wind and slept till morning. I did this to beat the Indian in his own cunning.

"Next morning I reached the summit [Mount Stirling] about nine o'clock, and had the grandest view I ever saw. I could see north and south almost forever. The surrounding region seemed lower, but much of it black, mountainous and barren. On the west the snow peak [Telescope Peak] shut out the view in that direction.

"To the south the mountains seemed to descend for more than twenty miles, and near the base, perhaps ten miles away, were several smokes, apparently from camp fires, and as I could see no animals or camp wagons anywhere I presumed them to be Indians. A few miles to the north and east of where I stood, and somewhat higher, was the roughest piece of ground I ever saw. It stood in sharp peaks and was of many colors, some of them so red that the mountain looked red hot, I imagined it to be a true volcanic point, and had never been so near one before, and the most wonderful picture of grand desolation one could ever see.

"Toward the north I could see the desert the Jayhawkers and their comrades had undertaken to cross, and if their journey was as troublesome as ours and very much longer, they might by this time be all dead of thirst. I remained on this summit an hour or so bringing my glass to bear on all points within my view, and scanning closely for everything that might help us or prove an obstacle to our progress.

"The more I looked the more I satisfied myself that we were yet a long way from California and the serious question of our ever living to get there presented itself to me as I tramped along down the grade to camp. I put down at least another month of heavy weary travel before we could hope to make the land of gold, and our stock of strength and provisions were both pretty small for so great a tax upon them. I thought so little about anything else that the Indians might

110

have captured me easily, for I jogged along without a thought of them.

"I thought of the bounteous stock of bread and beans upon my father's table, to say nothing about all the other good things, and here was I, the oldest son, away out in the center of the Great American Desert, with an empty stomach and a dry and parched throat, and clothes fast wearing out with constant wear. And perhaps I had not yet seen the worst of it. I might be forced to see men, and the women and children of our party, choke and die, powerless to help them. It was a darker, gloomier day than I had ever known could be, and alone I wept aloud, for I believed I could see the future, and the results were bitter to contemplate. I hope no reader of this history may ever be placed in a position to be thus tried for I am not ashamed to say that I have a weak point to show under such circumstances. It is not in my power to tell how much I suffered in my lonely trips, lasting sometimes days and nights that I might give the best advice to those of my party. I believed that I could escape at any time myself, but all must be brought to go through or perish, and with this all I knew I must not discourage the others. I could tell them the truth, but I must keep my worst apprehensions to myself lest they loose heart and faith needlessly.

"I reached the camp on the third day where I found the boys who went away with me and whom I had out-walked. I related to the whole camp what I had seen, and when all was told it appeared that the route from the mountains westerly was the only route that could be taken, they told me of a discovery they had made of a pile of squashes probably raised upon the place, and sufficient in number so that every person could have one. I did not approve of this for we had no title to this produce, and might be depriving the rightful owner of the means of life. I told them not only was it wrong to rob them of their food, but they could easily revenge themselves on us by shooting our cattle, or scalp us, by gathering a company of their own people together. They had no experience with red men and were slow to see the results I spoke of as possible.

"During my absence an ox had been killed, for some were nearly out of provisions, and flesh was the only means to

111

prevent starvation. The meat was distributed amongst the entire camp, with the understanding that when it became necessary to kill another it should be divided the same way. Some one of the wagons would have to be left for lack of animals to draw it. Our animals were too poor, and would not last long as food. No fat could be found on the entire carcass, and the marrow of the great bones was a thick liquid, streaked with blood resembling corruption.

"Our road led us around the base of the mountain. There were many large rocks in our way, some as large as horses, but we wound around among them and managed to get along. The feet of the oxen became so sore that we made mocassins for them from the hide of the ox that was killed, and with the protection they got along very well. Our trains now consisted of seven wagons. Bennett had two; Arcane two; Earhart Bros. one. Culverwell, Fish and others one; and there was one other, the owners of which I have forgotten. [This was the wagon of Harry Wade.] The second night we had a fair camp with water and pretty fair grass and brush for the oxen [Kwichup Springs].

"We were not very far from the snow line and this had some effect on the country. When Bennett retired that night he put on a camp kettle of the fresh beef and so arranged the fire that it would cook slowly and be done by daylight for breakfast. After an hour or so Mr. Bennett went out to replenish the fire and see how the cooking was coming on, and when he went to put more water in the kettle, he found that to his disappointment, the most of the meat was gone.

"I was rolled up in my blanket under his wagon and awoke when he came to the fire and saw him stand and look around as if to fasten the crime on the right party if possible, but soon he came to, and in a whisper said: 'Did you see anyone around the fire after we went to bed?' I assured him I did not, and then he told me some one had taken his meat. 'Do you think,' said he 'that any one is so near out of food as to be starving? I know the meat is poor, and who ever took it must be nearly starving.' After a whispered conversation we went to bed, but we both rose at daylight and, as we sat by the fire, kept watch of those who got up and came around. We thought we knew the right man, but were not sure, and could not imagine what might happen if stealing grub should begin and continue. It is a sort of unwritten law that in parties such as ours, he who steals provisions forfeits his life. We knew we must keep watch and if the offense was repeated the guilty one might be compelled to suffer. Bennett watched closely and for a few days I kept closely with the wagons for fear there might be trouble. It was really the most critical point in our experience. After three or four days all hope of detecting the criminal had passed, and all the danger was over out of any difficulty.

"One night we had a fair camp, as we were close to the base of the snow butte, and found a hole of clear or what seemed to be living water. There were a few minnows in it not much more than an inch long. This was among in a big pile of rocks, and around these the oxen found some grass.

"There now appeared to be a pass away to the south as a sort of outlet to the great plain which lay to the north of us, but immediately west and across the desert waste, extending to the foot of a low black range of mountains, through which there seemed to be no pass, the distant snowy peak lay still farther on, with Martin's pass over it still a long way off though steering toward it for a month. Now as we were compelled to go west this impassable barrier was in our way and if no pass could be found in it we would be compelled to go south and make no progress in a westerly direction.

"Our trail was now descending to the bottom of what seemed to be the narrowest part of the plain, the same one the Jayhawkers had started across, further north, ten days before. When we reached the lowest part of this valley we came to a running stream [Amargosa River], and, as dead grass could be seen in the bed where the water ran very slowly, I concluded it only had water in it after hard rains in the mountains, perhaps a hundred miles, to the north. This water was not pure; it had a bitter taste, and no doubt in dry weather was a rank poison. Those who partook of it were affected about as if they had taken a big dose of salts.

"A short distance above this we found the trail of the Jayhawkers going west, and thus we knew they had got safely across the great plain and then turned southward [about where the Longstreet Ranch was near Big Springs]. I hurried along their trail for several miles and looked over the country with field glass becoming fully satisfied we should find no water til we reached the summit, of the next range, and then fearing the party had not taken the precaution to bring along some water I went back to them and found they had none. I told them they would not see a drop of water for the next forty miles, and they unloaded the lightests wagon and drove back with everything they had which would hold water, to get a good supply.

"I turned back again on the Jayhawker's road, and followed it so rapidly that well toward night I was pretty near the summit [Furnace Creek Summit], where a pass through this rocky range had been found and on this mountain not a tree or shrub or spear of grass could be found—desolation beyond conception. I carried my gun along every day, but for the want of a chance to kill any game a single load would remain in my gun for a month. Very seldom a rabbit could be seen, but not a bird of any kind, not even a hawk, buzzard or crow made their appearance here.

"When near the steep part of the mountain, I found a dead ox the Jayhawkers had left, as no camp could be made here for lack of water and grass, the meat could not be saved. I found the body of the animal badly shrunken, but in condition, as far as putrefaction was concerned, as perfect as when alive. A big gash had been cut in the ham clear to the bone and the sun had dried the flesh in this. I was so awful hungry that I took my sheath knife and cut a big steak which I devoured as I walked along, without cooking or salt. Some may starve before eating such meat, but if they have ever experienced hunger till it begins to draw down the life itself, they will find the impulse of self preservation something not to be controlled by mere reason. It is an instinct that takes possession of one in spite of himself.

"I went down a narrow, dark cañon high on both sides and perpendicular, and quite so in many places [Furnace Creek Canyon]. In one of the perpendicular portions it seemed to be a varigated clay formation, and a little water seeped down its face. Here the Indians had made a clay bowl and fastened it to the wall so that it would collect and retain about a quart of water, and I had a drink of water, the first one since leaving the running stream. Near here, I stayed all night, for fear of Indians who I firmly believe would have taken my scalp had a good opportunity offered. I slept without a fire, and my supply of meat just obtained drove hunger away.

"In the morning I started down the cañon which descended rapidly and had a bed of sharp, volcanic, broken rock. I could sometimes see an Indian track, and kept a sharp lookout for them at every turn, for fear of revenge on account of the store of squashes which had been taken. I felt I was in constant danger, but could do nothing else but go on and keep eyes open trusting to circumstances to get out of any sudden emergency that might arise.

"As I recollect this was Christmas Day and about dusk I came upon the camp of one man and his wife and family, the Rev. J. W. Brier, Mrs. Brier, and two [three] sons. I inquired for others of his party and he told me they were somewhere ahead. When I arrived at his camp I found the reverend gentleman very cooly delivering a lecture to his boys on education. It seemed very strange to me to hear a solemn discourse on the benefits of early education when, it seemed to me, starvation was staring us all in the face, and the barren desolation all around gave small promise of the need of any education higher than the natural impulses of nature. None of us knew exactly where we were, nor when the journey would be ended, nor when substantial relief would come. Provisions were wasting away, and some had been reduced to the last alternative of subsisting on the oxen alone. I slept by the fire that night, without a blanket, as I had done on many nights before and after they hitched up and drove on in the morning I searched the camp carefully, finding some bacon rinds they had thrown away. As I chewed these and could taste the rich grease they contained, I thought they were the sweetest morsels I ever tasted.

"Here on the north side of the cañon were some rolling hills and some small weak springs, the water of which when gathered together made a small stream which ran a few yards down the cañon before it lost itself in the rocks and sand. On the side there stood what seemed to be one half of a butte, with the perpendicular face toward the cañon. Away on the summit of the butte I saw an Indian, so far away he looked no taller than my finger, and when he went out of sight I knew pretty well he was the very fellow who grew the squashes. I thought it might be he, at any rate.

"I now turned back to meet the teams and found them seven or eight miles up the cañon, and although it was a down grade the oxen were barely able to walk slowly with their loads which were light, as wagons were almost empty except the women and children. When night came on it seemed to be cloudy and we could hear the cries of the wild geese passing east. We regarded this as a very good sign and no doubt Owen's Lake, which we expected to pass on this route, was not very far off. Around in those small hills and damp places was some coarse grass and other growths, but those who had gone before devoured the best, so our oxen had a hard time to get anything to eat."

After his journey ahead to scout out a route behind the Jayhawkers and Briers, Manly returned to the Bennett-Arcan camp and reported what he had learned. It was not encouraging and the whole party was impatient at any further delay. They were almost out of all provisions and the thought of a great range of mountains made them fearful of the future. Manly now describes the entry of his little band into the Valley of Death and the terrifying experience that this entry was to them.

"Bennett and Arcane now concluded not to wait for me to go ahead and explore out a way for them to follow, as I had done for a long time, but to go ahead as it was evidently the best way to turn south and make our own road, and find the water and passes all for ourselves. So they hitched up and rolled down the cañon, and out into the valley and then turned due south. We had not gone long on this course before we saw that we must cross the valley and get over to the west side. To do this we must cross through some water, and for fear the ground might be miry, I went to a sand hill near by and got a mesquite stick about three feet long with which to sound out our way. I rolled up my pants, pulled off my moccassins and waded in, having the teams stand still till I could find out whether it was safe for them to follow or not by ascertaining the depth of the water and the character of the bottom.

116

"The water was very clear and the bottom seemed uneven, there being some deep holes. Striking my stick on the bottom it seemed solid as a rock, and breaking off a small projecting point I found it to be solid rock salt. As the teams rolled along they scarcely roiled the water. It looked to me as if the whole valley which might be a hundred miles long might have been a solid bed of rock salt. Before we reached this water there were many solid blocks of salt lying around covered with a little dirt on the top.

"The second night we found a good spring of fresh water coming from the bottom of the snow peak almost over our heads. The small flow from it spread out over the sand and sank in a very short distance and there was some quite good grass growing around."

In his account of the crossing of the salt beds on the floor of Death Valley, John Haney Rogers, Manly's companion, gave a version slightly different from Manly's and may have left us a clue as to what happened to the Earhart wagon:

"We then traveled down the valley till we struck the lake, and down the lake some fifteen or twenty miles where we concluded to cross at a point not over 25 or 30 yards wide. We got three of our wagons across alright and the fourth one broke through. Underneath the water was a crust of salt some six or eight inches thick. We struck then to the foot of the mountains, it being difficult to find drinking water, as it was all salt. We found a spring we could use."

Manly continued with his account:

"This was a temporary relief, but brought us face to face with stranger difficulties and a more hopeless outlook.

"There was no possible way to cross this high steep range of mountains anywhere to the north and the Jayhawkers had abandoned their wagons and burned them, and we could no longer follow on the trail they made. It seemed that there was no other alternative but for us to keep along the edge of the mountain to the south and search for another pass. Some who had read Fremont's travels said that the range im-

117

mediately west of us must be the one he described, on the
west of which was a beautiful country, of rich soil and having
plenty of cattle, and horses and containing some settlers, but
on the east all was barren, dry, rocky, sandy desert as far as
could be seen. We knew this eastern side answered well the
description and believed that this was really the range described, or at least it was close by.

"We had to look over the matter very carefully and consider all the conditions and circumstances of the case. We
could see the mountains were lower to the south, but they
held no snow and seemed only barren rocks piled up in lofty
peaks, and as we looked it seemed the most God-forsaken
country in the world.

"We had been in the region long enough to know the
higher mountains contained most water, and that the valleys had bad water or none at all, so that while the lower
altitudes to the south gave some promise of easier crossing it
gave us no promise of water, without which we must certainly perish. In a certain sense we were lost. The clear night
and days furnished us with the means of telling the points of
compass as the sun rose and set, but not a sign of life in
nature's wide domain had been seen for a month or more. A
vest pocketful of powder and shot would last a good hunter
till he starved to death for there was not a living thing to
shoot great or small.

"We talked over our present position pretty freely, and
everyone was asked to speak his unbiased mind, for we knew
not who might be right or who might be wrong, and some one
might make a suggestion of the utmost value. We all felt
pretty much downhearted. Our civilized provisions were getting so scarce that all must be saved for the women and
children, and the men must get along some way on ox meat
alone. It was decided not to waste a scrap of anything that
might sustain life. The blood, hide and intestines were all
prepared in some way for food. This meeting lasted until late
at night. If some of them had lost their minds I should not
have been surprised, for hunger swallows all other feelings.
A man in a starving condition is savage. He may be as
bloodshed and selfish as a wild beast, as docile and gentle as
a lamb, or as wild and crazy as a terrified animal, devoid of

affection, reason or thought of justice. We were none of us as bad as this, and yet there was a strange look in the eyes of some of us sometimes, as I saw by looking around, and as others no doubt realized for I saw them making mysterious glances even in my direction.

"Morning came and all were silent. The dim prospect of the future seemed to check every tongue. When one left a water hole he went away as if in doubt whether he would ever enjoy the pleasure of another drop. Every camp was sad beyond description, and no one can guide the pen to make it tell the tale as it seemed to us. When our morning meal of soup and meat was finished, Bennett's two teamsters, and the two of Arcane's concluded their chances of life were better if they could take some provisions and strike out on foot, and so they were given what they could carry, and they arranged their packs and bade us a sorrowful good bye hoping to meet again on the Pacific Coast. There were genuine tears shed at the parting and I believe neither party ever expected to see each other in this life again.

"Bennett's two men were named Silas Helmer and S. S. or C. C. Abbott, but I have forgotten the names of Arcane's men. Mr. Abbott was from New York, a harness maker by trade, and he took his circular cutting knife with him, saying it was light to carry and the weapon he should need. One of them had a gun. They took the trail taken by the Jayhawkers. All the provisions they could carry besides their blankets could not last them to exceed 10 days, and I well knew they could hardly get off the desert in that time.

"Mr. Abbott was a man I loved fondly. he was good company in camp, and happy and sociable. He showed no despondency at any time until the night of the last meeting and the morning of the parting. His chances seemed to me to be much poorer than my own, but I hardly think he realized it. When in bed I could not keep my thoughts back from the old home I had left, where good water and a bountiful spread were always ready at the proper hour. I know I dreamed of taking a draft of cool, sweet water from a full pitcher and then woke up with my mouth and throat as dry as dust. The good home I left behind me was a favorite theme about the campfire, and many a one told of the dream pictures, natural

119

as life, that came to him of the happy Eastern home with comfort and happiness surrounding it, even if wealth was lacking. The home of the poorest man on earth was preferable to this place. Wealth was of no value here.

"A hoard of twenty dollar gold pieces could now stand before us the whole day long with no temptation to touch a single coin, for its very weight would drag us nearer death. We could purchase nothing with it and we would have cared no more for it as a thing of value than we did for the desert sands. We would have given much more for some of the snow which we could see drifting over the peak of the great snow mountains over our heads like a dusty cloud.

"Deeming it best to spare the strength as much as possible, I threw away everything I could, retaining only my glass, some ammunition, sheath knife and tin cup. No unnecessary burden could be put on any man or beast, lest he lie down under it, never to rise again. Life and strength were sought to be husbanded in every possible way."

It probably was at Ash Meadows that the Briers and the Jim Martin party left their wagons. Martin killed oxen and dried as much meat as he and his men could carry. He gave the remaining oxen to the Briers. Forced at last to abandon their wagons, the Briers hurried on afoot having then the best traveling commissary of any party. In the first chapter of this work, we have read what Mrs. Brier wrote of her terrible struggle afoot, and with three small children, to bring these loose cattle into camp at what now is called Travertine Springs, about one half mile above the present Death Valley Inn on the hill at the mouth of Furnace Creek Wash.

Following the Briers, and still dragging their wagons, the old saddle mare, Pet, and the milch cow, Rosie, both tied to the tail gate, were the Wades. Harry Wade was keeping to himself, camping a day behind the rest and proceeding cautiously. In this way he lost no time and no energy in searching out the trail and he found the water holes cleaned out and full of clear water. The Royal Coachman was determined to go through on the cushions.

Here we now have all of the Death Valley '49ers safely out of southwestern Utah, scattered along Furnace Creek Wash and across Death Valley to what now is Jayhawker Spring, about seven miles southeast of present Stovepipe Wells Hotel. Their condition was hourly growing

120

worse. All parties had consumed all provisions except coffee and a few hoarded emergency rations. Even to the little children, they were entirely dependent on the dry meat of their staggering, starving cattle. Melissa Bennett remembered that some of them were given the remaining tallow candles to chew upon when they went supperless to bed.

It remains now to take up separately the various scattered groups, each frantic to escape from a situation far worse than any they had endured and with no nourishing food to carry them on. The dictionary has been exhausted of adjectives attempting to describe the plight and struggles of these Argonauts of '49 without conveying the realities of their experiences. In later years, those who endured those terrible hardships stated that the story could not be told; that, if it were written, it could not be printed. It is largely from their own letters and publications that this writer hopes to present a simple picture of the final stage of this greatest trek of all time.

CHAPTER EIGHT

THE FIRST CHRISTMAS IN DEATH VALLEY

It was a dismal Christmas, that first Christmas in Death Valley, more than one hundred and twenty-five years ago. We have read about the services held at Travertine Spring by Rev. J. W. Brier when his family, Manly and a few of the Mississippi Boys stood about thinking of the fine homes and well laden tables they had left more than eight months before.

An old cake, made by the mother of L. Dow Stevens before he left Galesburg, Illinois, and carried to their camp at Jayhawker Well on Salt Creek, was brought out. It brought back dear recollections, but was so dried and hard that it could scarcely be broken.

Sixty-three years later at a reunion, some of the Jay Hawks wrote a menu of such delicacies as they could have enjoyed that Christmas Day in Death Valley. Here it is:

JAYHAWK MENU
Pack Saddle Camp
Death   Valley   Christmas, 1849

Bull Hide Soup, tail accompaniment
Appetite Raisers,
Cactus and Greasewood Sprouts
Boiled Bull Ribs, Tarantula dressing
Roast Bull Beef with sand and salt

ENTREES
Rattlesnake, baked (in the sun)
Broiled Chuck Walla Lizard (ditto)
Roast Horned Toad
Roasted Centipedes (Mesquite Stuffing)
(Feet left on)
Blood Pudding Patties (In Bull's Ear)

EXHILARATORS
Old Cognac—non est
Champagne—nit
Aqua Sal Y Alkali—Galore
Cigars???
Chawed Plug Dried, with pipe (if you have one)
Toothpicks de cacti

Most of the Jay Hawks were camped at Jayhawker Well, southeast of present Stovepipe Wells Hotel. From that base they prospected the mountain range to the west looking for Martin's Pass, which then turned out to be no pass for their wagons. They decided that it would be impossible to take their wagons out of Death Valley except by traveling south, yet they still persisted in their determination to go directly west.

Following behind the Bennetts and Arcans, the Wade family had a Christmas dinner all their own.

After having denied every demand for a few dainties she had kept hidden away in the grub box under the wagon seat, Mrs. Wade brought out the makings of an English plum pudding. There, at a dry camp a few miles northwest of where Death Valley Junction now is located, Mrs. Wade prepared her Christmas dinner. True, it was cooked over a brush fire and in a three legged cast iron kettle. This same kettle had been stolen by the Indians while the Wades had been following the Platte River. But the following night, plucky Mary (Leach) Wade had crawled under the side of the Indian tepee and stolen it back. Mary was determined to have her kettle and just as determined to have her plum pudding. Harry Wade has been described by his descendants as a very determined man. His photo shows that their statements probably were true. But think of Mary Wade out on the Nebraska plains crawling into a tepee of hostile Indians to steal her kettle back, and you will decide that all of the courage and determination of the present-day Wades did not come from Harry. Mary's photo supports our belief in her determination. Anyway, the Wades needed all the determination they could muster and before they were to pull their wagon into Los Angeles they had used up quite a lot of it.

The Jay Hawk wagons had been cut into carts about two weeks earlier, probably near the head of Fortymile Canyon. Now the carts could be taken no farther. So all were busy at Jayhawker Well, cutting the bodies of the carts to pieces and making pack saddles for the starved and staggering oxen.

The poorest and weakest of the oxen were killed. In order to save time in drying the meat, the remaining parts of the wagons were burned and the meat placed on rocks over the fire. Tomorrow the Jay Hawks would start out afoot and lead the remaining oxen northwest around the shoulder of Tucki Mountain and west over the gap at the north end of the Panamints, the gap now known as Towne Pass.

It was at this salty spring, with no feed for oxen, about seven miles southeast of present Stovepipe Wells Hotel that William Lewis Manly came upon the Doty mess of Jay Hawks late in the night at the end of Christmas Day, 1849. The place long was known as McLeans Well but recently has been named Jayhawker Well.

About his meeting with Doty and the condition of the camp of downcast Jay Hawks, Manly wrote:

"Next morning after leaving the Bennett wagons I shouldered my gun and followed down the cānon keeping the wagon road, and when half a mile down, at the sink of the sickly stream, I killed a wild goose. This had undoubtedly been attracted here the night before by the light of our campfire.

"When I got near the lower end of the cānon, there wus a cliff on the north or right hand side which was perpendicular or perhaps a little overhanging, and at the base a cave which had the appearance of being continuously occupied by Indians. As I went on down I saw a very strange looking track upon the ground. There were hand and foot prints as if a human being had crawled upon all fours. As this track reached the valley where the sand had been clean swept by the wind, the tracks became more plain, and the sand had been blown into small hills not over three or four feet high.

"I followed the track till it led to the top of one of these small hills where a small well-lined hole had been dug and in this excavation was a kind of Indian mummy curled up like a dog. He was not dead for I could see him move as he breathed, but his skin looked very much like the surface of a well dried venison ham. I should think by his looks he must be 200 or 300 years old, indeed he might be Adam's brother and not look any older than he did. He was evidently crippled. A climate which would preserve for many days or weeks the carcass of an ox so that an eatable round steak

125

could be cut from it, might perhaps preserve a live man for a longer period than would be believed.

"I took a good long look at the wild creature and during all the time he never moved a muscle, though he must have known some one was in the well looking down at him. He was probably practicing on one of the directions for a successful political career looking wise and saying nothing. At any rate he was not going to let his talk get him into any trouble. He probably had a friend around somewhere who supplied his wants. I now left him and went farther out into the lowest part of the valley."

John Rogers left a slightly different account of this meeting with the old Indian. I reproduce it here just as Rogers dictated it for a news article in the *Merced Star* of April 26, 1894:

"Next morning Manley and myself started down the creek exploring. We went down to the mouth of the creek where it emptied out into the plains. There we found a big Indian camp. Their fires were still burning and the Indians gone, except an old man who was blind. He was crawling around on the ground. He had a little willow basket full of muddy water and had a sharp stick which he was using in digging up roots. Manly said he had a notion to shoot him. Says I, 'The duece you would. I would as leave shoot my father.' I took his willow basket and went to the creek and rinced it out and gave him some clean water. I gave him some meat and he raised his head and grunted as if he didn't know who was there. We started down into the valley. We traveled about ten miles and struck a bunch of willows and a spring of fresh water. In prospecting ten miles farther we struck a lake, after which we retraced our steps to camp.

"When we struck the Indian camp the old Indian was gone. I think he was left there for a purpose—to see what we would do with him. I think the kind treatment we gave that Indian saved our party. We moved camp to the spring at the willows. The ground was covered three or four inches deep with something like saltpetre or borax."

126

THE FIRST CHRISTMAS IN DEATH VALLEY

About the view of Death Valley from the mouth of Furnace Creek Wash and his visit to the Jay Hawks, Manly left the following interesting account:

"I could look to the north for fifty miles and it seemed to rise gradually in that direction. To the south the view was equally extended, and down that way a lake could be seen. The valley was here quite narrow, and the lofty snow-capped peak we had tried so hard to reach for the past two months now stood before me. Its east side was almost perpendicular and seemed to reach the sky, and the snow was drifting over it, while here the day sun was shining uncomfortably hot. I believe this mountain was really miles from its base to its summit, and that nothing could climb it on the eastern side except a bird and the only bird I had seen for two months was a goose I shot. I looked every day for some sort of game but had not seen any.

"As I reached the lower part of the valley I walked over what seemed to be boulders of various sizes, and as I stepped from one to another the tops were covered with dirt and they grew larger as I went along. I could see behind them and they looked clear like ice, but on closer inspection proved to be immense blocks of rock salt while the water which stood at their bases was the strongest brine. After this discovery I took my way back to the road made by the Jayhawkers and found it quite level, but sandy. Following this I came to a campfire soon after dark at which E. Doty and mess were camped. As I was better acquainted I camped with them. They said the water there was brackish and I soon found out the same thing for myself. It was a poor camp; no grass, poor water and scattering, bitter sage brush for food for the cattle. It would not do to wait long here, and so they hurried on.

"I inquired of them about Martin's Pass, as they were now quite near it, and they said it was no pass at all, only the mountains was a little lower than the one holding the snow. No wagon could get over it, and the party had made up their minds to go on foot, and were actually burning their wagons as fuel with which to dry the meat of some of the oxen which they had killed. They selected those which were weakest and least likely to stand the journey, and by drying it the food was much concentrated.

"They were to divide the provisions equally and it was agreed thereafter everyone must look out for himself and not expect any help from anyone. If he used his own provisions, he had no right to expect anyone else to divide with him. Rice, tea and coffee were measured out by the spoonful and the small amount of flour and bacon which remained was divided out as evenly as possible. Everything was to be left behind but blankets and provisions for the men were too weak to carry heavy packs and the oxen could not be relied on as beasts of burden and it was thought best not to load them so as to needlessly break them down.

"When these fellows started out they were full of spirit and the frolic and fun along the Platte River was something worth laughing at but now they were very melancholy and talked in the lowest kind of low spirits. One fellow said he knew this was the Creator's dumping place where he had left the worthless dregs after making a world, and the devil had scraped these together a little. Another said this must be the very place where Lot's wife was turned into a pillar of salt, and the pillar been broken up and spread around the country. He said if a man was to die he would never decay on account of the salt.

"Thus the talk went on, and it seemed as if there were not bad words enough in the language to properly express their contempt and bad opinion of such a country as this. They treated me to some of their meat, a little better than mine, and before daylight in the morning I was headed back on the trail to report the bad news I had learned of the Jayhawkers."

Rogers' account of their trouble with the Indians at Ash Meadows is also of interest:

"The next morning we went out to drive our cattle in. We found three of them shot with arrows, two of them had only one arrow in each, and the third was filled with them. We killed and skinned him and jerked the meat. We also found about twenty arrows sticking in the ground as if they had been shot upwards and dropped down.

"We had never stood guard since the train had bursted up. I suppose the Indians shot our cattle out of revenge for eating their squashes."

Returning to the Bennetts, Wades, Earharts and others, who were struggling down Furnace Creek Wash, Manly found more trouble. His predictions had come true. The Indians had retaliated for the theft of their corn and squashes, stolen several days before.

About the return from his visit to the Jay Hawk camp and the critical condition in which he found the trailing parties, Manly wrote as follows:

"As my road was now out and away from the mountains, and level, I had no fear of being surprised by enemies, so walked on with eyes downcast thinking over the situation, and wondering what would be the final outcome. If I were alone, with no one to expect me to help them, I would be out before any other man, but with women and children in the party, to go and leave them would be to pile everlasting infamy on my head. The thought almost made me crazy but I thought it would be better to stay and die with them, bravely struggling to escape than to forsake them in their weakness.

"It was almost night before I reached our camp, and sitting around our little fire I told, in the most easy way I could the unfavorable news of the party in advance. They seemed to look to me as a guide and advisor, I presume because I took much pains to inform myself on opposing opinion, they moved as I thought best. During my absence from camp for the two days the Indians had shot arrows into three of our oxen and one still had an arrow in his side forward of the hip which was a dangerous place. To be sure and save him for ourselves we killed him. Some were a little afraid to eat the meat thinking perhaps the arrow might be poisoned, but I agreed that they wanted meat themselves and would not do that. I told them if they got shot themselves it would very likely be a poisoned arrow and they must take the most instant measures to cut it out before it went into the blood. So we ventured to dry the meat and take it with us.

129

Mary Ann Wade, who was born January 2, 1851, in the family covered wagon under an oak tree near present Saratoga at the end of the covered wagon journey of Harry and Mary Wade from New York to Alviso, California. Photo courtesy of Mrs. J. Q. White and now in Bear State Library.

"Now I said to the whole camp, 'You can see how you have displeased the red men. Taking their little squashes, and when we get into a place that suits them for that purpose, they may meet us with a superior force and massacre us, not only for revenge but to get our oxen and clothing.' I told them we must ever be on guard against a surprise, as the chances were greatly against us.

"We pulled the arrows out of the oxen, and they seemed to sustain no great injury from the wounds. This little faint stream where we camped has since been named Furnace Creek and is still known as such. It was named in 1862 by some prospectors who built what was called an air furnace on a small scale to reduce some ore found near by, which they supposed to contain silver, but I believe it turned out to be lead and too far from transportations to be available."

And so the little band of stragglers wound down Furnace Creek Wash, now almost as much in fear of the Indians as they were of death by starvation and thirst.

By the end of Christmas Day the rest of the '49ers were strung across Death Valley and ascending the Panamint Range in order to melt snow and supply water for camp. The Savage-Pinney Party was probably dying daily as they staggered across the northern reaches of Death Valley or, possibly Saline Valley, west of Death Valley.

The Indians were fled from their camps at the mouth of Furnace Creek Wash and lay hidden among the rocks of the surrounding ranges marveling at the many wonders possessed by these strange intruders, but marveling most of all at their unbelievable horses, horses with big horns on their heads.

CHAPTER NINE

WITH THE JAY HAWKS TO INDIAN WELLS

Most dramatic of all escapes from Death in '49, was that of the Jay Hawks. They had taken the lead in breaking trails since the separation from Jefferson Hunt's party at Division Springs near where Enterprise, Utah, is now. They were not only the youngest of any party of '49; they were also the best equipped. At Salt Lake they had traded and purchased oxen until they had the finest outfit to leave Salt Lake that year. It was because of their youth and fine outfit that they felt confident of being able to penetrate the Great American Desert regardless of the sincere advice of plainsmen who had tried and failed, including such men as Jim Bridger, Pegleg Smith and Kit Carson. So, when the meeting was held at Mount Misery, they declared that they would go through to Owen's Lake and the San Joaquin mines or leave their bones bleaching on the Utah deserts in the attempt. This last possibility was later to fall little short of becoming an actual fact.

Leaving Meadow Valley the Jay Hawks plunged several days farther north than did any of the other parties. Rev. Brier, who traveled over much of the same country as did the Jay Hawks, stated that they went far north of present Pioche, Nevada. He wrote:

> "We traveled along the range 75 miles southward [?] before we got to the end. Streams and timber were plenty and so were the Indians. We were now a little south of what is now Pioche, Nevada."

Brier also stated that during the snowstorm of December 6, the Jay Hawks were in a branch of Fortymile Canyon. Turning south, they soon caught and passed the others and were lost in the distance. This foray was an easy trip for them. Both they and their cattle were strong. The plunge across the desert to the west wore them down a little, but they still were confident and more determined than ever when they again left the trail selected by Manly and the rest and struck westward across the southern portion of Emigrant Valley into the head of Fortymile   133

Canyon. But the dry lakes, the muddy puddles of alkali water and the many dry camps were beginning to take their toll.

Fortymile Canyon and nine successive dry camps ate deep into their supplies of food and into the strength of both the Jay Hawks and their oxen. It was the effects of this determined plunge to the west that placed them in such a terrible plight when they came out into the tremendous sink of Death Valley. This dogged determination to travel as nearly as possible directly in a westerly course was actually the cause of the difficulties of all the Death Valley parties of '49. At several points, by following the southern course of the valleys they were in, they could have reached the Spanish Trail over which was traveling the party under Captain Jefferson Hunt. If they had done this, their serious troubles would have been ended. But the "Sand Walking" (San Joaquin) Company was headed for Owen's Lake, the old Joe Walker Trail, Walker's Pass, Kern River and the San Joaquin Valley. And these lay directly to the west.

By the time the Jay Hawks had reached Jayhawker Well at the northeast foot of old Tucki Mountain they were in dire straights. Already they had endured enough hardships to have killed every member of an older or less well equipped party. Had it not been for the snow storm of December 9, all would have left their bones in Fortymile Canyon.

At Jayhawker Well the young Jay Hawks still were determined, but for the first time they realized their situation. Tom Shannon, Bill Rood and Alex Palmer climbed Tucki from the snowbank where others of their party were melting snow, fully expecting to see the Pacific Ocean from the summit. All they saw was more dry, desert valleys separated by two rocky mountain ranges more forbidding than any they had ever seen and, apparently one hundred miles from their station, a third towering, snowcapped range which they at once realized was absolutely impassable for wagons.

When this news was taken to the camp at Jayhawker Well it all but discouraged the little group which was making pack saddles of wagon boxes, slaughtering oxen and drying meat. On December 29 the Georgians gave the last of their oxen to the Briers and hurried on over the snow on the shoulder of Tucki Mountain.

A small party of Jay Hawks was on the shoulders of Tucki Mountain melting snow to secure fresh water on their journey westward from Jayhawker Well. The Georgians were miners. They recognized the 134 formation on which the Jay Hawks were sitting as an extremely rich deposit of silver-bearing ore. One of the Georgians picked up a piece of ore that he pronounced pure silver. J. W. Brier later wrote that at the Ducommun store in Los Angeles this silver was made into a gunsight, and provided the name for the later famous lost Gunsight Lead. Another authority stated that the gunsight was made in the mines at Mariposa.

Several of the '49ers are quoted as authorities that one of the Georgians had with him $5000 in gold coin. While at this camp on what they later referred to as Silver Mountain, he grew tired of carrying this gold coin. Finding no one willing to help him carry it to the Spanish settlements on shares, he went to one side of the camp, turned up a rock and dumped the gold coin under it. In 1890 Manly wrote the Jay Hawks about this incident:

> "The $5000 the Georgia boys buried will never be found, 40 years buries everything on that trail out of sight and that silver lead has been looked for every year since. There is no place for it only in the first range west of the place where you burned your wagons."

Both the gold and the silver lead probably have been found. Several rich silver mines were located on the shoulder of Tucki Mountain. Small pieces of pure silver float were not uncommon in that locality. He who turned over a rock with $5000 in gold coin under it was certain not to talk—and, as they used to say in those days, "The double eagles have no one's name on them."

As soon as each mess of the Jay Hawks prepared its packs, the men and oxen picked their way through the boulders of the alluvial fans of the canyons which spread around the north base of Tucki Mountain and began to climb the steep fan of Emigrant Wash. It is probable that the Jay Hawks were not again assembled in one group until February 5, thirty-seven days later, when the surviving stragglers found their way into Rancho San Francisquito near present Newhall.

On December 30 Sheldon Young wrote in his log:

> "Got our packs ready and started. Left at three o'clock. Went twelve miles and had a dry camp. Cattle acted like old hands at it."

Apparently the cattle had tamed down considerably since their long series of wild stampedes on the Platte.

On December 31 Young's mess "Went twenty-four miles and got to the top of a high mountain. Plenty of snow. Dry Camp."

On New Year's Day, 1850, the Young mess lay in camp at the summit of Towne Pass and melted snow for the oxen, leaving camp at noon January 2. They then went eight miles and descended into another valley. "Camped at the mouth of the cañon. West course. Lost one steer."

The Jay Hawks are now in the north end of Panamint Valley. It is logical to suppose that the Young party had traveled through what is now Towne Pass and down the same canyon now traversed by Highway #190. Present day travelers over the Jay Hawk route do not depend on snow storms. They are provided by the State Highway Department with fifty gallon drums filled with emergency water. At least there is water in the drums when they have not been punctured by the eager rifles of 1949ers.

One does not wonder what would have happened to that grave, struggling band of Jay Hawks had they attempted to traverse Towne Pass and Panamint Valley in the summer. It was a terrifying experience even in January (of 1849).

One group of Jay Hawks left Death Valley by way of what now is known as Jayhawker Canyon, the first canyon southwest of Emigrant Canyon. This course is proved by the fact that William B. Rood carved his initials and the date on a rock near Jayhawker Spring in this canyon. From the summit they went down through Nemo Canyon which runs into Wild Rose Canyon about one mile below the present service station. All missed the water which existed in Wild Rose from the present service station upstream. Continuing from the mouth of Nemo Canyon downstream they entered Panamint Valley south of the entry made by the party with Sheldon Young.

Following are several entries made by Sheldon Young in his log and covering the wanderings in Panamint Valley:

"January 3rd., Went eight miles to the bottom of a valley wholly destitute of grass. Plenty of water and some greasewood for browse.

"January 4th., Went ten miles down the valley. Water. No grass. Country looks hard ahead. Cattle are fast failing. Three was left today.

"January 5th., Went twenty-four miles South by East. We

have been seven days without seeing a bit of grass. Had a dry camp. Rained some. Weather warm.

"January 6., Went four miles east. Found wood and grass. Plenty of Indians. Horses have been here of late. Lay in camp the rest of the day.

"January 7., Lay in camp this day. Killed four oxen,—they had given out,—for beef. We are in a narrow valley, considerable grass, some salt water and brush for wood."

Here the Jay Hawks are at the camp known among the '49ers as the Mesquite Thicket, or Camp of the Horse Bones, in Panamint Valley. Note that the cattle were failing rapidly—seven died or were killed in three days. Note also that Young writes nothing of the condition of the Jay Hawks. His entire fear concerns the cattle, their traveling commissary. When the cattle were gone the men soon would go. Remember, they had been entirely out of all provisions except coffee since they entered Death Valley. Every day lost in this desolate valley where there was water, but no stock feed, reduced the chances of reaching the settlements in California. This is a point often overlooked by critics of Death Valley '49ers. A mad scramble was on, over rocky mountain ranges, barren of one spear of grass and across dry-lake-studded valleys and three mountain ranges to Rancho San Francisquito, two hundred and fifty miles distant.

This Camp of the Horse Bones was the terminus of an old Indian trail which began at the Spanish settlements and Missions around San Gabriel and San Fernando. Later on in their travels the Jay Hawks were to meet a band of stolen horses being driven by Indians. They were headed for this isolated camp near Death Valley. The Indian riders made a pass at the Jay Hawk oxdrove and stampeded all but a couple of oxen which were carrying packs and being led. The poor old starved oxen could run only a short distance. A few were recovered by the Jay Hawks.

Concerning the Camp of the Horse Bones, J. W. Brier many years later wrote as follows:

"The arrival at an Indian Village among the mesquite groves, in which only one of the villagers remained, an aged squaw, who scolded us in a language we did not understand.

"We entered the rectangular thatched huts, and found a   137 number of hair ropes and bridles but little furniture. Midway of the village was a vast heap of offal, and the bones of horses were scattered about freely, showing that the natives were accustomed to visit the great ranges of California for their regular supply of meat."

The Briers followed the Jay Hawks from Jayhawker Well to Rancho San Francisquito. Although they were not considered to be a part of the Jay Hawk organization they always camped near some of the Jay Hawk messes and were in later years adopted into that organization.

In 1916 John B. Colton dictated the following about Mrs. Brier and her part in helping the Jay Hawks from Panamint Valley into Rancho San Francisquito:

"Mrs. Brier was the only woman in the party and although of very slight physique and burdened with the care of her three children, she was through all the hardship which attended the trip. Her devotion and courage, her unfailing kindness to the remaining members of the party inspired them with the greatest love and admiration and to the end of her life she was affectionately known to the survivors as the little woman."

At another time Colton stated:

"When her husband was too weak to put the pack saddles on the oxen, it was Mrs. Brier who did the work. When a traveler fell by the trail, it was Mrs. Brier who encouraged him to make another effort.

"After we had been reduced to walking, Mrs. Brier carried one of the children in her arms, another on her back a great portion of the time and a third she led by the hand. There was never a murmur from this brave woman."

Wrote Sheldon Young on January 8,—"Went eight miles camping on the spring. Good grass. South East." Young noted the one all important item—grass. But all of the parties were gathering at what is now Indian Ranch, north of old Ballarat. The grass lasted only a few days. Then everyone began another race for more water and more grass, which 138 were not found together for almost two hundred miles.

J. W. Brier later gave the reason for moving from the Camp of the Horsebones to the spring at Indian Ranch, eight miles southeast.

> "As it might be dangerous to pass the night in the deserted village [probably the presence of the beligerent old squaw had something to do with the danger], we moved down to another spring and made camp."

Continuing the description of the physical condition of the Jay Hawks, Brier wrote that they had only dried beef "such as it was," but no bread.

> "The Jayhawkers were equally destitute, but one of their number was rich in the possession of a tallow candle, and this he ate in solitude—having fallen to the rear for this purpose."

The Slate Range proved a difficult barrier to the westward progress of the Jay Hawks. They skirted its eastern slopes looking for a pass over which their oxen could travel, for, where they went, the oxen must go. Argus Peak arose to an elevation of 6542 feet, 5500 feet above the floor of Panamint Valley. On Towne Pass they had reached a elevation of 5260 feet and more than a mile above the floor of Death Valley, which they had crossed a few days earlier.

While camped at Indian Ranch the Jay Hawks put out explorers who finally found two routes which they thought passable. Both routes were used. By this time Mr. Brier and his family had arrived. In later years he wrote that he located one of the canyons through which the Jay Hawks climbed to the summit of the Slate Range. This probably was present Manly Pass. The Briers followed this group. It was the greatest test yet endured by the Jay Hawks, and two of them failed to survive it. Forty-eight years later Mrs. Brier wrote the following about this experience:

> "The valley ended in a canyon with great walls rising up—oh, as high as we could see, almost. There seemed no way out, for it ended almost in a straight wall. I know many of the company never expected to leave that narrow gorge. By that time most of them could hardly stagger more than a few steps at a stretch; some were beyond even that. Mr. Brier

139

managed to keep erect with the aid of two sticks. Providence was with us that awful night, or the morning would have risen on the dead.

"Seeping up from the sand Mr. Brier found a little water, and by digging the company managed to scoop up about a pint an hour. Coffee and dried beef kept us alive till morning, but the moaning of the suffering cattle was pitiful. At daylight we managed to reach the lowest bench of the cliff by holding to the cattle. Father Fish came up holding to an ox's tail, but could go no further. That night he died. I made coffee for him but he was all worn out. Isham died that night too."

A large group of Jay Hawks rushed south to Searles Lake and to a salt well a short distance north of the lake shore. At the site of this salt well there has in recent years been developed water which is used at Valley Wells for a swimming pool and a recreation center for the town of Trona.

The Jay Hawks scooped up the slippery, reddish borax brine of which the lake was composed and tasted it. They could not swallow a drop of it or of the water from the salt well. Wearily they retraced their steps to the dry camp at the west edge of the Slate Range, exhausted and disheartened.

Before the entire party had crossed the Slate Range into the upper end of Searles Lake Valley ten men were down and due to perish. The Jay Hawks made a dry camp at the west edge of the Slate Range. From there they sent out scouts looking for water. Some of them had then been out three days without finding water.

For the Jay Hawk reunion of 1896 Rev. J. W. Brier wrote a long letter to be read to the assembly. As it is of great interest, not only in connection with this exit from Panamint Valley but as a picture of the fast failing little band, it is here given in full:

> "Antioc Jan 16   96
> "California

"Dear Old Comrades,

"Forty and six years have passed since we reached the San Francisco Ranch and a few of us are still on this side of the river. We are in our 82nd year both being born in 1814. Neither of us expect to see another anniversary. Well we are ready to go and are only waiting for the tide that will bear us out to sea. Death has not come into our homes the past year. You all remember that we went down Panamint Valley 2 days journey when we reached the great Mesquite swamp and camped 2 or 3 days at a pool where there were a number of Indian Wickiups then we went down some 5 or 6 miles farther south to the springs where we all tarried a few days longer. While here Capt Town and I explored the west rim of Panamint [referring to the east rim of the Slate and Argus ranges] where we found an Indian Trail over a very steep pass which I condemned as impassible [probably Water Canyon]. The Captain differed and turned back to camp. I went on south many miles farther and discovered a large canyon. [This probably was the canyon which led to Manly Pass.] I then returned to camp which I reached about 10 p.m. I found my wife baking the last of the flour which belonged to my companions. We had no ownership in it whatever. Old Capt. Haines sat by looking wistfully on, and a boy, I think his nephew or grandson [young John B. Colton] was all the evening getting fuel. At last the work was done and at midnight Mr. Maston and Crampton asked myself and family to eat one biscuit each and that was to be the last for us. All was silent as the grave.

"Capt. Haynes took out a five dollar gold piece and offered it to the men for one biscuit but they refused it. The Captain wept and said to me, 'I have the best 160 acres in Knott [Knox] Co., Ill, 100 stock hogs, and 2000 bushels of old corn in crib and here I cannot get one biscuit for love or money' and the boy looked sad and disappointed and went away to his blankets. Next morning the Jay Hawks packed up and started for the Condemned pass, but we remained until noon to assist our two comrades to pack up—Not one word was spoken all that fornoon (all too full) when ready they turned their faces away and reached out their hands. Not a word was said. As they receded my little group stood with eyes dimed with tears, and bitterly thought of the morrow. Well we gathered up our oxen and packed up and wearily followed on.

"At sunset we came to a part of the Jay Hawks and other stragglers who were waiting for us. These were Carter, John

Groscup, Harry Vance, M. Gould, Father Fish, and Isham. Well we slept at that point. The place was not only dismal in the extreme, but dangerous Indians were watching us from the heights of that I was aware, because I saw there fresh tracks in the wet sand in the canyon in the morning. They could have rolled rocks on us from above and have buried us. I was aware of the danger but said nothing.

"In the morning we found that about one half of our oxen had quietly passed us and as we supposed had returned to the last water. The oxen of Carter, Vance, Gould, Fish with two of mine were missing. Carter went back for the run away oxen and left Father Fish in the care of Harry Vance, for he was too weak to travel, and I took with me John Groscup and Isham. Before leaving Father Fish came to me weeping, and said I have this morning been guilty of a great sin will God forgive me? I said what is it? He said the boiler turned over and spilled the coffee. Isham said where is the coffee? and I said it is gone to the devil, I suppose. Oh! said he I have not said such a thing before in 40 years.

"It showed me the reality of the old man. This was his last talk with me. Well I started on with my family, Groscup and Isham. With much effort we got out of the canyon on my windrow of sand in an hour we were on the top of the pass. After going down the western slope in another canyon about 200 yards we suddenly came to a jumping off place of about 6 feet. Groscup and I built a stone bridge down to the level over which all passed in safety. Groscup then took the lead with his one ox and mine followed. He soon found other jumpoffs but the madcap did not wait for a bridge but forced his ox to jump and mine followed suit.

"So we went until about 3 P.M. we found ourselves facing what is now known as Borax Lake and right east of your camp. It looked to be about 3 miles away, but it was midnight when we reached the Jay Hawks camp. Isham being weary stopped to rest some 4 or 5 miles back, but did not come to camp. I now go back to our last camp in big canyon, Well, Carter found all the oxen near the mouth of the canyon. They packed up by noon and started.

"Father Fish took hold on the tail of his ox and was helped up the windrow out of the dismal canyon. He held on to the tail 3 or 4 hundred yards when he reeled and fell to rise no more. The boys were so excited that they forgot to leave him his blankets. I sent back for him the next day but he was found dead. The story of Ishams death you all remember. I have given you this little naration of 2 days in which we were separated. I am now giving to the public the whole naration from where we took the cutoff to the San Fransketo Rancho. It draws an audiance and holds it spellbound for 2 hours. I would go east and give it but cannot now. We have not yet put our book to the press, but still intend to do so. Now my Dear old Comrads this may be my last communication so fare you well. Meet us in Heaven where there will be no hunger or thirst or pain forever.

"Yours truly,
"Jas. W. Brier and Wife."

For the first time many of the Jay Hawks fell into the depths of despair. Ed Doty and one other scout returned late in the afternoon with the disheartening word that they had found no water. Only Luther Richards still was out looking for water.

Because of his many kindnesses to his companions Richards was known as The Little Deacon. He was a small, wiry, tireless fellow and remained out until sundown that night searching the north end of Searles Lake Valley.

As The Little Deacon was about to turn back to camp he heard a call. Looking up to the top of a nearby bluff he saw several Indians. They had called to him. He held up his open hands to show that he was not armed and motioned for the Indians to come down to him. After much hesitation the Indians came. Richards attempted to show by all the signs he could conceive that he was terribly in need of water. But the Indians showed no signs of understanding him. They wanted his shirt. The shirt was old and torn and dirty, but it was soon off Richards' back and on the back of a Pah-ute Indian.

In return for the shirt the Pah-ute placed his own blanket around Richards' shoulders. Richards carried this blanket for a year and prized it more than anything he possessed only to have it stolen from him in the mines.

When the exchange of wearing apparel was made the Indians led The Little Deacon to a water hole. By pretending that they were drinking and then spitting out water they made him understand that the water 143 was poison. They then led Richards to another hole of water in the rocks close to the base of the Argus Range where it joins the Slate Range near the head of Searles Lake Valley. By pantomime the Indians assured Richards that this was good water.

The Little Deacon was undoubtedly about famished. Did he hurriedly get down and take a drink of water? If we are to credit the accounts of several Jay Hawks we must believe that he did not. They stated that he immediately turned and ran about four miles to call to his companions, "I've found water." This seems almost unbelievable, but with ten men down along the back trail, two to arise no more, perhaps the Little Deacon's first thought was of them.

Most remarkable of all was the situation at the Jay Hawk dry camp. Mrs. Brier had come in, leaving Fish and Isham exhausted on the desert. She had been unable to encourage them to take another step. At the Jay Hawk camp, full of courage and optimism, she was still at work. She lectured the disheartened Jay Hawks about keeping up their spirits. She said, "Take courage boys, the darkest hour is always just before the dawn." In a few minutes The Little Deacon ran into camp with his cry, "I've found water."

The Little Deacon immediately turned and led some of the stronger Jay Hawks to the water. They built a fire of desert brush. By its guidance the rest of the party followed.

There was no rest for Richards or for those who were strong enough to follow him. Filling canteens with water they went back over the trail giving water to those who were down and helping them to get started to the newly found water.

But the rescuers were too late to aid Isham or "Father Fish" who was the fiddler at their initiation ceremonies at Salt Lake. After Mrs. Brier had left Isham he crawled more than four miles on his hands and knees. Falling from a rock he was too exhausted to move and perished where he lay. A low mound of sand was scraped over the body of Isham. Ten years later William Lewis Manly found the bones of Fish lying where there was not a handful of earth to cover them. The struggling band had thrown away almost every article but food, including their knives and almost all of their guns, and had no implements with which to dig a grave. Of the Jay Hawks only Ed Doty and Tom Shannon are known to have carried their guns all of the way to Rancho San Francisquito.

This spring, discovered so providentially by The Little Deacon, was named by the Jay Hawks, Providence Spring. Some of them revisited it many years later when they were searching for the Gunsight Lead. It

144

probably was known later as Indian Joe's Spring and, if so, was located in Indian Joe's Canyon north of present Wilson Canyon.

The Jay Hawks had suffered terribly in Panamint Valley and in crossing the Slate Range. Some of them had been without water for three days. Others had been out from the water at the Camp of the Horse Bones a full five days before water was discovered by The Little Deacon. Considering the more than thirty days of constant struggle and thirst since the Jay Hawks had passed from Emigrant Valley into the head of Fortymile Canyon, it is remarkable that any of them were able to continue. But continue they did—for almost thirty days more. Many persons have perished in less than a week on the Nevada and California deserts surrounding Death Valley. To nothing but indomitable courage and willpower can be attributed the survival of the Jay Hawks for almost two months beyond the time when they should have perished, for they staggered into Rancho San Francisquito on the 4th and 5th of February, 1850, little more than walking skeletons; skin and a few ligaments holding together shriveled entrails and bones, the marrow of which, like those of the oxen, had been reduced to bloody water. It was this continuing and slowly worsening struggle which led Manly and others to despair of ever presenting a true word picture of their epic journey through the Valley of Death and across the deserts.

The journey from Providence Spring led over the Slate Range, which is the southern branch of the Argus Range, into the basin in which China Lake is located. The Jay Hawks recorded little about China Lake. After having been so deeply disappointed by Searles Lake they knew what to expect at this second lake which came into view as they emerged from the rocky canyon of the Slate.

From the Slate Range it is about twenty miles airline to Indian Wells where the Jay Hawks found the next water. From Deacon Richards' Providence Spring it was thirty-five miles airline to Indian Wells. The route traveled by the Jay Hawks must have measured at least forty miles. Some of the Jay Hawks were four days in traveling this distance. Others were five days. There was no living water to be had throughout the entire distance.

The existence of Indian Wells, toward which the Jay Hawks traveled, was unknown to them at the time. They were heading for the snow-capped Sierra, at the base of which they expected to find running streams of water. It was a steady climb of more than twenty miles up a sandy, ashy, brush-covered alluvial fan from the Slate Range to Indian Wells. When the foremost Jay Hawks approached the base of the Sierra 145 they found no water but they did discover a well-defined trail which ran parallel with the Sierra and which had been traveled by horses. This was the Joe Walker Trail, of which they had heard in Salt Lake. They followed the trail south to a hole on a bench-land high above Indian Wells Valley. This water hole was walled up with rock and had been found in that condition by the first white travelers over that route. Today (1949) it is being developed into a health resort. A reservoir has been constructed and a bathhouse and other improvements are being built nearby. The old spring has been tunneled far back into the bank and again walled with rock. This place is on the west side of Highway #6, two-tenths of a mile north of Homestead Service Station and four miles west and slightly north of the village of Inyokern.

If the trip from Panamint Valley to Providence Spring was an exhausting ordeal to the Jay Hawks, the trail from there to Indian Wells was worse. Although no lives were lost the constant tramp through five days of dry camps took a heavy toll of the fast ebbing strength of both oxen and men. There was no water with which to cook any portion of the slaughtered oxen. When the throat of an ox was cut the Jay Hawks crowded around and held their little frying pans, each to catch his share of the watery blood. This they drank before it curdled. It was their only means of moistening their lips and throats so they could eat a meal of the poor stringy, tough sinew; all that remained of the flesh of the starved, staggering cattle.

Each Jay Hawk was expected to stand his turn in furnishing an ox for slaughtering. When it came Tom Shannon's turn his pet animal had to go. To shoot this poor old bag of bones was Tom's most difficult act of the entire trip.

Every particle of the carcass of an ox was saved. It was all either eaten at once or dried over a fire. The more repulsive portions were carried along to be eaten when the starved Jay Hawks were forced to it. When they arrived in the canyon above Rancho San Francisquito to headquarters these loathsome portions were all the rations that remained. They were quietly discarded behind trailside brush as the juicy fresh beef was handed out to the famished Jay Hawks.

In 1894 a newspaper reporter interviewed the Jay Hawks at their reunion and quoted them as follows about their starved cattle:

> "The main body of Jayhawkers kept their cattle, for they
> were their only hope; on these they lived, and the cattle lived
> on the bitter sage brush and greasewood, except when they

occasionally found an oasis with salt, alkali or nitre water and a little grass upon it. The feet of the cattle were worn down until the blood marked every step. Then the boys wrapped their feet in raw hides, as they did their own.—But for their cattle not a man could have lived through that awful journey. They ate the hides, blood, the refuse and picked the bones in camp, making jerked beef of the balance to take along with them."

When the rawhide moccasins worn by both Jay Hawks and their oxen wore through they did not throw them away. They were carried along until water was obtained; when they were boiled, the soup drunk and the hide parched over a brush fire and eaten. In the absence of water the entrails of the cattle were prepared "by well shaking" and then parched over the fire. These and the hide contained the most nourishment of any portion of the feeble oxen. In 1893 one of the Jay Hawks stated:

"The cattle were all poisoned by the alkali and sulphur of the deserts, and what flesh they had was covered with a yellow slime and could scarcely be eaten, even by the hunger crazed gold hunters, even to the marrow in their bones, which was but like blood and water. The hides were singed [held hair side down over a brush fire], boiled into a soup, then burned over the fires and made into soup again. This soup made of rawhide, was the chief subsistence of the party toward the last."

On this struggle across Indian Wells Valley, Asa Haynes, Captain of the Jay Hawks, came near perishing. He was one of the oldest men in the party. Having been born in 1804, he was forty-five years of age. He was badly overcome with hunger as far back as the Indian Ranch camp in Panamint Valley. There he had watched Mrs. Brier baking the last of the flour into little, hard, unleavened biscuits, the last bread seen by any of the Death Valley '49ers until they reached Rancho San Francisquito. Concerning this incident E. F. Bartholomew in 1885 wrote to Captain Haynes:

"There is no visit I had rather make, than the one to meet the boys of '49 at their reunion, and especially the one this

147

year at your house, you, the Captain of our little band of lost Jayhawkers. Many are the times I have thought of you, feeble and old as you were then, and starving for want of some nourishing food. I can see in your hand that five dollar gold piece you held out so pitifully for that little, hard, dried-biscuit, not two inches in diameter."

Other details of this incident have previously been presented on these pages.

While crossing Indian Wells Valley, John B. Colton became sick from drinking poison water. He was so weakened that he lay down to die. Charles Mecum came up to him and placed him on an ox. He was so weak that it was necessary to tie him on the ox. In 1892 Urban P. Davidson wrote of this incident:

"John Colton fell by the wayside and could go no farther. Charlie came up with an ox having two eyes, a little hide and some bones left [called a steer] boosted the boy on and persuaded the critter to carry him into camp. Some fell and then crawled into camp about midnight. Some never came."

In writing to Colton, Mecum reminded him of his desperate condition on the desert and stated that the steer, if turned upside down would have made a better harrow than a steer. It is within reason to imagine that Colton's back was just as bony as was the steer's, for, upon reaching Los Angeles he was to weigh just sixty-four pounds. His knee joints were great knots below thighs as small as his forearm had been when he left Illinois, and his features were so shrunken and ghastly that the form of his teeth could be seen through his thin lips.

When Ed Doty took charge of this faltering band of Jay Hawks he began to urge them to greater efforts. His spirit was infectious. Instead of lying down to die as they were ready to do, they began to joke about their appearance and spread out in small groups through the brush to search for water. In this way they traveled to the Joe Walker Trail.

CHAPTER TEN

THE JAY HAWKS ESCAPE

William Lewis Manly and John Haney Rogers, on their way to the Spanish settlements to get provisions for the parties stranded in Death Valley, came upon the Jay Hawks when they were camped at Indian Wells. They first saw a smoke and thought it might be from the camp fires of Indians. So they used great caution in approaching the little smoke. About this meeting Manly wrote:

"We took a circuitous route and soon saw that the persons were on a little bench above us and we kept very cautious and quiet listening for any sounds that might tell us who they were.

"If they were Indians we should probably hear some of their dogs, but we heard none, and kept creeping closer, till we were within fifty yards without hearing a sound to give us any idea of who they were.

"We decided to get our guns at full cock and then hail the camp, feeling that we had a little the advantage of position. We hailed and were answered in English. 'Don't Shoot' said we, and they assured us they had no idea of such a thing, and asked us to come in. We found here to our surprise, Ed Doty, Tom Shannon, L. D. Stevens, and others whom I do not recollect, the real Jayhawkers. They gave us some fresh meat for supper, and near the camp were some water holes that answered well for camp purposes.

"Here an ox had given out and they had stopped long enough to dry the meat, while the others had gone on a day ahead.

"Coming around the mountain from the north was quite a well defined trail, leading to the west and they said they were satisfied some one lived at the end of it, and they were going to follow it if it lead to Mexico or anywhere else. They said that Mr. Brier and his family were still on behind, and

149

alone. Every one must look out for himself here, and we could not do much for another in any way.

"We inquired of them about the trail over which they had come, and where they had found water, and we told them of our experience in this respect. We then related how our train could not go over mountains with wagons, how they had returned to the settlements to obtain relief while they waited for our return. We explained to them how they must perish of starvation. We told them how nearly we came to the point of perishing that very morning, of thirst, and how we were saved by finding a little patch of ice in an unexpected place, and were thus enabled to come on another days travel.

"These men were not as cheerful as they used to be and their situation and prospects constantly occupied their minds. They said to us that if the present trail bore away from the mountains and crossed the level plain, that there were some of them who could not possibly get along safely to the other side. Some were completely discouraged, and some were completely out of provisions and dependent on those who had either provisions or oxen yet on hand. An ox was frequently killed, they said, and no part of it was wasted. At a camp where there was no water, for stewing a piece of hide would be prepared for eating by singeing off the hair and then roasting in the fire. The small intestines were drawn through the fingers to clean them, and these when roasted made very fair food.

"They said they had been without water for four or five days at a time and came near starving to death, for it was impossible to swallow food when one became so thirsty. They described the pangs of hunger as something terrible and not to be described. They were willing to give us any information we desired and we anxiously received all we could, for on our return we desired to take the best possible route, and we thus had the experience of two parties instead of one. They told us about the death of Mr. Fish and Mr. Isham, and where we would find their bodies if we went over their trail.

"In the morning we shouldered our packs again and took the trail leading to the west, and by night we had overtaken the advance party of the Jayhawkers, camped in an cañon where there was a little water, barely sufficient for their use.

We inquired why they did not take the trail leading more directly west at the forks, and they said they feared it would lead them into deep snow which would be impassable. They said they considered the trail they had taken as altogether the safest one.

"We met Bennet and Arcane's teamsters, and as we expected they were already out of grub and no way to get anymore. When the party killed an ox they had humbly begged for some of the poorst parts, and thus far were alive. They came to us and very pitifully told us they were entirely out and although an ox had been killed that day they had not been able to get a mouthful. We divided up our meat and gave them some although we did not know how long it would be before we would ourselves be in the same situation.

"Thus far we had not seen anything to shoot, big or little although we kept a sharp lookout.

"The whole camp was silent, and all seemed to realize their situation. Before them was a level plain which had the appearance of being so broad as to take five or six days to cross. Judging by the look from the top of the mountain as we came over, there was a little to hope for in the way of water. We thought it over very seriously. All the water we could carry would be our canteens full, perhaps two drinks apiece and the poor meat had so little nourishment that we were weak and unable to endure what we once could.

"We were along, Rogers and I, in interest at any rate, even if there were other men about. For the time it really seemed as if there was very little hope for us and I have often repeated the following lines as very closely describing my own feelings at that time.

> Oh hands, whose loving, gentle grasp I loosed.
> When first this weary journey was begun.
> If I could feel your touch as once I could.
> How gladly would I wish my work undone.
>
> Harriet Kenyon.

During the evening, I had a talk with Capt. Asa Haines, in which he said he left a good home in Illinois, where he had everything he could wish to eat, and every necessary comfort, and even some to spare, and now he felt so nearly worn out that he had many doubts whether he could live to reach the mountains, on the other side. He was so deeply impressed that he made me promise to let his wife and family know how I found him and how he died, for he felt sure he would never see the California mines. I said I might not get through myself, but he thought we were so young and strong that we would struggle through. He said if he could only be home once more he would be content to stay. This was the general tenor of the conversation. There was no mirth, no jokes, and every one seemed to feel that he was very near the end of his life, and such a death as stood before them, choking, starving in a desert was the most dreary outlook I ever saw.

"This camp of trouble, of forlorn hope, on the edge of a desert stretching out before us like a small sea, with no hope for relief except at the end of a struggle which seemed almost hopeless, is more than any pen can paint, or at all describe. The writer had tried it often. Picture to myself, dear reader the situation and let your own imagination do the rest. It can never come up to the reality.

"In the morning, as Rogers and I were about to start, several of the oldest men came to us with their addresses and wished us to forward them to their families if we got within the reach of mails. These men shed tears, and we did also as we parted. We turned silently away and again took up our march."

Striking directly south on the old Walker Trail the Jay Hawks soon came to a place where the trail forked. A branch led westward over a pass in the Sierra. This they recognized as Walker's Pass, for which they had been heading since leaving Captain Jefferson Hunt at Division Springs in what is now the extreme southwest corner of Utah. But the trail leading to the west was faintly defined and the starving party was afraid to follow it. They felt certain that the heavily traveled trail would lead them to some settlement. So they continued southward.

Crossing the south end of Indian Wells Valley, the Jay Hawks entered Last Chance Canyon and through it crossed El Paso Mountains into the desert valley northeast of present Cantil. On the way through Last Chance the Jay Hawks passed near the Petrified Forest, now visited by all Rock Hounds who covet agatized wood. In the south end of

152

the canyon they passed over the vast deposit of volcanic ash or seismo-tite from which Dutch Cleanser long was made.

From the mouth of the canyon at the south edge of El Paso Mountains the little band could see a clump of willows about four miles to the southwest. When they arrived at the willows they found a fine large flowing spring. The clump of willows had been cut away in the center and made into a corral. This old spring on the old trail of the Indian horse thieves stands today in an alfalfa field about a mile and a quarter east of the village of Cantil. It appears much as it did one hundred and twenty-five years ago, and is known as Desert Spring. It now is an official California landmark.

The water from Desert Spring flowed out upon the desert and created a small meadow. There the Jay Hawks recruited their famished cattle with both feed and water. This was the first feed except sage that the oxen had tasted since leaving Indian Wells, seven days earlier. Even Sheldon Young was encouraged by Desert Spring. On January 23 he wrote in his log:

"Went five miles South-West [from the El Paso Moun-tains]. Found grass, water and plenty of willows. The coun-try begins to have a different look. We are now in hopes of getting out soon."

So certain was Sheldon Young's mess of better times ahead that they again headed southwest eighteen miles to high country.

Continuing twenty-four miles south they still were climbing over a table land. This day, January 25, they passed the site of present Mojave. Wrote Sheldon Young:

"Camped by some puddle water. Grass. Weather continues cold and stormy on the mountains."

One hundred years later to a day the weather was the same on the same mountains and the desert about Mojave was covered with almost a foot of snow.

The next day, after a short march, the Jay Hawks reached Willow Springs. Wrote Sheldon Young on January 26:   153

"Went three miles south and came to a beautiful spring of water. Wood. Had our two oxen killed."

On January 27 the party lost the trail. Apparently there were several trails leading from Willow Springs in southerly directions. The Jay Hawks traveled ten miles; they then found they were lost. A party went back to Willow Springs and found the main trail. The rest cut westward to the trail and then followed it southward.

To the mountains south of Willow Springs were many miles more than the Jay Hawks had estimated. Certain that their troubles would soon be over they had not stopped long enough at either Desert Spring or Willow Springs to properly recruit either themselves or their oxen. After making a dry camp the night of January 27 and traveling sixteen miles to the mountains, they had covered about thirty-five miles from Willow Springs and were confronted with another range of mountains, the northern end of the San Gabriels. In their eagerness the Jay Hawks overreached their endurance. Across Indian Wells Valley they had been covering from five to eight miles a day. In the last three days they had covered more than ten miles a day. Here, at almost the very end of their journey, they lost two of their party. This was the most tragic experience in their entire struggle through deserts and mountain ranges.

William Robinson was weaker than the rest. On January 27 he told Mrs. Brier that he felt he would never reach California. Remember that none of these '49ers knew they had then been in California more than a month. Forty-eight years later on December 20, 1898, Mrs. Brier wrote:

"When near the place where Mojave is now Robinson said to me: 'Mrs. Brier, I have a presentiment I shall never reach California.' None of us knew then that we were well across a section of the state. 'Oh, Yes, you will: don't give up,' I said to cheer him. The next day he fell off his pony and died. The men dug a shallow grave with their knives and laid him to rest."

Of this day Sheldon Young wrote:

"Bore West of South, Struck trail again. Went sixteen miles to the mountains. Struck a large cañon. Found grass and water. Horse and ox bones about here plenty. Wm.

Walker's Pass, showing the present highway following the route taken by the parties of Death Valley '49ers who took that shortcut to the San Joaquin Valley and the Southern Mines. In the foreground is the site of Coyote Holes. Where the highway makes the first curve to the right is Soldier Well. In the middle distance, between two peaks, is the highest point reached in Walker's Pass.

Photo Courtesy Ray Geers and now in Bear State Library.

155

Descendants of Death Valley '49ers at a reunion held February 4, 1930, at the site of del Valle home on Rancho San Franscisquito. Men in the front row are, left to right: Frank and Henry Doty, sons of Jay Hawk Captain Edward Doty, and E. W. Mecum, son of C. B. Mecum. In the background stands a portion of the milk house where the Death Valley '49ers feasted on milk and cheese for the first time since leaving Salt lake five months before.

Photo courtesy Mrs. Frank Doty and now in Bear State Library.

Robinson brought into camp. Died in the evening from the effects of drinking too much cold water after having been without part of the day."

The Jay Hawks had found a spring in the mountains near the head of Soledad Canyon through which the railroad now runs. It was at this spring where poor Robinson had his last drink of water. Unable to walk he was placed on an ox. Two brother Jay Hawks held him on. When near the camp he assured his comrades that he could ride without help. When within fifty feet of the campfire he fell from the ox. As the others rushed to his aid he begged them not to touch him, telling them that he was too tired and exhausted to be moved and that he would come on in to camp as soon as he had rested. The boys covered Robinson with a blanket and went to the fireside. When they returned to help him into camp a short time later he was dead.

The shock of Robinson's death was doubly hard on the now frantic Jay Hawks. A few miles back they had lost another comrade, one from whom they had no word for more than sixteen years.

When approaching the San Gabriel Mountains the Jay Hawks met a band of horses being driven by Indians. Thinking to stampede the poor, starved Jay Hawk oxen the Indians ran their horses near them and yelled. Except for two oxen which were being led, they all ran off into the desert. Only a few of them were recovered. One of these stampeded oxen was carrying a pack. In this pack were all of the belongings of a Jay Hawk known only as Frenchy, or Old French. He ran after his fleeing ox and was soon lost to sight. The Jay Hawks thought that Frenchy had been killed by the Indians. Sixteen years later a band of desert Indians were found in possession of a feeble-minded Frenchman who answered the description of Frenchy. Many years later this man died at an advanced age in the San Bernardino County Hospital.

On this day, January 30, Sheldon Young entered the following in his log:

"Went six miles south-west. Plenty of signs of wilde cattle and deer. Stopped at noon. Cattle took a stampede. Camped. No water. Bunch grass. Cedar wood."

On January 31 the Jay Hawks searched for their stampeded cattle. They were in desperate straights. On February they left camp at noon. Sheldon Young wrote:

"Found part of the cattle. Four head not yet found. Struck into a large cañon. Found stream of water,—suppose it to be the head of Kern River. [They were on the head of the Santa Clara River, which empties into the ocean near Ventura.] It is lined with plenty of timber and grass. It looks like home. Plenty of signs of game, but none killed yet."

It was not until the forenoon of February 3 that the Jay Hawks killed any game. This proved to be a cow belonging to the herds of del Valle, or Rancho San Francisquito, as it properly was known. The Argonauts were in the worst condition endured during the entire journey. It was this fact, contrasted with their feasting in the midst of plenty the very next day, that made the Jay Hawks remember February 4 and celebrate its memory more than seventy-one years later.

First of the Jay Hawks to prepare for the trip to California, John B. Colton was also first to see the Spanish settlements near Newhall. On February 4 he had recovered from the weakness which overcame him in Indian Wells Valley. With Tom Shannon that morning he had crowded ahead of the rest of the party. As they started out Colton remarked that he felt as though they were going "to strike something soon." They came upon some small trees. Soon they saw larger trees. At last they looked through the drooping branches of an oak tree and saw a red object, the tile roof of an adobe house. It was the home of the widow of Antonio del Valle, on Rancho San Francisquito. This adobe was located on the south bank of the Santa Clara River about one half mile due south of the present junction of Highway #99 and Highway #1, the second of which leads to Ventura and Santa Barbara. It was later to become famous as the birthplace of Ramona, heroine of the novel by Helen Hunt Jackson. Today the site is reached by a private road which leaves Highway #99 at its junction with the Newhall road which connects with Highway #6.

The Jay Hawks were split into several parties, Colton and Stevens being ahead of all others. One group saw a mare and two colts. These they killed. The mare was eaten on the spot. "Nothing was left but the bones and hoofs." Another group came on some cattle that belonged to Sr. del Valle. They shot several and began cutting them up and eating the flesh raw. Crowded around the slaughtered animal with chunks of bloody meat in their hands and blood on their faces, hands and clothing, the Jay Hawks presented a terrible appearance to the San Francisquito

158   yaqueros.

José Sálazar, who later married the widow del Valle, and several vaqueros were attracted by the sound of rifle shots and rode up to the feasting party. Tom Shannon had been in the Mexican War and could speak some Spanish. He explained the situation that the Jay Hawks were in. Little explanation was necessary as Manly and Rogers already had visited the Rancho and told of the condition of these starving people. Besides, the wasted bodies and wolfish hunger of the little group was explanation enough.

Sálazar rode to the ranch house to have food prepared for the Jay Hawks. Some of his vaqueros took meat and bread back along the trail and revived those who were down. Mrs. Brier stated that eight men, including her husband, were down that morning and if not rescued, would have died. Considering the statements of others and the fact that they had lost two men during the preceeding three days, it seems that her statement was well grounded.

In 1893 the *San Francisco Chronicle* published a long account of the Jay Hawks' sufferings. Most of the material for the story was furnished by John B. Colton. Here is what was published about the condition of the perishing party when they reached Rancho San Francisquito:

> "When Salazar learned of the approach of the starving band of pioneers he set things moving at once. Horsemen were dispatched to bring in the wanderers. Others were ordered to round up some fat young cattle for the slaughter, that the unfortunate American might be feasted.
>
> "Salazar's wife herself, and other women went forth to meet the feeble travelers. When they saw the survivors they wept at their pitiful appearance. Big strong men had lost more than 100 pounds, and were nothing but wrinkled skin clinging over visible skeletons. Their very teeth showed in exact outline beneath the clinging parchment cheeks. Their temples were sunken, their eyes were caved far into their heads, their noses pinched and drawn, their necks shrunken to the primal tendons, and their hands ashen and clawlike in their terrible thinness."

Colton, a young man about six feet in height, weighed sixty-four pounds when he arrived in Los Angeles after more than a week of feasting at the del Valle home.

After arriving at Rancho San Francisquito and eating heartily of 159

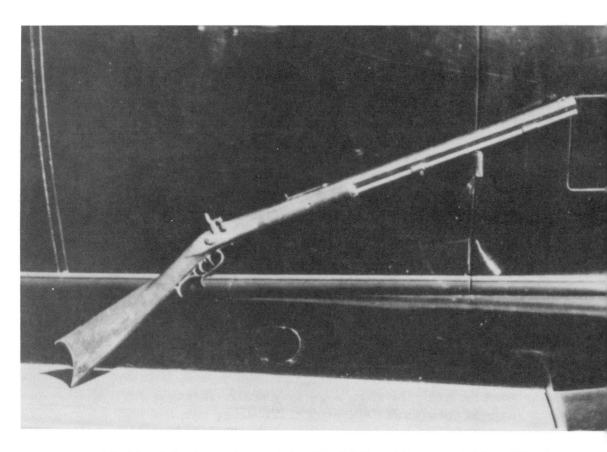

The Muzzle loading rifle which Jay Hawk Edward Doty carried from Illinois to California.
Photo courtesy Mrs. Frank Doty and now in Bear State Library.

tortillas, beans and fresh meat the whole party became violently ill. Colton wrote that he got up several times during the first night and roasted more meat. He could not sleep for thinking of how good it tasted. In 1885 Edward Bartholomew wrote:

"And again at San Francisquito Ranch: those eight days we lay there suffering. Oh! I can hear those groans till yet, from all parts of that camp, and more particularly from that mess under the tree where our Captain (Asa Haines) lay."

After the week of feasting at the del Valle home most of the Jay Hawks made their way down the Santa Clara River to Ventura and to the mines by way of San Luis Obispo, San Jose, Livermore and Altamont Passes. Ed Doty bought some cattle from the Briers who went on into Los Angeles. He later returned to Santa Barbara and died there. Lorenzo Dow Stevens and Tom Shannon lived many years at San Jose.

Within a few months Lou West made up a party and returned to Death Valley, searching for the Lost Gunsight Lead. A number of other Jay Hawks including Wm. G. Rood also returned at one time or another to search for the Gunsight.

In 1851 Deacon Richards and Harrison B. Franz were living in San Jose. Both left California; Richards to return to his home in Illinois and Franz to mine for more than fifty years, most of this time in Baker County, Oregon.

Alonzo Clay mined at Bidwell's Bar on the Klamath River and at Reddings Diggin's. He returned to his old home in Illinois.

Charles B. Mecum mined at Bidwell's Bar, made his "pile" in a short time and returned to Galesburg.

Urban Davison mined at Bidwell's Bar and left California. He died at Thermopolis, Wyoming.

Most active of all Jay Hawks was John B. Colton. In the mines he heard a familiar voice. Dropping his tools he climbed across gravel piles to another claim where he presented himself to Captain Jefferson Hunt. Hunt had no knowledge of the escape of any of the party which separated from him at Division Springs. Colton experienced much satisfaction in assuring Hunt that almost all of them did escape.

Having been born August 11, 1831, Colton was seventeen years and eight months of age when he left his home at Galesburg, Illinois, April 1, 1849. When he arrived at Ranch San Francisquito, February 4, 1850, he was eighteen years and six months of age. He was the youngest 161

Death Valley '49ers descendants reunion at the del Valle home site on Rancho San Francisquito, February 4, 1930. Left to right: second, Henry Doty, holding the gun which was carried to California in 1849 by his father, Edward Doty; third, Chester Doty (son of Henry); sixth, Frank Doty; seventh, E. W. Mecum; ninth, Wm. A. Wiley.
Photo courtesy Mrs. Frank Doty and now in Bear State Library.

162

member of the Jay Hawk band, or of any of the parties, except those which included the children of the Wade, Bennett, Arcan and Brier families. He was a tall, slender boy and became the poorest and skinniest of all the men who staggered into the del Valle home that February morning in 1849.

Colton worked his way to the mines by helping a party of Mexicans who were going to the Sonoran Camp, later the town of Sonora. He mined around Sonora and Columbia and became interested in a ditch company. In 1851 or early in 1852 he returned to Illinois after having been more than ordinarily successful in the mines. He was one of the last Jay Hawks to die. One would expect that the terrible experiences in Death Valley and on the deserts of Nevada would have shortened the lives of all those pioneers, but some of them lived to be almost one hundred years of age. Harrison B. Franz lived to an advanced age. John Groscup lived to be eighty-nine. Asa Haynes, the oldest Jay Hawk, died in the eighty-fifth year. Charles B. Mecum died at the age of eighty-three. The "Little Deacon" Richards lived to be eighty-one. Tom Shannon was seventy-eight when he died after having served in both the Mexican and Civil Wars. John Lewis West was eighty; Sheldon Young, the ex-sailor who kept the log, lived to be seventy-seven. Lorenzo Dow Stevens was last of all the Jay Hawks to die, aged ninety-four when he passed away in 1921. He lived to observe the seventy-first anniversary of the Jay Hawk trek through Death Valley. Others lived well into the sixties and seventies. In fact, from the percentage of aged who survived the Death Valley trek of '49, it would seem that the desert experience was beneficial to their health.

John B. Colton became the historian of the Jay Hawks. In 1872 he called a reunion of the old gang at his home in Galesburg, Illinois. He attended a reunion every subsequent year until his death in 1919, a total of forty-seven anniversaries. He became known as the *Historian of the Jay Hawks.* He arranged for the meetings of the Jay Hawks, collected photographs of them, corresponded with every Jay Hawk who would write to him and filed every newspaper clipping he could secure relating to early mining or to the Death Valley parties of '49. His gatherings, now in the Huntington Library at San Marino, California, fill a large photograph album, hundreds of folders and more than a dozen scrapbooks, some of them more than four inches in thickness. Colton was actually one of the most untiring historians of all time, for he made the Death Valley trek of '49 probably the best documented single incident in American History.

163

Pasted in one of Colton's well-thumbed scrapbooks is the following poem which probably brought many memories to his mind and many tears to his eyes during the years when he sat in his armchair and read over his collection:

"Hello." "Hel-lo!" "Why, Jim!" "Why, Dan!"
　"Good Lord! I want to know!"
"Well, well! old fel! give us your han'—
　But, Jim how does it go?"

"Oh, sometimes gay and sometimes rough:
　an, how's it go with you?"
"Well, turns jus' now's a little tough
　Up here in I-da-ho."

"But where ye been, Jim, ever since
　We left the Stanislow,
And pull up stakes down that at Dent's
　Twenty eight years ago."

"Well, sence that time that we put out
　on that stampede from Stoney,
Ben most the tme knockin' about.
　Down into Air-e-zony.

"Only been back a month or so,
　And thought I'd take a tramp
Through the old diggin's, long with Jo,
　Who stops at Nigger Camp.

"Started from Alpha on our trip,
　And passed up the Divide,
Through Tangle-Leg and Let-Er-Rip
　Red Dog and Whisky Slide.

"Then after hearing that we went
　Down by the Tail-Holt Mill,
Crost Greenhorn Mountains to Snow Tent,
　And up to Gouge Eye Hill.

THE JAY HAWKS ESCAPE

"From Gouge Eye down to Esperance,
   Slap Jack and Ora Fin:
Through Deadwood and Last Chance,
   Root Hog and Last Ravine.

"From Petticoat to Shirt-Tail flat,
   And on by the Murder's Bar,
Crost Bloody Run and thro' Wild Oat,
   To Poker and Lone Star.

"From Angels Camp down by Rawhide,
   We took a run one night,
Through Chinese Roost and Satan's Pride
   Across to Hell's Delight.

"Then came along to Poverty,
   Dead Broke and Bottle Range,
To Hangtown, Poor Man and Lone Tree,
   Garrote and Smash-Up Bridge.

"Through Nip and Tuck and Old Bear Trap,
   Coon Hollow and Fair Play,
Along the Scorpion and Fur Cap,
   Kanaka and El Rey.

"We stopped one day at Never Sweat,
   Another up at Ophir,
Then moved our boots into You Bet,
   And Struck the Gopher.

"To Sucker near Grass Widow Bend,
   Where as 'twas getting late,
We brought our jouney to an end,
   Down by the Devil's gate."

"Wal, Jim, you must uv seen a heap;
   I'd like to make the rounds,
As you have done, and cast a peep
   Through the old stamping grounds."

"Y-e-s, but I tell you what it is,
    The times they ain't no more,
In Californy as they was
    'Way back in Fifty-four."

But most impressive of all is the last and longest entry in the log of the Jay Hawk ex-sailor, Sheldon Young, written February 5, 1850, after he had trailed the remainder of the Jay Hawks to their last camp:

"Went seven miles west. Had a dry camp. Plenty of grass and a wide timber and a wide cãnon. We are in a country where there is plenty of wild cattle and horses. There was such a bellowing of cattle that it was hard sleeping last night. Went out to shoot some,—killed one cow. Got caught at it. Found a ranch six miles from camp. Had thousands of cattle, sheep and horses and we have got out of trouble at last."

Death Valley '49ers' descendants standing on the ruins of the adobe walls of the del Valle home near present Castaic Rancho. The tower to the right of center marks the site of Highway number 99 and the Ventura Highway. Highway 99 leads to the San Joaquin Valley through the canyon which shows at the left elbow of Chester Doty. Left to right: Wm. A. Wiley, Chester Doty (son of Henry Doty), Henry Doty, Frank Doty and E. W. Mecum.

Photo courtesy of Mrs. Frank Doty and now in Bear State Library.

CHAPTER ELEVEN

THE BRIERS AND WADES

Probably the most determined party among the Death Valley '49ers were the Briers: Rev. James Welsh Brier; his wife, Juliette Brier; and their three sons, Christopher Columbus Brier, John Welsh Brier and Kirk White Brier. When the party jumped off into the Great American Desert in November of 1849 the oldest son was aged eight years and seven months, the second was six years and two months and the third, four years and two months. The Rev. Brier was born in 1814, so was thirty-five years of age and Mrs. Brier, born in 1813, was thirty-six. The ages of the Briers have been variously given by other writers, but the above are from data furnished by the Briers themselves.

It is important to keep the above ages in mind, for Mrs. Brier and her husband, too, accomplished one of the most exhausting journeys ever undertaken by a similar family in the history of the settlement of America. According to an account left by Mrs. Brier they were forced to abandon their wagon in Fortymile Canyon and to walk the rest of the way, about four hundred miles, to Rancho San Francisquito. In scouting for feed and water Rev. Brier must have walked an additional hundred miles. John B. Colton has already told us that for much of this distance Mrs. Brier carried Kirk on her back, John in her arms and led Columbus by the hand.

At this point the writer is at a loss to know how familiar are his readers with the four hundred miles between the head of Fortymile Canyon and Rancho San Francisquito. Beyond stating that almost every foot of that distance was composed of brush-covered, loose sand or light ashy soil and sharp-edged rocky mountains, some of the last practically perpendicular, adjectives mean very little. To simply state, as has been done, that theirs was one of the most unbelievable journeys ever undertaken in the settlement of America also leaves much to the imagination. No writer yet, from William Lewis Manly down to date, has accomplished anything in describing the terrors of that trek of '49. Mrs. Brier has come nearest of any to having us see them as they plodded across the Great American Desert.

Juliette W. Brier, John Welsh Brier and Rev. James Welsh Brier, from a photograph made about 1890.
Photo courtesy Huntington Library and now in Bear State Library.

THE BRIERS AND WADES

In approaching the story of Death Valley '49ers always we are brought face to face with that little lady who much of the way carried those two little starving boys, together weighing almost as much as she did. We find very little about her husband, except in her letters. One of only three unpleasant phases of the history of the men and women who made that journey of '49 concerns Preacher Brier.

Almost every writer has been free in condemning the man who, at the site of the later Mountain Meadow Massacre, preached a sermon, taking as his text "There Shall Be No More Death." Also they have been free to criticize Brier as one who could talk on any subject whether he knew anything about it or not. They have condemned him for having had a falling out with work and of allowing his wife to bring through the oxen and wagons and to carry the children much of the way. Manly criticized his sermon at Travertine Springs in Furnace Creek Wash as a "lecture on education.—It seemed very strange to me to hear a solemn discourse on the benefits of early education when, it seemed to me, starvation was staring us all in the face, and the barren desolation all around gave small promise of the need of any education higher than the natural impulses of nature." In fact, there is little concerning the journey of '49 for which Brier has not been condemned. This writer's father, also a minister and well acquainted with Rev. Brier, was several times heard to roundly criticize him.

Brier was heartily condemned by many of the Jay Hawks, whom he had insisted on following against their stiff opposition. He was mimicked and ridiculed in the Jay Hawk camp. The lead in this was taken by Tom Shannon. Tom had been in the Mexican War and was probably the only Jay Hawk besides Sheldon Young who ever had been away from his home before starting for California. Shannon's imitations of Brier and his parodies of Brier's sermons provided much entertainment for the Jay Hawks.

In 1898, shortly before Rev. Brier died, he learned of Shannon's entertainment at his expense. He wrote to Deacon Richards when Richards was preparing for the Jay Hawk reunion of that year, with the request "That our names may no longer appear in the list of Jay Hawkers, for we never had any connection with that company."

After acknowledging the friendship and worthiness of many of the Jay Hawks, Brier continued with his condemnation of Tom Shannon!

"I remember that when your old stampede oxen left you in a bad fix that I lent you 3 or 4 of mine to help you on, and I further remember that I sold to Capt. Doty, as a favor, my 7 splendid oxen for $115 [taking Doty's note], when on the same day I could have taken $200 in coin. I did this little act to help the Jay Hawks but Tom Shannon that blackard of your company has paid me in full for my little unselfish act of kindness.—While I was helping the Jay Hawks [note that Brier does not use the word 'Jayhawker'!] I suppose these slanders were being bandied through the Jay Hawk camp."

Also, Brier was much offended at the way he was handled by Manly in his book, *Death Valley in '49*. His letter raves at Manly:

"See Louis Manly's book, So called.

"And who is Louis Manly! He was only Bennet's ox driver. [Manly never was one of Bennett's ox drivers. Bennett had only one wagon and his driver was John Haney Rogers.] I did not know him but I recollect that he and John Rodgers passed us on the desert and they filled themselves with my jerk [dried beef] and that this same ox driver came to me at Los Angeles strapped and I took him into my home and gave him employment and wages, and by recommending him highly, got him in with two of our friends who took him to the mines. Well he has paid me—the vile ingrate. This would have been a joy to me to this day [Brier here means his association with the Jay Hawks] had I not since learned of the dirty scoundrelism that was at that very time being practiced in your camp.

"As a matter of course we do not hold any of you accountable for the doings of these wicked men. I was a minister and that was sufficient for them. I hope these facts will not dampen the joy of your meeting. A few more winds will cover our tracks. Please drop our names from your list. It is painful for me to name these things but you should know them.

"Farewell

"J. W. Brier, Sr."

It was terribly unfortunate that someone told Rev. Brier of the horse-play that went on in the Jay Hawk camps concerning his part in the struggle to reach California. Undoubtedly the Jay Hawks felt justified in their criticisms. Certainly there is nothing but truth in the statements made by Rev. Brier.

It is not the duty of this writer to try Rev. Brier or Tom Shannon, but to present all of the facts. As the story of the Briers is unfolded on these pages the reader surely will remember that it was common practice to poke fun at ministers and to refer to their "falling out with work". The reader will also notice that Rev. Brier in his own way constantly was helping by scouting for water and feed.

In order to evaluate properly the struggle made by the Briers several other things must be known. At one place and one place only in the Jay Hawk records reference is made to a pony which the Briers are there stated to have brought with them and to the fact that Mrs. Brier occasionally rode it. Certainly no pony was available after the Briers left their wagons in the head branch of Fortymile Canyon. Mrs. Brier and both her husband and son, John Welsh Brier, and several others left written accounts covering in detail their experiences between Ash Meadows and Rancho San Francisquito. In none of these accounts is any mention made of such a pony. Certainly Mrs. Brier would not have been carrying Kirk on her back, John in her arms and leading Columbus if a pony had been available.

A second fact of interest is that the Briers had two helpers, perhaps ox drivers, with them, Patrick and Loomis St. John. These men are mentioned frequently. We know that they were with the Briers when they left the Jay Hawk camp at Jayhawker Well and also, probably, when they traveled from Ash Meadows to Jayhawker Well. Mrs. Brier made no mention of driving the oxen when coming into Travertine Spring in Furnace Creek Wash on Christmas Day. Undoubtedly Patrick and St. John were behind, driving the cattle. Rev. Brier was ahead, following the Jay Hawks.

Always there has been some doubt as to whether the Briers came through Fortymile Canyon or left the Jay Hawks and followed the groups guided by Manly around the southeast tip of the Specter Range *via* Indian Springs.

Both Rev. and Mrs. Brier wrote that they left their wagons on a branch of Fortymile Canyon. This does not necessarily mean that they continued on down Fortymile Canyon behind the Jay Hawks. They may have turned southward ahead of the Manly-led groups.

In his history of the Brier's epic journey to California, John Welsh Brier does not clear up this uncertainty. He gives no details about the route from the south end of Emigrant Valley to Ash Meadows. Following is what he wrote concerning this early portion of their travels: 173

Juliette W. Brier, from a photo made about 1880.
Photo courtesy California State Library and now in Bear State Library.

"By a sweep to the north and west we entered a north-and-south valley, bounded on the west by Timpahute mountain. We should have doubled this mountain on the north, but our magnet drew us southward. Our course lay for miles among conical stacks, containing the seed of a species of bunch grass, gathered for food by the natives. The scene was exceedingly picturesque; and the grain would have proved most serviceable to us in the days to come. We respected the rights of the red man, but he was not equally considerate. Two riding animals were missing on the morning of our departure, and their unhappy owners had the misfortune of seeing them pursued by naked savages along the base of the distant mountain. [This may have been what became of the Brier pony.] Before disappearing from view the exultant natives made their adieus by executing a grand salaam in the reverse order.

"We journeyed fifty miles with the Timpahute, and descended into the first real desert I had ever seen, and saw here, for the first time, the mirage. We had been without water for twenty-four hours, when suddenly there broke into view to the south a splendid sheet of water, which all of us believed was Owen's Lake. As we hurried towards it the vision faded, and near midnight we halted on the rim of a basin of mud, with a shallow pool of brine. From this point I remember little of our westward course across the great desert until we rested at the mouth of a deep-walled fissure, and two Indians were brought into camp, captured at the extremity of the cleft. Questioned by signs as to the direction of the great water, they pointed to the southwest, and one of them led two of our young men to a beautiful mountain spring. During the night both escaped."

At this point Brier is in error. This discovery occured many days farther west. It was the "Little Deacon" Richards who was led to the beautiful mountain spring, probably now known as Indian Joe Spring. Deacon was apparently the only person in all of the parties who could approach the Indians or obtain any information from them.

John Welsh Brier's account continues with a very interesting discription of their trials. It is well to remember that John was only six years and two months of age when the party left Division Springs. So most of the story he tells was obtained either from his mother or his father, both of whom were living when his story was published.

> "From the escape of the captives to the abandonment of our wagons my memory is utterly at fault. The latter event is vividly recalled—the drifting sand, the cold blast from the north, the wind-beaten hill, the white tent, my lesson in the Testament, the burning of wagons as fuel, the forsaking of nearly every treasured thing, the packing of oxen, the melancholy departure. [All of this took place in Fortymile Wash.] (Twelve years afterward Gov. Blaisdell found the things we had abandoned in a remarkable state of preservation.) The walking, now made necessary, was hard upon the women and children, but the short rations were more trying for all.
>
> "After many days of bitter travel, we reached the Amargosa and camped in its dry channel, counting ourselves fortunate to find a muddy pool of water. The end of the next day found us, with our canteens empty, at the summit of a pass where there was no water, no grass, no fuel—nothing but a low, tubular plant, mottled with pale red and purple, that rattled desolately in the north wind. Early the next morning, from the top of a neighboring crag, my father looked across the furrowed hills into a deep valley reaching westward to a lofty mountain range, and in it, seeming scarcely two leagues away, a beautiful oasis of grass and springing water. All that day we hurried toward it, hardly able to keep pace with the eager animals down the well-beaten trail, and it was midnight (of Dec. 24, 1849) before we reached the oasis. For the last six miles my father carried my younger brother."

Continuing with his narrative, Brier set down some pertinent facts concerning his father.

> "By this time the physical condition of the party had become about as bad as it could be. There was not a vigorous man among us, and two or three had reached a stage beyond which there was nothing but death. My mother came of a Vermont stock, fit alike for adversity and prosperity. My father had always been active, enterprising and irrepressi-

ble. He had spent his manhood in self-sacrificing labors, and had never known what it meant to be discouraged. Now, however, we could see that he was failing, while, under an acute disorder, it was hard for him to perform the ordinary duties of the camp. Still, he continued to explore, as he had always done, until his infirmity forced him to the rear."

The march from the miserable saline water at Jayhawker Well took a heavy toll on the reserve strength of the Briers. In 1898, Mrs. Brier wrote:

"When we reached the Jayhawker's camp [present Jayhawker Wells] they were about to burn their wagons [carts] and pack their oxen to hurry along. That made us still gloomier, but none complained. The men realized that to stop or go back meant death, and they determined to struggle on while strength and life lasted, trusting tomorrow to bring them to the land of plenty. Then we struggled through the salty marsh for miles and through the dry sand. Oh, it was terrible. We would sink to our shoetops and as water gave out we were nearly famished. I have heard since that Governor Blaisdell of Nevada found our tracks there twelve years later and still encrusted in the hardened salt.

"A march over twenty miles of dry sand brought us to the foot of the mountains, with hope almost gone and not a drop of water to relieve our parched lips and swollen tongues. The men climbed up to the snow and brought down all they could carry, frozen hard. Mr. Brier filled an old shirt and brought it to us. Some ate it white and hard and relished it as though it was flowing water, but enough was melted for our cattle and camp use.

"Here we lived on jerked beef and miserable pancakes. Some of the company told us they were going to leave their cattle, bake up their provisions and push ahead as a last resort. Dr. Carr broke down and cried when we would not go back to the springs [Travertine Springs]. I felt as bad as any of them, but it would never do to give up there. Give up—ah, I knew what that meant—a shallow grave in the sand."

Here again there is still some question as to which route the Briers 177 took into Panamint Valley. As most of the Mississippi Boys left them in the north end of Panamint Valley and passed over the north end of the Argus Range by way of present Darwin Canyon perhaps it is safe to assume that all traveled over Towne Pass.

In a letter written January 23, 1879, Rev. J. W. Brier stated that the most of the Mississippi boys left them at the head of the Panamint Valley. They cut west by way of the later Modoc Mine and hit Darwin Wash above the falls. Here is what Brier wrote about this party:

> "You recollect when some of the Mississippi boys with little West and Tom and Joe, the darkies, left us and steered for a canyon on the west side of the valley. The canyon is now called Darwin's, and at the mouth of it is a large mining town called Darwin City."

In 1898 Mrs. Brier wrote the following:

> "We went over the pass through the snow into what they named Panamint Valley, and found a deserted Indian village among the mesquite trees. We were rejoiced by seeing hair ropes and bridles and horse bones, thinking we had reached civilization. The men ahead, however, could only report more sand and hills. After two days here we struggled away into the desert, carrying all the water possible. We grew more fearful of our provisions and watched each mouthful, not daring to make a full meal. Coffee and salt we had in plenty. The salt we picked up in great lumps in the sand before coming over the last mountains. Our coffee was a wonderful help and had that given out I know we should have died."

It was while the Briers were camped at Indian Ranch north of later Ballarat that the last of the Mississippi boys left them. In his letter of 1898 Mr. Brier wrote the following:

> "Now my family, Captn. Towne, Mr. Marsten, and Crumpton and the two Turner boys went with the Jay Hawks down to the Mesquite Swamp. There these 5 men left us and struck off west."

178   It was at Indian Ranch that Mrs. Brier cooked the last of the flour

possessed by any of the party. It belonged to Masterson and Crumpton who were preparing to leave, as stated above. While this cooking was going on young John B. Colton gathered wood for the fire and poor old Asa Haynes, weak and sick, looked on hopefully. When the cooking was done a biscuit apiece was given to all of the Briers. Asa Haynes offered a five dollar gold piece for one biscuit and was refused. With tears streaming down his cheeks Haynes told of his fine home in Illinois and of the well-stocked pantry there. He ended by decrying the fact that he could not buy even one biscuit for gold. And the boy Colton, who had so hopefully gathered wood, went away hungry to his blankets.

Also it probably was at Indian Ranch camp that the Briers parted company with Edward Croker, although it is not definitely stated. Of his leaving, Mrs. Brier wrote the following:

"Before the bread gave out one man, Croker, who was in our party, complained of the short allowance of bread. I told him we must save it as long as possible, and he said with an oath, that he would have it while it lasted. 'You shall,' I said, 'but that won't be long,' and it wasn't. Then he left our mess. Before we were through that journey, I heard that man begging for even the entrails of a crow."

Of all the descriptions of the wanderings of the various parties in and while leaving Panamint Valley, that of Mrs. Brier is the best. We continue from the same article quoted next above:

"New Year's day was hardly noticed. We spent it resting at the head of Panamint Valley. Sometimes we went south and again north, not knowing whether or not we should get out of that death hole of sand and salt. On January 6 two of our mess decided to leave us and take their provisions.

"These men—Masterson and Crumption—owned the only flour we had, so they baked up their dough, except a small piece, which I made into twenty-two little crackers and put away for an emergency. Then with tearful eyes they gave us their hands, with averted faces, and turned away without a word. That was our last bite of bread until we reached San Francisquito Ranch, six weeks later. From that time on my husband I and the poor children and St. John and Patrick lived on coffee and jerked beef, except when we killed an ox

179

for a new supply. Even then there was not an ounce of fat in one and the marrow in their bones had turned to blood and water.

"It was always the same—hunger and thirst and an awful silence, so I'll just tell of one or two more experiences.

"Everybody knows how the company went across the Mojave Desert and finally reached San Francisquito Ranch. Our greatest suffering for water was near Borax [Searles] Lake. We were for forty-eight hours without a drop. A mirage fooled us. We went to bed hoping against hope.

"In the morning the men returned with the same story. 'No water.'

"Even the stoutest heart sank when nothing but sagebrush and dagger trees greeted the eye. There were wails and lamentations from lips that had never murmured before. My husband tied little Kirk to his back and staggered ahead. The child would murmur occasionally, 'Oh father, where's the water?' His pitiful, delirious wails were worse to hear than the killing thirst. It was terrible. I seem to see it all over again. I staggered and struggled wearily behind with our other two boys and the oxen. The little fellows bore up bravely and hardly complained, though they could barely talk, so dry and swollen were their lips and tongue. John would try to cheer up his brother Kirk by telling him of the wonderful water we would find and all the good things we could get to eat. Every step I expected to sink down and die. I could hardly see.

"At last we came upon two Germans of the company, who had gone ahead. They were cooking at a tiny fire.

" 'Any water?' asked my husband.

" 'There's vasser,' one said, pointing to muddy puddle.

"The cattle rushed into it, churning up the mud, but we scooped it up and greedily gulped it down our burning, swollen throats. Then I boiled coffee and found the pot half full of mud, so you can see what the water was like. It was awful stuff, but it saved our lives. A little later we came to a beautiful cold spring. Oh, how good it was; I have always believed Providence placed it there to save us, for it was in such an unlikely place."

180

The Briers were fooled by the borate waters of Searles Lake. John Welsh Brier wrote:

> "At the end of a most discouraging afternoon, we suddenly emerged upon a scene as wonderful as it was unexpected—a great body of water shining only a few miles across the desert. Long past midnight we came up to it, and found only a basin of slime strongly impregnated with borax, on the banks of which were camped the Jayhawkers from whom we had parted days before. They had brought a little water with them, however, and generously shared with us."

In a letter written to Deacon Richards in 1898, Rev. Brier tells of meeting Patrick and Loomis St. John somewhere in Indian Wells Valley, probably between the Argus Range and Indian Wells. Brier recorded the following:

> "Farther on, Patrick and Lummis St. John overtook us and were utterly destitute. I took them in."

From this point on, both Patrick and St. John worked as ox drivers and camp attendants for the Briers. This last information is contained in a long letter which Mrs. Brier wrote in January of 1905. In it she stated:

> "Patrick and Loomis St. John, who came to us at Providence Springs in a state of starvation, asked for help. Mr. Brier told them they would be welcome to such as we had, meat and coffee, and asked them to assist me with the oxen which they were most willing to do."

Of the Indian Wells Valley portion of the trek Mrs. Brier left a touching account of her fears and struggles. She wrote:

> "Sometimes we found water and grass in plenty, but never a thing to eat—. And the silence of it all! At night I would go to bed praying for God to help us through. 'Oh,' I thought, 'if I could only see something to show the end of our journey.' But I didn't dare speak of it for fear of alarming the children.

181

"But I never lost hope. I couldn't give up. We needed all
our hope and faith. I knew before starting we would have to
suffer, but my husband wanted to go, and he needed me."

After the futile trip to Searles Lake, the Briers made a dry camp with
the Jay Hawks. They moved to Providence Spring when that water was
discovered by the Little Deacon. They stayed there two days, killing an
ox and jerking the meat.

John Welsh Brier described the days spent on the trip across Indian
Wells Valley as among the worst of the journey:

"—Once our lives were only saved by a pool of turbid water
on the edge of the Mojave Desert, from which we drank,
caring little for the deposit of yellow mud at the bottom of the
coffee pot and not knowing that within a mile was a spring of
pure water."

This may have been any of three springs: Indian Wells, Desert
Springs or Willow Springs, for that entire area was treated in a sketchy
manner by the Briers in their written accounts. But it was probably
near Willow Springs that they found the pool of muddy water, for
Manly and Rogers lost their way in that area, missed Willow Springs
and found just such a pool.

For the Briers the last day of their journey was the most trying. In
1905 Mrs. Brier wrote the following touching words about their leave-
taking of the camp of February 3:

"Although the sad morning seemed more dubious to me
that those preceeding, as it became necessary to help my
husband rise from his place of rest and he told me he must
walk on before. He feared he should not be able to keep up.
Trails were in every direction and I feared he might take a
wrong one and get lost. He assured me he would keep in
sight of the train and started on. We followed as soon as
possible, assisted by two boys, Patrick and Loomis St. John.
Well, the next time I saw my husband after his early start
[was] when we overtook him. He was standing amid a crowd
with a large piece of meat in his hand. His first words to me
were, 'No more starvation, Julie. We are here at last'!"

THE BRIERS AND WADES

After the death of Robinson and the entry into the head of Soledad Canyon in the San Gabriel mountains south of Antelope Valley John Welsh Brier gave more details of their journey and their experiences at Rancho San Francisquito.

"From this point [the grave of Robinson], the prospect grew better with every mile, and the discovery of a stream flowing westward added to our relief, even though we had to wade it at every turn. The grass grew stronger and more varied; evidences of animal life began to appear, and about noon of the second day we killed a mare and two foals. What a banquet they furnished no one can appreciate who has not lived for months on the flesh of diseased and thirst-wasted oxen. Here we also experimented with acorn bread—which proved, literally, a bitter disappointment. Our shoes had long ago worn out, and many of us wore moccasins of green raw-hide, which, with our generally ragged outfit and skeleton plight, gave us a very grotesque appearance.

"At length, we entered a glad, perfectly level and lawn-like, studded with live oaks and sycamores. We had fallen into a deep trail, and I do not remember that anyone suggested our possible proximity to human habitation. Immediately on our left were the smooth hills, rich in wild oats and clover, while before us the dale seemed to expand; but the trees concealed from view what lay beyond.

"Here early in the evening, we went into camp. When the morning dawned a mist lay upon the hills.

"The party was well strung out, and, at the distance of half a mile, our family brought up the rear. Patrick brought down a hawk, and carefully stowed it away for his dinner. At the moment we were startled by the report of fire-arms. The mist cleared away, there was a burst of sunshine, and we heard the confusing bawling of a host of cattle. Hastening along the trail, we presently saw our men, drawn up in the order of battle, and towards them rode a small body of horsemen. Arrived on the scene, we found ourselves in the presence of the venerable proprietor of this magnificient estate, and a number of his vaqueros. The old man had flung his reata over the head of a coyote, which he had dragged to its death.

Presuming the cattle to be ownerless, our men had killed one of them; but the face of the Spaniard expressed no resentment, on the contrary, astonishment and compassion.

"Patrick—who had served in the Mexican War—was able to talk with him, and his brief explanations were abundantly confirmed by our appearance; but, as a diplomatic stroke, he designated my father as 'un Padre,' whereupon the old Catholic reverently removed his sombrero, and repeated in a broken voice, 'Padre! Padre! Pobrecito Padre!'

"We were cordially invited to proceed, at once, to the hacienda. My brothers and myself were caught up by the three swarthy vaqueros, who quickly carried us across the valley in spite of our squeals. We were at the base of the hill on which stood the adobe house and corrals of the Rancho de San Francisquito. Presently two vaqueros led in a coal-black bullock and slaughtered it for our use. Others rode down from the house with squashes, beans, corn meal and milk, and there were tortillas for immediate eating. We fed like hungry animals, and some of us would have died from the sickness which followed, had not Dr. Irving, of Los Angeles, arrived most opportunely. Through those of our former association who had already reached Los Angeles, the Doctor had learned of our wanderings, and had come out to help rescue us."

For a description of what happened at the del Valle home, we are indebted to Mrs. Brier:

"We looked more like skeletons than human beings. Our clothes hung in tatters. My dress was in ribbons, and my shoes hard, baked, broken pieces of leather. Some of the company still had the remains of worn-out shoes with their feet sticking through, and some wore pieces of ox hide tied about their feet. My boys wore oxhide moccasins. It was like coming back from death to life again. It was a long, long, weary walk, but thank God, he brought us out of it all."

Readers will remember that this little lady, weighing only one hundred and fifteen pounds when she began her fearful journey through Death Valley, lost almost no weight and lived to be almost one hundred years of age.

Four generations of the Wade Family. Left to right: Margaret Higgins; Mrs. Lydia Almira (Ortley) Hunter, aged 90; Jay Ward; Mrs. Ward, daughter of Mrs. Hunter. The small great-grandchild is not identified.

Photo by F. F. Latta and now in Bear State Library.

CONTINUED HISTORY OF THE WADES

While we already know much of the story of the Wade family there remain a few interesting details of their unique part in the chronicle of Death Valley '49ers.

Many readers of William Lewis Manly's book, *Death Valley in '49*, have been puzzled that he treated the Wade famiy so briefly. He stated that both the Wades and Earharts traveled by themselves and camped apart. When he and Rogers returned from their long-forced journey of twenty-six days to Los Angeles and return he disposed of the Wades, whom he had left with the Bennetts, in a few sentences. Most of his information about them is contained in the following:

"Some did not stay more than a week after we were gone, but took their oxen and blankets and started on. They could not be content to stay idly in camp with nothing to occupy their minds or bodies—so they packed their oxen and left in separate parties, the last some two weeks before."

Neither Manly nor any other early writer about Death Valley '49ers went to any trouble to learn what had happened to either the Wades or "Earharts," or the Frenchman who accompanied them. All of this was in spite of the fact that there never was any mystery about what became of the Wades. They lived for more than fifty years at Alviso within a few miles of Manly, Dow Stevens and Tom Shannon. Descendants still live there. The Wades were at Alviso as early as 1851. From 1856 on a number of Jay Hawks, Bennetts and others, were in the immediate vicinity. Dow Stevens wrote a booklet titled *Life Sketches of a Jayhawker of '49*. In it he makes no mention of the Wades although he knew them and, in 1884 shortly after Harry Wade died, he wrote a letter to John B. Colton telling him of Mr. Wade's death. In that he also stated:

"Wade had taken his family and struck South down that Valley [Death Valley] and struck the Old Spanish Trail at the Mojaves, which is the way we ought to have went."

As Stevens published his booklet in 1916 it seems strange that he overlooked mentioning his neighbors, the Wades.

186   The Briers operated a boarding house in Los Angeles for several

Elizabeth Wade and the old Alviso homestead near the little village of Alviso. This house was built about 1860. Elizabeth Wade was a daughter of Charles and Stefana (Alviso) Wade. She was born in this old home and was the last Wade to own it.

Photo by the author and now in Bear State Library.

months immediately after arriving there from Rancho San Francisquito. Rogers worked for the Briers for more than a month during that time. During that same time Harry Wade and his son, Harry George Wade, freighted between Los Angeles and San Pedro making their headquarters on Los Angeles River just below the old Plaza. It is inconceivable to this writer that this situation could have existed without both Manly and the Briers meeting and talking with the Wades. Yet they, the most prolific writers about the experiences of the Death Valley '49ers, avoid even mentioning the Wades.

In addition, there appeared in 1894 in the *Plainsfield Enterprise,* (Plainsfield, Illinois) a long account of the experiences of the Wades and the others in Death Valley and on their trip to Los Angeles. In December, 1894, shortly before Manly's book went to press this newspaper article was reprinted in a San Jose historical publication named *The Pioneer.* Manly had been a contributor to *The Pioneer* over a period of several years. The more this writer worked on *Death Valley '49ers* the more mystified he became by the absence of mention of the Wades in accounts written by the Briers and Stevens and, in particular, those by Manly.

A lesser mystery surrounded the later history of both the Bennetts and Arcans. Manly wrote that Mrs. Bennett died in San Jose in the 1850s but he gave no information about what became of the rest of the family.

In preparing this manuscript any mystery surrounding the later history of the Bennetts, Wades and Arcans was cleared by interviewing the descendants of those families.

The mystery of the Earharts still is a mystery. William Rice, who spent many years in Death Valley and the surrounding deserts, stated to this writer that he thought the name was not Earhart, but De Hart. Rice gathered much data concerning Death '49ers but most of it was destroyed at the time of his death in 1930. Rice lived in Death Valley with a man named De Hart who claimed to have been with the party which camped with Bennett while Manly and Rogers went to Los Angeles for supplies. Rice felt that De Hart knew too much about the Death Valley parties to have manufactured the story. But to date no descendant of either this Earhart or a De Hart has been located.

According to the many references to the Earharts, including Captain Culverwell who accompanied them a short distance when they left Death Valley, they first attempted to take their wagon up one of the
canyons of the Panamints, following Manly and Rogers. When their

wagon broke down they packed their oxen and left Death Valley afoot. It generally has been supposed that the Earharts left by the southern route, but this is not certain. The Wades saw nothing of them after they left Bennett's Long Camp. They may have continued on the trail of Manly and Rogers. Captain Culverwell could not keep up with them and perished by the trail. On their return from Los Angeles Manly and Rogers found the dead body about eight miles from the Bennett camp.

Regardless of all speculation nothing definite has been recorded anywhere as to what actually became of the Earharts.

In San Bernardino Mrs. Agnes Lindner, aged 90 years, told the history of the Bennetts. Mrs. Lindner was the only child of little Melissa Bennett. She attached no mystery to any of the Bennett family. When Mrs. Bennett died the youngest child was placed in the care of the Scotts of Scott's Valley, near Santa Cruz. Martha married a man named Johnson and settled in Wilmington where she and her children lived for many years. Melissa married Judge Rolfe, of San Bernardino, and had by him one child; the Mrs. Lindner who furnished this data.

There even was no mystery about the subsequent history of Asabel Bennett. It has been thought by some that the terrible experience he suffered in crossing the deserts of Nevada and California affected his mind. He never was satisfied to stay in any one place more than a few weeks. Also, he never was able to live on good terms with any of his children or acquaintances any longer. He trailed his '49er son, George, and a younger son, John Rogers Bennett, with him about the west in a covered wagon until George died and John left him somewhere in Utah. The two girls refused to become covered wagon addicts, so left their father and married young. Neither they nor their husbands ever were on friendly terms with their father.

If an affectation of the mind caused Asabel Bennett to travel about in a covered wagon, the journey across the plains to California affected the minds of almost all. This obsession to be always on the move, never to let the oxen get more than a few hundred yards from camp, to die or to see what was on the other side of the nearest mountain, was the most marked characteristic of all pioneers interviewed or known by this writer. This includes the writer's own father. If mother had not "stayed put" we children would all have been covered wagon addicts. The Bennett daughters had no mother "to stay put" for them. They either had to follow their father and to become virtual wagon tramps or to break with him. They chose the latter course.

But the most inexcusable actions of Asabel Bennett were those in   189 connection with his subsequent trips to Death Valley. About ten years after he was rescued by Manly and Rogers from his Long Camp at the base of Telescope Peak he returned to Death Valley with a party of Mormon miners and a man named Alvord. The Mormons became enraged at Alvord, claiming he was holding out on them a rich silver find. So they abandoned Alvord, probably somewhere near Anvil Springs in Butte Valley directly south of Telescope Peak. In fact, Anvil Springs is thought to have obtained its name from an anvil left there by this party. When the Mormons left Alvord, Bennett left with them.

When Manly learned what had been done by the Mormon-Bennett party he at once formed a rescue party composed of himself, a man named Twitchell and Bennett, as guide.

After finding Alvord they planned to prospect for the Lost Gunsight Lead and other lost mines which were thought to be in that part of California. Alvord soon was found and the prospecting was begun. As the provisions became low a camp was made in a canyon, probably on the west slope of the Argus Range.

Bennett and Twitchell took the mules and started to San Bernardino after groceries. Neither of them ever returned to Indian Wells Valley. In a forced march afoot westward over the old trail of '49, Manly and Alvord reached Indian Wells out of provisions, sick and lame. They were rescued and taken from the country by Dr. George of Porterville. This was the third time Manly had made this journey under the most trying circumstances.

Thirty years later Manly met Twitchell and asked him why he and Bennett had not returned. The excuse given by Twitchell was that they were delayed by a snow storm and then concluded that Manly and Alvord had either left the desert or had starved to death, the last of which they came very nearly doing. Manly recorded that it required a considerable amount of grace finally to forgive Bennett and Twitchell for abandoning Alvord and himself after all that Rogers and he had done for Bennett in '49.

Bennett went to Salt Lake, married a Mormon woman, got into serious trouble with the Mormons and considered himself lucky to escape to Los Angeles. He stayed with his daughter in Wilmington only a short time and went to Idaho, dying at Idaho Falls in 1891 in his eighty-fourth year. His descendants know nothing about his life outside of California.

History of the Wades was cleared when the writer interviewed Mrs. J. Q. White, her sisters and her cousins, all descendants of Harry and

190

Margaret J. (Wade) Higgins, daughter of Harry George Wade, in front of a house in Alviso, California. This house was framed on the east coast, shipped around the Horn to Alviso and erected there in the early 1850s. It was owned only by two persons, Mrs. Higgins and her father.
Photo by author and now in Bear State Library.

Mary Wade. They and their ancestors have been living in and around Alviso and San Jose for more than one hundred years. When he was writing his book William Lewis Manly often drove in his fringe-topped surrey to the Ortley home near Alviso. There he visited with Almira (Wade) Ortley and obtained from her many facts about the wanderings and sufferings of the entire train of '49ers from the time they left Division Springs in extreme southwestern Utah to the time when the Wades settled at Alviso. Living near where Manly interviewed Almira (Wade) Ortley there were living, in 1960, four generations of Almira's descendants. The writer visited with them and learned the above facts from them.

When Manly wrote his book he used what material he obtained from Almira, all but that which related to the Wade escape from Death Valley and to their subsequent history. The reader naturally wonders why Manly avoided this most interesting Wade history.

If it were left for this writer to explain Manly's omissions, his explanation would be simple. With all of his wonderful character, William Lewis Manly was only human. It would have spoiled a good story, that of his and John Haney Rogers' twenty-six day journey to Los Angeles after aid for those starving at the Long Camp, to show that the Wades simply yoked their oxen and drove into Los Angeles. Of course, the escape of the Wades was not as simple as that. But, in the opinion of this writer, it was too simple in comparison to justify in Manly's mind the heroic journey made by himself and Rogers.

Manly was wrong in his omission. Attitudes have changed in the last one hundred years, and we know that he was justified in the course that he took to rescue those left in Death Valley. He had climbed a peak in the Panamints, probably the one now known as Gold Hill, and had scanned the country to the south, using J. B. Arcan's powerful telescope. In it he saw to the south only the low, barren and desolate hills, the like of which in his past experience all had proved absolutely dry. The course which he selected was watered. To the north was sky-high Telescope Peak covered with snow. To the west were more and still higher peaks covered for a visible one hundred miles with snow. In that direction lay water and probably game and ox feed.

Depending on the judgment of Manly were the lives of the seven Bennett and Arcan women and children. If we count the Wades we must include one more woman and two more small children. When he left them Manly undoubtedly supposed he was going to bring aid to the

Wades as well as to the others. If the Wades had remained they most certainly would have been among the rescued. Certainly Manly used the best judgment possible when he went west for help. And just as certainly the Wades and "Earharts" were taking in their hands what uncertain life they then possessed when they started to drive out of the south end of Death Valley.

It is true that the area surrounding the southern exit from Death Valley is comparatively well watered. But, in 1850 the location of that water was not known and it, for the most part, was then in places that were inaccessible. Even with water there was no stock feed worthy of the name. Since Christmas Day the Wades had been out of almost all provisions and it was about the fifteenth of January when they left the Long Camp of the Bennetts. The five cattle and the saddle mare were their only possible source of food. The animals constituted a traveling commissary. But they had to be kept traveling if the party was to escape. If the animals had been eaten probably the entire party would have perished.

All of the above statements are well justified in the light of existing records and the facts related by Wade descendants.

Most troublesome of all records, from which this account was prepared, is the article before mentioned and reprinted in *The Pioneer,* December 15, 1894. It is titled *Across the Plains in 1849* and is signed, Mrs. Edward Burrell [nee Louisa Hannibal]. All statements in the article were represented as having been obtained from Almira Wade. While this article contains many statements of known accuracy it also contains many statements which, through Mrs. Burrell, are from a third-hand source and some of which have long been known to be inaccurate.

Most disturbing of all statements in the Burrell article was the following:

> "He [Mr. Wade] said that 'If Mr. Manly and Mr. Rogers could go on foot for help, he and his family could go on foot for help.' So the wagon cover was made into pack saddles and the family started on foot, still bearing south."

No statement that could have been made concerning a journey out of Death Valley in '49 would be any sooner questioned. With no food of any kind the Wades just simply could not have walked to Los Angeles, or to San Bernardino, where they were long thought to have gone.

The full story of the Wade escape from Death Valley was long in 193

Charles Elliott Wade, born August 12, 1838. He was eleven years of age when he accompanied his parents through Death Valley to Los Angeles. He married Stefana Alviso and has many descendants in Santa Clara County. Photo courtesy Mrs. J. Q. White and now in Bear State Library.

coming to light. In 1949 this writer sat behind the large plate glass window in Furnace Creek Inn at the mouth of Furnace Creek Wash in Death Valley and heard a portion of the story from Mrs. J. Q. White, youngest child of Almira Wade. Then he drove to Alviso and heard more of it from Mrs. Lydia Hunter, Mrs. White's then ninety-year-old sister, and oldest child of Almira. From descendants of Harry George Wade more details were learned. From the Jay Hawk records several items gave more light.

After Manly and Rogers left for Los Angeles, the Wades and Earharts argued among themselves the advisability of remaining in Death Valley. One of them said, "If those boys ever get out of this cussed hole, they are d---d fools if they ever come back to help anybody." So the Wades and Earharts decided to follow Manly and Rogers. They made the wagon bows and covers into pack-saddles and abandoned their wagons and all started afoot up Six Springs Canyon behind Manly and Rogers. Far up the canyon they came to a dry fall over which the cattle could not be taken. Badly discouraged they returned to the Long Camp. After more argument it was decided that it would be better to travel a few miles each day and thus come closer and closer to the Spanish Settlements than to sit in camp and starve. So the oxen again were yoked to the wagons and a start was made to drive out of the south end of Death Valley.

With the Wades was a Frenchman, not mentioned by Manly or any other writer concerning these parties, who went south when they entered Death Valley. The Frenchman was hired to help fourteen-year-old Harry George Wade drive the team and care for the stock in camp.

Shortly after this party left the Bennett Long Camp the Earhart wagon broke down and had to be abandoned. The Earharts rigged up their packs on the oxen and started on afoot. Captain Culverwell was with the Earharts but was too old and too weak to keep up, so turned back and perished by the trail. The Wades do not report having seen the Earharts again after their wagon broke down.

It was no easy journey that this most unique of all '49ers parties made out of Death Valley and to Los Angeles. All came near perishing from starvation. The oxen fared best of all, being able to eat the sage and other brush along the way. But when the Wades started out of Death Valley there were only four oxen, a milk cow, and a saddle mare, enough for one team, and none of them could be killed. After talking with the Wade descendants, this writer feels certain that none of the Death Valley '49ers suffered any more from hunger than did the Wades. 195

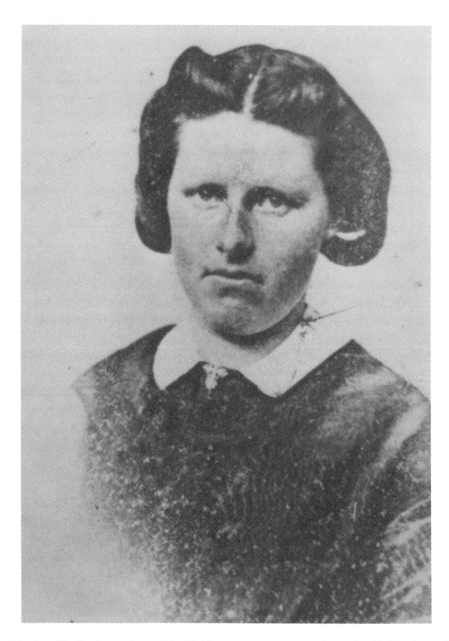

Almira Wade, born June 21, 1840, was nine years of age in 1849 when she accompanied her parents to California. She married John J. Ortley and lived all of her life in Alviso, California. She had three daughters and a son who lived in or near Alviso. Almira was the first white discoverer of Saratoga Springs in the south end of Death Valley.

Photo courtesy of Mrs. J. Q. White and now in Bear State Library.

Tears still come into the eyes of Almira's descendants when they force themselves to recount the terrible condition into which the entire family fell before they reached help of any kind.

Leaving the Bennett Long Camp the Wades traveled southeast over about the same route as the present road on the west side of Death Valley. At the end of the third day they made a dry camp near the eastside hills at the southern end of the valley. Here, as soon as they were unyoked at this third dry camp the stock all stampeded over the back trail toward the nearest water they knew, the Tule Spring where the Bennetts and Arcans were camped. The Frenchman, Mr. Wade and Harry George all started in pursuit of the thirsty stock. They were gone all night, returning at daylight with the stock but scarcely able to place one foot ahead of the other.

The Wades were in a most serious position. From their camp we know that, with one exception, it was many miles in any direction to any drinkable water. And also they were almost entirely without food. The expedition would have ended there except for a most unlooked-for happening.

Little Almira Wade was sitting on the wagon seat. Her mother and little Richard were in the back of the wagon. It was almost dark. Almira saw a pair of desert ravens swoop down from the sky and disappear behind a sand dune about three hundred yards from the wagon.

It immediately occurred to Almira that the ravens might be going to water at a spring hidden behind the sand dune. So she investigated. Many readers of these lines have climbed that same sand dune and have seen what Almira Wade saw when *she* climbed it.

Behind the sand dune was a great spring of good water, its overflow forming a lake of fresh water covering several acres. This place is what now is known as Saratoga Springs, and Almira Wade was undoubtedly the first white discoverer of it.

There is an interesting thought connected with the experience of the Wades at Saratoga Springs. Those of us who have been led to believe that animals smell water at a great distance have our beliefs severely tried when we learn that the Wade oxen stampeded from within three hundred yards of a lake of water and raced away from it in the direction of water they had left three days before. Perhaps there was a wind blowing the odor of the water away from the oxen. Regardless, the discovery of Saratoga Springs was a windfall for the Wades for they recruited their stock and took new heart from that discovery.

But the Wades could not stay at the newly found springs. They could 197

Richard Angus Wade, born October 19, 1844, and five years of age when he accompanied his parents through Death Valley to Los Angeles. He spent almost his entire life in Alviso and San Jose.

Photo courtesy of Mrs. J. Q. White and now in Bear State Library.

not stop anywhere for, day by day, they were getting weaker and weaker and were slowly starving to death. They hurried on.

Mrs. Margaret Higgins, daughter of Harry George Wade, told this author that the Wades carried in their wagon more than 50 gallons of water, besides a full canteen for each member of the family. This water was in several cans, one much larger than the others. Mrs. Higgins stated that her father carried the largest of these cans, filled with water, in his wagon when he was freighting from Alviso and San Jose around the Santa Clara Valley.

Although she was not certain of this, Mrs. Higgins thought Harry Wade obtained these cans from some Mormon dairyman south of Salt Lake who was alarmed by the dry country into which the party was heading. She said that none of the Wades would depend on wooden barrels for a supply of water when traveling. Mrs. Higgins had checked this with Mrs. Hunter, oldest daughter of Almira Wade. She remembered about the cans and of having seen several of them at the old Wade home at Alviso. Mrs. Lowe, Mrs. White and Elizabeth Wade remembered hearing about the cans but did not remember ever having seen any of them. All were first cousins of Mrs. Hunter but all were many years younger. Mrs. Hunter stated that the cans had a small neck, like a modern milk can, but that the lid fitted down over the neck, unlike that of a modern milk can.

Skirting the dry lakes, the Wades followed a route quite close to the present Highways #127 and #91.

Near the site of present Baker they struck the Old Spanish Trail which they had left at Division Springs, Utah, months before. But they did not know this. The trail was broad and plain, and there was water at intervals along it. But there was no food for the Wade family. If they had not been able to ride in the wagon much of the time, and to have a half cup of milk daily from Rosie, the cow, some of them would have perished.

They passed the site of present Baker, striking the Mojave River near the site of present Barstow. From there they had better traveling and somewhere in this vicinity they met a party of miners who gave them a pail of flour and told them that they were on the Old Spanish Trail. This flour and the knowledge that at last they were on a certain trail to California encouraged the starving family beyond expression.

West of San Bernardino the Wades met some native California cattlemen who took them to a cattle camp. This was on the Cucamonga Ranch, near the present village of that name. The cattlemen were 199 killing cattle and rendering tallow. They made tortillas and gave them to the starving people and showed them how to roll them and dip them in the boiling tallow. Almira Wade later said that this was the best meal she ever tasted.

As the Wades neared Los Angeles it began to rain and, in contrast to the many months of drying on the deserts, they were thoroughly soaked. It rained continuously until they reached Los Angeles.

February 10, 1850, the Wades always have considered their day of deliverance from starvation on the Great American Desert. They then reached Rowland's Mills, the first improved settlement on the road into Los Angeles "and", as Sheldon Young wrote in his log, "—we have got out of trouble at last."

CHAPTER TWELVE

TO THE SPANISH SETTLEMENTS FOR HELP

No incident of travel to California has woven about it more of the romance of heroism than has that memorable trip of William Lewis Manly and John Haney Rogers from the Bennett Long Camp at the base of Telescope Peak in Death Valley to Los Angeles and return. At first estimated to be a ten day journey, it resolved into a heartbreaking twenty-six day struggle during which time the lives of both men several times were in the balance. After several days without water they once were saved by a few thin flakes of ice, part of which they ate and the rest of which they melted in a camp kettle and poured into their canteens.

Neither Manly nor Rogers was related or indebted to any person who was waiting for them at their starvation camp in Death Valley. At least some of the people at that camp felt certain that if the two were once fortunate enough to escape from that awful sink hole, they never would be foolish enough to return to it. There was no possible reward they could expect for such a sacrifice. They went out of the goodness of their hearts and returned because they could think of doing nothing else.

It is extremely fortunate that William Lewis Manly was interested enough to work for many years preparing a written account of his experiences on the way to California. He wrote such an account in 1877 and again in 1888, but the most valuable of all records of travel to California in '49 is Manly's *Death Valley in '49*. It is an ungarnished story by an untrained writer, but it is in a class by itself as a portrayal of western life and travel. Although Manly and his companions claimed that he left the story half untold, one marvels today at the accuracy with which Manly described more than eight hundred miles of unmapped, unsettled desert between Salt Lake and Los Angeles, most of which he traveled over only once.

Manly's book was made possible by a number of facts not often presented. In the first place, during his journey west, Manly kept a diary. From his later writing we know that this diary must have been an accurate detailed account of the happenings of each day and a 201 faithful description of the territory through which he passed. In the second place, Manly returned home not long after he reached California. Some distance before he reached home he was frozen in for the winter. He used this time—which would have been entirely wasted by most persons—and with his diary as a guide, to write a long narrative of his experiences. Unfortunately this narrative and the diary were burned long before Manly wrote his book, but the fact that he had gone over the whole account and had set down all the events in detail impressed them on his memory so that he never forgot them.

But many of Manly's statements about the desert area in and surrounding Death Valley are not based on this far-removed contact. During the early 1860s he made no less than three journeys into that territory and, as previously has been noted, walked twice across Panamint Valley, the Slate and Argus Ranges and Searles and Indian Wells Valleys, over the old trail he had traveled three times in January, February and March of 1850. All of this made it possible for Manly's naturally active and more than ordinary retentive mind to bring to him almost everything he had seen and done forty-five years before.

It is from Manly's *Death Valley in '49* that most of this chapter will be taken. No rehashing that this or any other may do can compare with that simple, forceful, gripping story. We take up Manly's account as he was consulting with the Bennett and Arcan families at their Long Camp. Probably this location was at what now is Tule Springs, north of the ruins of the old Eagle Borax works in southwestern Death Valley. We must remember that the present Bennett's Well was not in existence in 1850. It was dug in the 1890s by another Bennett:

"This night we had another meeting to decide upon our course and determine what to do. At this meeting no one was wiser than another, for no one had explored the country and knew what to expect. The questions that now arose were 'How long can we endure this work in this situation?' 'How long will our oxen be able to endure the great hardship on the small nourishment they receive?' 'How long can we provide ourselves with food?'

"We had a few small pieces of dry bread. This was kept for the children, giving them a little now and then. Our only food was in the flesh of the oxen, and when they failed to carry themselves along we must begin to starve. It began to look as if the chances of leaving our bones to bleach upon the desert were the most prominent ones.

"One thing was certain we must move somewhere at once. If we stay here we can live as long as the oxen do, and no longer, and if we go on it is uncertain where to go, to get a better place. We had guns and ammunition to be sure, but of late we had seen no living creature in this desert wild. Finally Mr. Bennett spoke and said:—

" 'Now I will make you a proposition. I propose that we select two of our youngest, strongest men and ask them to take some food and to go ahead on foot to try to seek a settlement, and food, and we will go back to the good spring we have just left and wait for their return. It will surely not take them more than ten days for the trip, and when they get back we shall know all about the road and its character and how long it will take us to travel it. They can secure some other kind of food that will make us feel better, and when the oxen have rested a little at the spring we can get out with our wagons and animals and be safe. I think this is the best and safest way.

" 'Now what do you all say?' After a little discussion all seemed to agree that this was the best, and now it remained to find the men to go. No one offered to accept the position of advance messengers. Finally Mr. Bennett said he knew one man well enough to know that he would come back if he lived, and he was sure he would push his way through. 'I will take Lewis (myself) if he will consent to go.' I consented, though I knew it was a hazardous journey, exposed to all sorts of things, Indians, climate and probable lack of water, but I thought I could do it and would not refuse. John Rogers a large strong Tennessee man was then chosen as the other one and he consented also.

"Now preparations began, Mr. Arcane killed the ox which had so nearly failed, and all the men went to drying and preparing the meat. Others made us some new mocassins out of rawhide, and the women made us each a knapsack.

"Our meat was closely packed, and one can form an idea how poor our cattle were from the fact that John and I actually packed seven-eights of all the flesh of an ox into our knapsacks and carried it away. They put in a couple of spoonfuls of rice and about as much tea. This seemed like robbery to the children, but the good women said that in case of sickness even that little bit might save our lives. I wore no coat or vest, but took half of a light blanket, while Rogers wore a thin summer coat and took no blanket. We each had a small tin cup and a small camp kettle holding a quart. Bennett had me take his seven-shooter rifle, and Rogers had a good double barreled shot gun. We each had a sheath knife, and our hats were small brimmed, drab affairs fitting close to the head and not very conspicuous to an enemy as we might rise up from behind a hill into possible views.

"We tried on our packs and fitted the straps a little so they would carry easy. They collected all the money there was in camp and gave it to us. Mr. Arcane had about $30 and others threw in small amounts of money from forty cents upward. We received all sorts of advice. Capt. Culverwell was an old sea faring man and was going to tell us how to find our way back, but Mr. Bennett told the captain that he had known Lewis as a hunter for many long years, and that if he went over a place in the daytime he could find his way back at night every time. Others cautioned us about the Indians and told us how to manage. Others told us not to get caught in deep snow which we might find on the mountains.

"This advice we received in all the kindness in which it was given, and then we bade them all good bye. Some turned away, too much affected to approach us and others shook our hands with deep feeling, grasping them firmly and heartily hoping we would be successful and be able to pilot them out of this dreary place into a better land. Every one felt that a little food to make a change from the poor dried meat would be acceptable. Mr. and Mrs. Bennett and J. B. Arcane and wife were the last to remain when the others had turned away. They had most faith in the plan and felt deeply. Mrs. Bennett was the last, and she asked God to bless us and bring some food to her starving children.

"We were so much affected that we could not speak and silently turned away and took our course again up the canyon we had descended the night before.

"After a while we looked back and when they saw us turn around, all the hats and bonnets waved us a final parting.

204

"Those left in the camp were Asabel Bennett and Sarah his wife, with three children, George, Melissa, and Martha; J. B. Arcane and wife with son Charles. The youngest children were not more than two years old. There were also the two Earhart brothers, and a grown son, Capt. Culverwell, and some others I cannot recall; eleven grown people in all, besides a Mr. Wade, his wife and three children who did not mingle with our party, but usually camped a little distance off, followed our trail, but seemed to shun company. We soon passed round a bend of the cañon, and then walked on in silence.

"We both of us meditated some over the homes of our fathers, but took new courage in view of the importance of our mission and passed on as fast as we could.

"By night we were far up the mountain, near the perpendicular rough peak, and far above us on a slope we could see some bunches of grass and sage brush. We went to this and found some small water holes [Anvil Springs?] No water ran from them they were so small. Here we staid all night. It did not seem very far to the snowy peak to the north of us. Just where we were seemed the lowest pass, for to the south were higher peaks and the rocks looked as if they were too steep to be got over.

"Through this gap came a cold breeze, and we had to look round to get a sheltered place in which to sleep. We lay down close together, spoon fashion, and made the little blanket do as cover for the both of us. In the morning we filled our canteens, which we had made by binding two powder cans together with strips of cloth, and started for the summit near by. From this was the grandest sight we ever beheld. Looking east we could see the country we had been crawling over since November 4th. 'Just look at the cursed country we have come over!' said Rogers as he pointed over it. To the north was the biggest mountain we ever saw [Telescope Peak] peaks on peaks with snow covering which was apparently everlasting.

This mountain seemed to have very few trees on it, and in extent, as it reached away to the north seemed interminable. South was a nearly level plain, and to the west I thought I could dimly see a range of mountains that held a little snow

Death Valley and the far-reaching desert and mountainous country to the east. At the left are the Black Mountains, described by William Lewis Manly as the roughest country he ever had seen. In the center are Furnace Creek Ranch, Furnace Creek Inn and the mouth of Furnace Creek Wash. Beyond are the Amargosa Desert and Ash Meadows. To the right is the Funeral Range and, beyond, the Charleston Range with Mount Stirling at the northern and highest end. It was through the territory shown in the center of the view that our Death Valley '49ers staggered and found their way down Furnace Creek Wash to the Valley of Death.

Photo courtesy of Clark Mills and now in Bear State Library.

upon their summits [the Sierra], but on the main range to the south there was none. It seemed to me the dim snowy mountains must be as far as 200 miles away, but of course I could not judge accurately. After looking at this grand, but worthless landscape long enough to take in its principal features we asked each other what we supposed the people we left behind would think to see mountains so far ahead.

"We knew that they had an idea that the coast range was not very far ahead, but we saw at once to go over all these mountains and return within the limits of fifteen days which had been agreed upon between us, would probably be impossible, but we must try as best we could, so down the rocky steep we clambered and hurried on our way. In places the way was so steep that we had to help each other down, and the hard work made us perspire freely so that the water was a prime necessity. In one place near here, we found a little water and filled our canteens, besides drinking a good present supply. There were two low, black rocky ranges directly ahead of us which we must cross [Slate and Argus Ranges].

"When part way down the mountain a valley or depression opened up in that direction up which it seemed as if we could look a hundred miles. [From Manly's statements, it is probable that they descended a ridge.] Near by and a short distance north was a lake of water and when we reached the valley we crossed a clear stream of water flowing toward the lake.

"Being in need of water, we rushed eagerly to it and prepared to take a big drink, but the tempting fluid was as salt as brine and made our thirst all the more intolerable. Nothing grew on the bank of this stream and the bed was of hard clay, which glistened in the sun. [They are now in Panamint Valley. It is a mystery how they missed the water at both the Camp of the Horse Bones and Indian Ranch.]

"We now began the ascent of the next ridge, keeping a westerly course, and walked as fast as we could up the rough mountain side [the Slate Range]. We crossed the head of a cañon near the summit about dark, and here we found a trail, which from indications we knew to be that of the Jayhawkers, who had evidently been forced to the southward of the course they intended to take. They had camped here

Panamint Valley, Mount Argus, the Slate and Argus Ranges as seen from the summit of Telescope Peak. Beyond the Argus Range is Indian Wells Valley, walled in on the west by the towering Sierra. To the left is Searles Lake Valley and El Paso Range. To the right the Owens Range and the Little Lake lava flow. Death Valley '49ers struck directly through this desolation to the Sierra at Indian Wells.

Photo courtesy of Clark Mills and now in Bear State Library.

and had dug holes in the sand in search of water, but had found none [probably in Water Canyon].

"We staid all night here and dug around in some other places in the bottom of the cañon, in the hope to have better luck than they did, but we got no water anywhere.

"We seemed almost perishing for want of water, the hard exercise made us perspire so freely. In the morning we started on, and near the summit we came to the dead body of Mr. Fish, laying in the hot sun, as there was no material near here with which his friends could cover the remains. This Mr. Fish was the man who left camp some two weeks before in company with another and who carried the long whiplash wound about his body, in hope he could somewhere be able to trade it for bread. No doubt in this very place where he breathed his last, his bones still lie.

"As we came in sight of the next valley [Searles Lake Valley] we could see a lake of water some distance south of our western course [Searles Lake].

"We had followed the Jayhawkers trail thus far, but as we found no water in small holes in the rocks as we were likely to do when we were the first to pass, we decided to take a new route in the hope to find a little water in this way, for we had no hope to find a little water in this way, or any other. This valley we now crossed seemed to come to an end about ten miles to the north of us. To the south it widened out, enclosing the lake spoken of. This valley was very sandy and hard to walk over. When about halfway across we saw some ox tracks leading toward the lake, and in the hope we might find the water drinkable we turned off at right angles to our course and went that way also. Long before we reached the water of the lake, the bottom became a thin slimy mud which was very hard on our mocassins. When we reached the water we found it to be of a wine color, and so strongly alkaline as to feel slippery to the touch, and under our feet.

"This side trip, had cost us much exertion and made us feel more thirsty than ever.

"We turned now west again, making for a cañon [in the Argus Range, northwest of Trona], up which we passed in the hope we should at some turn find a little basin of rain water in some rock. We traveled in it miles and miles, and

209

our mouths became so dry we had to put a bullet or a small smooth stone in and chew it and turn it around with the tongue to induce a flow of saliva. If we saw a spear of green grass on the north side of a rock, it was quickly pulled and eaten to obtain the little moisture it contained.

"Thus we traveled along for hours, never speaking, for we found it much better for our thirst to keep our mouths closed as much as possible, and prevent the evaporation. The dry air of that region took up water as a sponge does. We passed the summit of this ridge without finding any water, and on our way down the western side we came to a flat place where there was an Indian hut made of small brush. We now thought there surely must be some water near and we began a thorough search. The great snow mountain did not seem far off, but to the south and southwest a level or inclined plain extended for a long distance [Indian Wells Valley]. Our thirst began to be something terrible to endure, and in the warm weather and hard walking we had secured only two drinks since leaving camp.

"We were so sure that there must be water near here that we laid our knapsacks down by the little hut and looked around in every possible place we could think of. Soon it got dark and then we made a little fire as a guide and looked again. Soon the moon arose and helped us some, and we shouted frequently to each other so as not to get lost.

"We were so nearly worn out that we tried to eat a little meat, but after chewing a long time, the mouth would not moisten it enough so we could swallow, and we had to reject it. It seemed as if we were going to die with plenty of food in our hand, because we could not eat it.

"We tried to sleep but could not, but after a little rest we noticed a bright star two hours above the horizon and from the course of the moon we saw the star must be pretty truly west of us. We talked a little, and the burden of it was a fear that we could not endure the terrible thirst a while longer. The thought of the women and children waiting for our return made us feel more desperate than if we were the only ones concerned. We thought we could fight to the death over a water hole if we could only secure a little of the precious fluid. No one who has ever felt the extreme of thirst can imagine the distress, the dispair, which it brings. I can find no words, no way to express it so others can understand.

"The moon gave us so much light that we decided we would start on our course, and get as far as we could before the hot sun came out, and so we went on slowly and carefully in the partial darkness, the only hope left to us being that our strength would hold out till we could get to the shining snow on the great mountain before us. We reached the foot of the range we were descending about sunrise. There was here a wide wash from the snow mountain, down which some water had sometime run after a big storm, and had divided into little rivulets only reaching out a little way before they had sunk into the sand.

"We had no idea we could now find any water till we at least got very near the snow, and as the best way to reach it we turned up the wash although the course was nearly to the north. The course was up a gentle grade and seemed quite sandy and not easy to travel. It looked as if there was an all day walk before us, and it was quite a question if we could live long enough to make the distance. There were quite strong indications that the water had run here not so very long ago, and we could trace the course of the little streams round among the little sandy islands. A little stunted brush grew here but it was so brittle that the stems would break as easy as an icicle.

"In order to not miss a possible bit of water we separated and agreed upon a general course, and that if either one found water he should fire his gun as a signal. After about a mile or so had been gone over I heard Roger's gun and went in his direction. He had found a little ice that had frozen under the clear sky. It was not thicker than window glass. After putting a piece in our mouths we gathered all we could and put it into the little quart camp kettle to melt. We gathered just a kettle full, besides what we ate as we were gathering, and kindled a little fire and melted it.

"I can but think how providential it was that we started in the night for in an hour after the sun had risen that little sheet of ice would have melted and the water sank into the sand. Having quenched our thirst we could now eat, and found that we were nearly starved also. In making this meal

211

we used up all our little store of water, but we felt refreshed and our lives renewed so that we had better courage to go on. [This incident took place in the area south of the Little Lake lava flow. They now start southwest to the Sierra.]

"We now took our course west again taking a bee line for a bluff that lay a little to the south of the big snow mountain. On and on we walked till the dark shadow of the great mountain in the setting sun was thrown about us, and still we did not seem more than half way to the bluff before us.

"All the way had been [up] hill and very tireseome walking. There was considerable small brush scattered about, here and there, over this steeply inclined plain.

"We were still several miles from the base of this largest of the mountains and could now see that it extended west for many miles. The buttes to the south were low, black and barren, and to the west as far as we could see there were no mountains with any snow. As the sun got further down we could see a small smoke curling up near the base of the mountain, and we thought it must be some signal made by the Indians, as we had often seen them signal in that way, but we stopped and talked the matter over, and as we were yet a long way from the bluff which had been our objective point, we concluded we would investigate the smoke signal a little closer. So we set off toward it in the dusk and darkness and when within about a mile we found we were in a tract that had been somewhat beaten. Feeling with my fingers I was quite sure I could distinguish ox tracks, and then was quite sure that we had overtaken the Jayhawkers, or at least were on their trail. And then I thought perhaps they had fallen among the Indians, who now might be feasting on their oxen and it became clear to us to use great caution in approaching the little smoke."

Here Manly describes his meeting with the now desperate and hopeless Jay Hawks. They begged him to notify their families that they had perished in the desert. The site of the spring now is Indian Wells, on Highway #6, about five miles northwest of Inyokern. On July 9, 1950 there was dedicated at this site a monument marking Indian Wells as California Historic Landmark #457. In the next paragraph Manly is describing their passage through Last Chance Canyon:

"As we went down the cañon we came to one place where it was so narrow, that a man or a poor ox could barely squeeze through between the rocks, and in a few miles more reached the open level plain. When three or four miles out on the trail and not far from the hills we came to a bunch of quite tall willows. The center of the bunch had been cut out and the branches woven in so as to make a sort of corral. In the center of this was a spring of good water and some good grass growing around. This was pretty good evidence that some one had been here before. We took a good drink and filled our canteens anew, for we did not expect to get another drink for two or three days at least. [This site is the place long known as Desert Spring, one-half mile east of present Cantil. It is now California Historic Landmark #476.]

"We took the trail again and hurried on as the good water made us feel quite fresh. After a few miles we began to find the bones of animals, some badly decayed and some well preserved. All the heads were those of horses, and it puzzled us to know where they came from. As we passed along we noticed the trail was on a slight up grade and somewhat crooked. If we stepped off from it the foot sank in about two inches of dirt finer than the finest flour. The bones were scattered all along, sometimes the bones of several animals together. Was it the long drive, poison water, or what? It was evident they had not been killed but had dropped along the way. [They are following the Old Indian Horse Thief Trail, a portion of the Joe Walker Trail. In crossing the vast desert to the south, these animals had perished before reaching Desert Spring].

"It was a dreary trail at best, and these evidences of death did not help to brighten it in the least. We wondered often where it led to and what new things would be our experience. After walking fast all day we came to quite an elevation, where we could stand and look in all directions. The low black range where we left the Jayhawkers was in sight, and this spur of the great snowy mountains extended a long way to the south, and seemed to get lower and lower, finally ending in low rocky buttes, a hundred miles away [the Tehachapi Range]. Some may think this distance very far to see, but those who have ever seen the clear atmosphere of that region will bear me out in these magnificent distances. Generally a mountain or other object seen at a distance would be three or four times as far off as one would judge at first sight, and peak after peak extending away to the north, all of them white with snow. Standing thus out in the plain we could see the breadth of the mountain east and west, and it seemed as though it must have been nearly a hundred miles. The south end was very abrupt and sank as one into a great plain in which we stood, twenty miles from the mountain's base.

"To the northwest we could see a clay lake [Rosamond Dry Lake], or at least that was what we called it, and a line of low hills seemed to be an extension of the mountain in a direction swinging around to the south to enclose this thirsty, barren plain before us, which was bounded by mountains or hills on this side. To the south this snow-capped range seemed to get higher, and we could see some mountains to the south of our westerly course.

"The low mountains as those seen in the northwest direction is the same place now crossed by the Southern Pacific Railroad, and known as the Tehachipi pass, the noted loop, in which the railroad crosses itself, being on the west slope and Ft. Tejon being on the same range a little further south where the Sierra Nevada mountains and the Coast Range join. The first mountain bearing snow, south of our course was probably what is known as Wilson's peak, and the high mountains still farther south, the San Bernardino mountains. There were no names there known to us nor did we know anything of the topography of the country except that we supposed a range of mountains was all that separated us from California. [At this point they were about twenty miles southeast of Willow Springs.]

"We were yet in the desert, and if we kept our due west course, we must cross some of the snow before us which if steep gave us some doubts whether we could get through or not.

"We did not know exactly what the people left behind would do if we were gone longer than we intended, but if they started on it was quite plain to us they would be lost, and as seven days had already passed we were in serious trouble for fear we could not complete the trip in the time allotted to us.

We surveyed the plain and mountains to learn its situation and then started on, following our trail. As we went on we seemed to be coming to lower ground, and near our road stood a tree of a kind we had not seen before. The trunk was about six or eight inches through and six or eight feet high with arms at the top quite as large as the body, and at the end of the arms a bunch of long, stiff bayonet shaped leaves [Joshua trees].

"It was a brave little tree to live in such a barren country. As we walked on these trees were more plentiful and some were much larger than the first. As we came to the lowest part of the valley there seemed to be little faint water ways running around little clouds of stunted shrubs, but there was no signs that very much water ever run in them. We thought that these were the outlet of the big sandy lake which might get full of water and overflow through these channels after some great storm.

"As this low ground was quite wide we lost our trail in crossing it, and we separated as we went along, looking to find it again, till nearly dark when we looked for a camping place. Fortunately we found a little pond of rain water, and some of our strange trees that were dead gave us good material for a fire, so that we were very comfortable indeed, having both drink and fire.

"Starting on again our course was now ascending slightly, and we came across more and more of the trees, and larger ones than at first. We saw some that seemed to have broken down with their own weight. The bayonet shaped leaves seemed to fall off when old and the stalk looked so much like an old overgrown cabbage stump that we named them 'Cabbage trees,' but afterward learned they were a species of Yucca. We were much worried at loosing our trail and felt it would be unsafe to try to cross the mountain without finding it again, so we separated, Rogers going northwest, and I southwest, agreeing to swing round so as to meet again about noon, but when we met, neither of us had found a trail, and we were still about 10 miles from the foothills. Rogers said he had some of the people say that the trail leading from Salt Lake to Los Angeles crossed such a mountain in a low pass, with very high mountains on each side, and he supposed that the high mountain to the south of our course must be the one where the trail crossed, but as this would take us fully fifty miles south of our course as we supposed it was we hesitated about going there, and concluded we would try the lowest place in the mountain first, and if we failed we could then go and try Roger's route, more to the south.

"So we pushed on, still keeping a distance apart to look out for the trail, and before night, in the rolling hills, we saw here and there faint traces of it, which grew plainer as we went along, and about sundown we reached some water holes and from some old skulls of oxen lying around the ground showing that it had at some previous time been a camping ground. [This is probably the spring at which Jay Hawk, William Robinson, later died.] We found some good large sage brush which made a pretty good fire, and if we could have had a little fresh meat to roast we thought we were in a good position for supper. But that poor meat was pretty dry food. However it kept us alive, and we curled up together and slept, for the night was cool, and we had to make the little blanket do its best. We thought we ought to find a little game, but we had not seen any to shoot since we started.

"In the morning the trail led us toward the snow, and as we went along, a brave old crow surprised us by lighting on a bush near the trail, and we surprised him by killing him with a charge of shot. 'Here's your fresh meat,' said Rogers as he put it into his knapsack to cook for supper, and marched on. As we approached the summit we could see, on the high mountains south of us, some trees, and when we came near the highest part of our road there were some juniper trees near it, which was very encouraging. We crossed over several miles of hard snow, but it moistened up our moccassins and made them soft and uncomfortable. After we had turned down the western slope we killed a small hawk. 'Here's your meat,' said I, as the poor thin fellow was stowed away for future grub, to cook with the crow.

"When we got out of the snow we had lost the trail again but the hills on the sides were covered with large brush, and on a higher part of the mountain south, were some big trees, and we began to think the country would change for the better pretty soon. [Here they are entering the head of Soledad Canyon where the railroad and highway now run. They

216

passed south of Elizabeth Lake.] We followed down the ravine for many miles, and when this came out into a larger one, we were greatly pleased at the prospect, for down the latter came a beautiful running brook of clear pure water, singing as it danced over the stones, a happy song and telling us to drink and drink again, and you may be sure we did drink, for it had been months and months since we had had such water, pure, sweet, free from the terrible alkali and stagnant taste that had been in almost every drop we had seen. Rogers leveled his shot gun at some birds and killed a beautiful one with a top knot on his head, and colors bright all down his neck. It was a California quail. We said birds always lived where human beings did, and he had great hopes born to us of a better land. I told John that if the folks were only there now I could kill game enough for them.

"We dressed our three birds and got them boiling in the camp kettle, and while they were cooking, talked over the outlook which was so flattering that our tongues got loose and we rattled away in strange contrast to the ominous silence of a week ago. While eating our stew of crow and hawk, we could see willows, alders and big sage brush around and we had noticed what seemed to be cottonwoods farther down the cañon, and green trees on the slope of the mountain. We were sure we were on the edge of the promised land and were quite light hearted, till we began to tell of plans to get the good people out who were waiting for us beside the little spring in the desert.

"We talked of going back at once, but our meat was too near gone, and we must take them something to encourage them a little and make them strong for the fearful trip. As to these birds—the quail was a superb morsel as ever a man did eat; the hawk was pretty fair and quite good eating; but that abominabel crow! His flesh was about as black as his feathers and full of tough and bony sinews. We concluded we did not want any more of that kind of bird, and ever since that day, when I have heard people talk of 'eating crow' as a bitter pill, I think I know all about it from experience.

"There seemed to be no other way for us but to push on in the morning and try to obtain some relief for the poor women and children and then get back to them as fast as ever we could, so we shouldered our packs and went down the cañon as fast as we could. We came soon to evergreen oaks and tall cottonwoods, and the creek bottom widened out to two hundred yards. There were trees on the south side and the brush kept getting larger and larger. There was a trail down this cañon, but as it passed under fallen trees we knew it could not have been the same one we had been following on the other side of the summit, and when we discovered a bear track in a soft place we knew very well it was not a track intended for human beings, and we might be ordered out almost any moment.

"On the high bold grassy point about four hundred yards we saw two horses that held their heads aloft and gave a snort, then galloped away out of sight. About 10 o'clock I felt a sudden pain in my left knee, keen and sharp, and as we went along it kept growing worse. I had to stop often to rest, and it was quite plain that if this increased or continued I was sure enough disabled, and would be kept from helping those whom we had left. Nerved with the idea we must get help to them, and that right soon, I hobbled along as well as I could, but soon had to say to Rogers that he had better go on ahead and get help and let me come on as fast as I could, for every moment of delay was a danger of death to our party who trusted us to get them help. Rogers refused to do this, he said he would stay with me and see me out, and that he could not do much alone, and had better wait till I got better. So we worked along through the tangled brush, being many times compelled to wade the stream to get along, and this made our mocassins soft and very uncomfortable to wear. I endured the pain all day, and we must have advanced quite a little distance in spite of my lameness, but I was glad when night came and we camped in the dark brushy cañon, having a big fire which made me quite comfortable all night, though it was quite cold, and we had to keep close together so as to use the blanket. I felt a little better in the morning and after eating some of our poor dried meat, which was about as poor as crow, but a little worse, we continued on our way.

"The tangle got worse and worse as we descended, and at times we walked in the bed of the stream in order to make more headway, but my lameness increased and we had to go

218

very slow indeed. About noon we came to what looked like an excavation, a hole four feet square or more it looked to be, and on the dirt thrown out some cottonwood trees had grown, and one of the largest of these had been cut down sometime before. This was the first sign of white men we had seen and it was evidently an attempt at mining, no one knows how long ago. It encouraged us at any rate, and we pushed on through brush and briers, tangles of wild rose bushes and bushes of every sort, till all of a sudden we came out into an open sandy valley, well covered with sage brush and perhaps a hundred yards wide; probably more.

"The hills on the south side had on them some oak trees and grassy spots, but the north side was thickly covered with brush. Our beautiful little brook that had kept us company soon sank into the dry sand out of sight, and we moved rather slowly along every little while we spoke of the chances of wagons ever getting through the road we had come, and the hope that my lameness might not continue to retard our progress in getting back to the place of our starting, that the poor waiting people might begin to get out of the terrible country they were in and enjoy as we had done, the beautiful running stream of this side of the mountain. If I did not get better the chances were that they would perish, for they never could come through alone, as the distance had proved much greater than we had anticipated, and long dry stretches of desert were more than they would be prepared for. As it was we feared greatly that we had consumed so much time they would get impatient and start out and be lost.

"I continued to hobble along down the barren valley as well as I could and here and there some tracks of animals were discovered, but we could not make out whether they were those of domestic cattle or elk. Soon, on the side of a hill, rather high up a pack of prairie wolves were snarling around the carcass of some dead animal, and this was regarded as another sign that more and better meat could be found, for these animals only live where some sort of game can be found, and they knew better than we that it was not for their health to go into the barren desert.

"Before us now was a spur from the hills that reached

nearly across our little valley and shut out further sight in that direction and when we came to it we climbed up over it to shorten the distance. When the summit was reached a most pleasing sight filled our sick hearts with a most indiscribable joy. I shall never have the ability to describe the beauty of the scene as it appeared to us, and so long as I live that landscape will be impressed upon the canvas of my memory as the most cheering in the world. There before us was a beautiful meadow of a thousand acres, green as a thick carpet of grass could make it, and shaded with oaks, wide branching and symmetrical, equal to those of an old English park, while all over the low mountains that bordered it on the south and over the broad acres of luxuriant grass was a herd of cattle numbering many hundreds, if not thousands. They were of all colors and shades and sizes. Some were calmly lying down in happy rumination, others rapidly cropping the sweet grass, while the gay calves worked off their superflous life and spirit in vigorous exercise or drew rich nourishment in the abundant mother's milk.

"All seemed happy and content, and such a scene of abundance and rich plenty and comfort bursting thus upon our eyes which for months had seen only the desolation and sadness of the desert, was like getting a glimpse of Paradise, and tears of joy ran down our faces. If ever a poor mortal escapes from this world where so many trails come, and joys of a happy Heaven are opened up to him, the change cannot be much more than this which was suddenly opened to us on that bright day which was either one of the very last of December 1849 or the first of January 1850, I am inclined to think it was the very day of the new year, but in our troubles, the accuracy of the calendar was among the least of our troubles. If it was, as I believe the beginning of the year, it was certainly a most auspicious one and one of the most hopeful of my life.

"And now if the others were only here, was the burden of our thought, and a serious awakening from the dream of beauty and rich plenty spread out before us. This ring-streaked and speckled herd might be descended directly from Jacob's famous herd, blessed of the Lord, and while we could not keep our thoughts from some sad doubts as to the fate of those whom we had left behind, we tried to be generally hopeful and courageous and brightened up our steps to prepare for a relief and return to the hot dry plain beyond the mountains where they were awaiting us, no doubt with much tribulation.

"I now thought of myself and my failing knee and we sat down under the shade of an oak to rest, and after a little, better feeling seemed to come. Down by a gulley cut by the rains a yearling steer was feeding and I took the rifle and crawled down near him and put first one ball through him, and then another, before he fell dead on the other side of the wash, when we sprang with all the agility of a deer. We quickly got some good meat and had it roasted and eaten almost quicker than can be told.

"We hardly realized how near starved we were till we were satisfied for once and till we had plenty before us again. We ate till we were satisfied, and for the first time in many long dreary weeks. We kindled a fire and commenced drying the meat, one sleeping while the other kept the fire, and changing off every four hours. What a rest that was! One who has never been nearly worn out and starved, down nearly to the point of death can never know what it is to rest in comfort. No one can tell. It was like a dream, a sweet, restful dream where troubles would drown themselves in sleep. How we felt the strength come back to us with that food and the long draughts of pure clear water.

"The miserable dried meat in our knapsacks was put away and this splendid jerked beef put in its place. The wolves came to our camp and howled in dreadful disappointment at not getting a meal. Rogers wanted me to shoot the miserable howlers, but I let them have their concert out, and thought going without their breakfast must be punishment enough for them. As our mocassins were worn out we carefully prepared some sinews from the steer and made new foot gear from the green hide which placed us in shape for two or three week's walking.

"The morning was clear and pleasant. We had our knapsacks filled with good food we had prepared, and were enjoying the cool breeze which came up the valley, when we heard faintly the bark of a dog, or at least we thought we did. If this

221

were true there must be some one living not very far away and we felt better. I was still very lame and as we started along the walking seemed to make it worse agin, so that it was all I could do to follow John on the trail down the valley. As we went along a man and woman passed us some distance on the left, and they did not seem to notice us, though we were in plain sight. They were curiously dressed. The woman had no hoops nor shoes, and a shawl wound around her neck and one end thrown over her head, was a substitute bonnet. The man had sandals on his feet, with white cotton pants, a calico shirt, and a wide rimmed, comical, snuff-colored hat. We at once put them down as Spaniards, or then descendents of Mexico, and if what we had read about them in books was true, we were in a set of land pirates, and blood thirsty men whom we might have occasion to be aware of. We had never heard a word of Spanish spoken, except a word or two upon the plains which some fellow knew, and how we could make ourselves known and explain who we were was a puzzle to us.

"Difficulties began to arise in our minds now we were in an apparent land of plenty, but in spite of all we went along as fast as my lame knee would permit me to do. A house on higher ground soon appeared in sight. It was low, of one story with a flat roof, gray in color, and of a different style of architecture from any we had ever seen before. There was no fence around it, and no animals or wagons in sight, nor person to be seen. As we walked up the hill toward it I told John our mocassins made of fine green hide would betray us as having recently killed an animal, and as these people might be the owners and detain us by having us arrested for the crime, and this would be especially bad for us just now. We determined to face the people, and let the fact of our close necessities be a sufficient excuse for us, if we could make them understand our circumstances. [Here Manly and Rogers are the first Death Valley '49ers to reach the del Valle home, on Rancho San Francisquito, about one-half mile south of Newhall Ranch Service Station at the junction of Highway #99 and the Ventura Highway.]

"As we came near the house no person was seen, but a mule tied to a post told us there was some one about, and a man soon made an appearance, dressed about the same style as the one we had passed a short distance behind. As we came near we saluted him, bidding him good morning, and he in turn touched his hat politely, saying something in reply which we were not able to understand. I showed him that I was lame, and taking out some money pointed to the mule, but he only shook his head and said something I could not comprehend. Rogers now began looking around the house, which was built of sundried bricks about one by two feet in size, and one end was used as a storehouse. As he looked in, a man came to him and wanted a black, patent leather belt which Rogers wore, having a watch-pocket attached to it. He offered a quart or more of coarse corn meal, and Rogers made the trade.

"We tried to inquire where we were or where we ought to go, but could get no satisfactory answer from the man, although when we spoke San Francisco he pointed to the north. This was not very satisfactory to us and we seemed as badly lost as ever, and where or which way to go we did not seem very successful in finding out. So we concluded to go on a little way at least, and I hobbled off in the direction he pointed, which was down the hill and past a small, poorly fenced field which was sometimes cultivated, and across the stream which followed down the valley. As we passed on a mile or two we stopped on a big patch of sand to rest.

"I told Rogers I did not think this course would lead us to any place in a month, and just now a delay was ruinous to us and to those who were waiting for us, and it would not do for us to go off to the north to find a settlement. While I was expressing my opinion on matters and things, Rogers had wet up a part of his meal with water and put it to bake on the cover of his camp kettle. There was a fair sized cake for each of us, and it was the first bread of any kind we had eaten in months, being a very acceptable change from an exclusively meat diet. Looking up the valley we could see a cloud of dust, thick and high, and soon several men on horseback who came at a rushing gallop. I told Rogers they were after us, and believed them to be a murderous set who might make trouble for us. I hastily buried our little store of money in the sand, telling them [him] that if they got us, they would not get our money. Putting our guns across our laps in an easy position we had them cocked and ready for business, and our knives where we could get them handy, and awaited their arrival."

CHAPTER THIRTEEN

BACK TO THE VALLEY OF DEATH

It was a terrible shock to the hopes of both Manly and Rogers when they had just reached a land of plenty to find themselves unable to explain their mission and to secure the aid for which they had struggled so far. If they were ever to think of abandoning the little starved band in Death Valley and go on to the mines alone, here was the time when such thoughts must have come to them. Stranded and besieged by a gang of charging strangers, they must have felt helplessly alone and unable even to save themselves. But, just as their problems seemed overwhelming, help was at hand. Read what William Lewis Manly wrote of his and his co-hero, John Haney Rogers', experience with the Californians and of their trying journey back into the Valley of Death:

"They came on with a rush until within a short distance and halted for consultation just across the creek, after which one of them advanced toward us and as he came near us we could see he was a white man, who wished us good evening in our own language. We answered him rather cooly, still sitting in the sand and he no doubt saw that we were a little suspicious of the crowd. He asked us where we were from, and we told him our circumstances and condition and that we would like to secure some means of relief for the people we had left in the desert, but our means were very limited and we wanted to do the best we could. He said we were about 500 miles from San Francisco, not far from 100 miles from the coast and thirty miles from Los Angeles. We were much afraid we would not be able to get anything here, but he told us to go across the valley to a large oak tree which he pointed out, and said we would find an American there, and we should wait there till morning. He said he would go back and stay at the house we had passed, and would do what he could to assist us to go to Los Angeles where we could get some supplies. Then he rode away, and as we talked it over we saw no way but to follow the directions of our new-found friend.

"It seemed now that my lameness had indeed been a blessing. If I had been able to walk we would now have been well on toward the seashore, where we could have found no such friend as this who had appeared to us. The way seemed clearer to us, but the time for our return was almost up and there was no way of getting back in fifteen days as we had agreed upon, so there was great danger to our people yet. It seemed very likely to take us twenty-four or thirty days at best, and while they probably had oxen enough to provide them with food for so long a time they might take a notion to move on, which would be fatal.

"At the big oak tree we found an American camper, who was on his way to the gold mines. He was going a new route and said the mines could be reached much quicker than by going up the coast by way of San Francisco. A new company with wagons was soon to start out to break the road, and when they reached the east end of the valley he would follow them. [This is the Hudgins party which broke the road by way of San Francisquito Canyon, Elizabeth Lake and Grapevine Canyon into the San Joaquin Valley.] I think this man's name was Springer. He had come by way of the Santa Fe Route, and the people of Los Angeles had told him this route was an easy one being often traveled by saddle horses, and if the company could make it possible for wagons they could have all the cattle they wanted to kill along the road as their pay for doing the work. Our new friend lay down early, and as he saw we were scant in blankets he brought some to us for our use, which were most thankfully received.

"As soon as we were alone Rogers mixed up some more of the meal which we baked in our friend's frying pan, and we baked and ate and baked and ate again, for our appetites were ravenous, and the demand of our stomachs got the better of the judgment of our brains.

"It was hard to find time to sleep, we were so full of the plans about the way, which we must manage to get relief for the people. We had many doubts if animals could ever come over the route we had come over, from deliberation we decided that by selecting a route with that idea in our minds, we could get mules and perhaps horses over the country. We perhaps could go more to the north and take the Jayhawkers trail, but this would take us fully a hundred miles farther and four or five days longer, at the very best, and every moment of delay was to be carefully avoided as a moment of danger to our friends.

"Thus, again, our sleep was troubled from another cause. Being so long unaccustomed to vegetable food, and helped on, no doubt, by our poor judgment in gauging the quantity of our food, we were attacked by severe pains in the stomach and bowels, from which we suffered intensely. We arose very early and with a very light breakfast, for the sickness admonished us, we started back for the house we had first passed, at which our friend on horseback, said he would spend the night and where we were to meet him this morning. He said he could talk Spanish all right and would do all he could to help us.

"Our suffering and trouble caused us to move very slowly, so that it was nine or ten o'clock before we reached the house, and we found they had two horses all ready for us to go to Los Angeles. There were no saddles for us, but we thought this would be a good way to cure my lameness. The people seemed to be friends to us in every way. We mounted, having our packs on our backs, and our guns before us, and with a friendly parting to the people who did not go, all four of us started on a trip of thirty miles to the town of Los Angeles.

"When we reached the foot of the mountain which was very steep but not rocky, John and I dismounted and led our animals to the top, where we could see a long way west and south, and it looked supremely beautiful. We could not help comparing it to the long wide, desert we had crossed, and John and myself said many times how we wished the folks were here to enjoy the pleasant sight, the beautiful fertile picture.

"There appeared to be one quite large house in sight, and not far off, which the man told us was the Mission of San Fernando, a Roman Catholic Church and residence for priests and followers. The downward slope of the mountain was as steep as the other side and larger, and John and I did not attempt to mount till we were well down on the level

227

ground again, but the other two men rode up and down without any trouble. We would let our leaders get half a mile or so ahead of us and then mount and put our horses to a gallop till we overtook them again. We had walked so long that riding was very tiresome to us, and for comfort alone we would have preferred the way on foot, but we could get along a little faster, and the frequent dismounting kept us from becoming too lame from riding.

"We passed the Mission about noon or a little after, and a few miles beyond met a man on horseback who lived up to the north about a hundred miles. His name was French and he had a cattle range at a place called Tejon (Tāhón). Our friends told him who we were, and what assistance we needed. Mr. French said he was well acquainted in Los Angeles and had been there some time, and that all the travelers who would take the Coast route had gone, those who had come by way of Salt Lake had got in from two to four weeks before, and a small train which had come to Los Angeles and had come the Santa Fe Route was still upon the road. He said Los Angeles was so clear of emigrants that he did not think we could get any help there at the present time.

" 'Now,' said Mr. French—'You boys can't talk Spanish and it is not very likely you will be able to get any help. Now I say, you boys turn back and go with me and I will give you the best I have, I will let you have a yoke of gentle oxen, or more if you need them, and plenty of beans, which are good food for I live on them; besides this I can give you an Indian guide to help you back. Will that do?' After a moment we said we doubted if oxen could be got over the road, and they were fat now they would soon get poor, and perhaps not stand it as well as the oxen which had became used to that kind of life, and of those they had in camp all they needed. We wanted to get something for the women and children to ride, for we knew we must abandon the wagons, and could not walk so far over that dry, rough country.

" 'Well,' said Mr. French:—'I will stop at the place you were this morning—I know them well—and they are good folks, and I am sure when I tell them what you want they will help you if they possibly can. This looks to me to be the most sensible course.' After talking an hour our two compan-

228

ions advised us that the proposition of Mr. French seemed the most reasonable one that appeared. But for us to go clear back to his range would take up so much valuable time that we were almost afraid of the delay which might mean destruction to our friends. French said he had a pack saddle with him, taking it home, and we could put it on one of our horses, and when we came back to Los Angeles could leave it at a certain saloon or place he named and tell them it belonged to him and to keep it for him. I have forgotten the name of the man who kept the saloon. We agreed to this, and bidding our two companions farewell, we turned back again with Mr. French.

"When night came we were again at the Mission we had passed on the way down. We were kindly treated here, for I believe Mr. French told them about us. They sent an Indian to take our horses, and we sat down beside the great house. There were many smaller houses, and quite a large piece of ground fenced in by an adobe wall. The roof of the buildings was like that of our own buildings in having eaves on both sides, but the covering was of semi circular tiles made and burned like brick. Rows of these were placed close together, the hollow sides up, and then another course over the joints, placed with the round side up, which made a roof that was perfectly waterproof, but must have been very heavy. These tiles were about two feet long. All the surroundings, and general make up of the place were new to us and very wonderful. They gave us good dried meat to eat and let us sleep in the big house on the floor, which was as hard as granite, and we turned over a great many times before daylight, and were glad when morning came. We offered to pay them, but they would take nothing from us, and we left leading our horses over the steep mountain, and reaching the house again late in the day. They turned our horses loose and seemed disposed to be very friendly and disposed to do for us what they could.

"We were very tired and sat down by the side of the house and rested, wondering how we would come out with our preparations. They were talking together, but we could not understand a word. A dark woman came out and gave each of us a piece of cooked squash. It seemed to have been roasted in the ashes and was very sweet and good. These were all signs of friendship and we were glad of the good feeling.

"We were given a place to sleep in the house, in a store room on a floor which was not soft. This was the second house we had slept in since leaving Wisconsin, and it seemed rather pent-up to us.

"In the morning we were shown a kind of mill like a coffee mill, and by putting in a handful of wheat from a pile and giving the mill a few turns we were given to understand we should grind some flour for ourselves. We went to work with a will, but found it hard, slow work.

"After a little, our dark woman came and gave us each a pancake and piece of meat, also another piece of roasted squash for our breakfast, and this, we thought, was the best meal we had ever eaten. The lady tried to talk to us but we could not understand the words, and I could convey ideas to her better by the sign language than any other way. She pointed out the way from which we came and wanted to know how many day's travel it might be away, and I answered by putting my hand to my head and closing my eyes, which was repeated as many times as there had been nights on our journey, at which she was much surprised that the folks were so far away. She then placed her hand upon her breast and then held it up, to ask how many women there were, and I answered her by holding up three fingers, at which she shrugged her shoulders and shook her head. Then pointing to a child by her side, four or five years old, and in the same way asked how many children, I answered by holding up four fingers, and she almost cried, opening her mouth in great surprise, and turned.

"I said to Rogers that she was a kind, well meaning wo- man, and that Mr. French had no doubt told her something of our story. Aside from her dark complexion, her features reminded me of my mother, and at first sight of her I thought of the best woman on earth my own far off mother, who little knew the hardships we had endured. We went to work again at the mill and after a while the woman came again and tried to talk and to teach us some words of her own language. She placed her finger on me and said ombre and I took out my little book and wrote down ombre as meaning man, and in

230

the same way she taught me that mujer, was woman; trigo, wheat; frijoles, beans; carne, meat; calazasa, pumpkin; caballo, horse; vaca, cow; muchacho, boy; and several other words in this way.

"I got hold of many words thus to study, so that if I ever came back talk a little and made myself understood as to some of the common objects and things of necessary use. Such friendly, human acts shown to us strangers, were evidences of the kindest disposition. I shall never forget the kindness of those original Californians. When in Walker's camp and finding he was friendly to Mormonism we could claim that we were also Mormons, but the good people though well known Catholics, did not so much as mention the fact nor inquire whether we favored that sect or not. We were human beings in distress and we represented others who were worse even that we, and those kind acts and great good will, were given freely because we were fellow human beings.

"The provisions we prepared were, a sack of small yellow beans; a small sack of wheat, a quantity of good dried meat, and some of the coarse, unbolted flour we had made at the mills. They showed us how to properly pack the horse, which was a kind of work we had not been used to, and we were soon ready for a start. I took what money we had and put it on a block, making signs for them to take what the things were worth. They took $30 and we were quite surprised to get two horses, provisions, pack-saddles and ropes, some of the latter made of rawhide and some of hair, so cheaply, but we afterward learned that the mares furnished were not considered of much value, and we had really paid a good fair price for everything. To make it easy for us they had also fixed our knapsacks on the horses.

"The good lady with the child, came out with four oranges and pointed to her own child and then to the East, put them in the pack meaning we should carry them to the children. With a hearty good bye from them, and a polite lifting of our hats to them we started on our return, down toward the gentle decline of the creek bottom, and then up the valley, the way we came. Toward night we came to a wagon road crossing the valley, and as we well knew we could not go up the tangled creek bed with horses we took this road to the north, which took a dry ravine for its direction, and in which there was a pack trail, and this the wagons were following. [They are now traveling up San Francisquito Canyon.] We kept on the trail for a few miles, and overtook them in their camp, and camped with them over night. We told them we considered our outfit entirely too small for the purpose intended, which was to bring two women and four children out of the desert, but that being the best we could get, we were taking this help to them and hoped to save their lives. Our mission became well known and one man offered to sell us a poor little one-eyed mule, its back all bare of covering from the effect of a great saddle sore that had very recently healed. He had picked it up somewhere in Arizona where it had been turned out to die, but it seemed the beast had enough of the good Santa Ana stock in it to bring it through and it had no notion of dying at the present time, though it was scarcely more than a good fair skeleton, even then. The beast became mine at the price of $15 and the people expressed great sympathy with us and the dear friends we were going to try to save.

"Another man offered a little snow-white mare, as fat as butter, for $15, which I paid, though it took the last cent of money I had. This little beauty of a beast was broken to lead at a halter, but had not been broken in any other way. Rogers said he would ride her where he could, and before she got to the wagons she would be as gentle as a lamb. He got a bridle and tried her at once, and then there was a scene of rearing, jumping, and kicking that would have made a good Bufalo Bill circus in these days. No use, the man could not be thrown off, and the crowd cheered and shouted to Rogers to—'Hold her level.'

"After some bucking and backing on the part of the mare and a good deal of whipping and kicking on the part of the man, and a good many furious dashes in lively, but very awkward ways, the little beast yielded the point, and carried her load without further trouble.

"The people gave us a good supper and breakfast, and one man came and presented us with 25 pounds of unbolted wheat flour. They were of great assistance to us in showing us how to pack and sack our load, which was not heavy and could be easily carried by our two animals which we had at first. However we arranged a pack on the mule and this gave me a horse to ride and a mule to lead, while Rogers rode his milk-white steed and led the other horse. Thus we went along and following the trail soon reached the summit from which we could see off to the east a wonderful distance, probably 200 miles, of the dry and barren desert of hill and desolate valley over which we had come.

"The trail leading still to the north from this point, we left and turned due east across the country, and soon came to a beautiful lake of sweet fresh water situated well up toward the top of the mountain. This lake is now called Elizabeth Lake. Here we watered our animals and filled our canteens, then steered a little south of east among the Cabbage trees, aiming to strike the rain water hole about noon and here found the Jayhawkers trail, which we took. They had evidently followed us and passed down the same brushy cañon while we having taken a circuitous route to the north, had gone around there. Getting water here for ourselves and horses, we went back to the trail and pushed on as fast as the animals could walk, and as we now knew where we could get water, we kept on till after dark, one of us walking to keep the trail, and some time in the night reached the Willow corral I have spoken of before. [Here Manly has undoubtedly not counted one day of travel. They are at Desert Spring, one half mile east of present Cantil.] There was good water here, but the Jayhawker's oxen had eaten all the grass that grew in the little moist place around, and our animals were short of feed. One of us agreed to stand guard the fore part of the night and the other later, so that we might not be surprised by Indians and lose our animals. I took the first watch and let the blaze of the fire go out so as not to attract attention and as I sat by the dull coals and hot ashes I fell asleep. Rogers happened to wake and see the situation, and arose and waked me again saying that we must be more careful or the Indians would get our horses. You may be sure I kept awake the rest of my watch.

"Next day we passed the water holes at the place where we had so stealthily crawled up to Doty's camp when coming out

233

Reginaldo del Valle, who was a small boy when the Death Valley '49ers arrived at Rancho San Francisquito. He served for a time as a State Senator and lived to welcome descendants of Death Valley '49ers to a reunion held at the ruins of the old home.

Photo courtesy of Security First National Bank of Los Angeles and now in Bear State Library.

234

Tom Wilson, aged Panamint Indian who saw the Death Valley parties of '49 and who furnished much information about the courses they took through the territory in and about Death Valley.
Photo courtesy of Clark Mills and now in Bear State Library.

235

[Indian Wells]. These holes held about two pails of water each, but no stream run away from them. Our horses seemed to want water badly for then they drank they put their head in up to their eyes and drank ravenously.

"Thirty miles from here to the next water, Doty had told us, and night overtook us before we could reach it, so a dry camp was made. Our horses began now to walk with drooping heads and slow, tired steps, so we divided the load among them all and walked ourselves. [They are now at the west slope of the Argus Range, northeast of present China Lake.] The water, when reached proved so salt the horses would not drink it, and as Doty had told us the most water was over the mountain ahead of us, we still followed their trail which went up a very rocky cañon in which it was hard work for the horses to travel. The horses were all very gentle now and needed some urging to make them go. Roger's fat horse no longer tried to unseat its rider or its pack, but seemed to be the most downhearted of the train. The little mule was the liveliest, sharpest witted animal of the whole. She had probably traveled on the desert before and knew better how to get along. She had learned to crop every spear of grass she came to, and every bit of sage brush that offered a green leaf was given a nip. She would sometimes leave the trail and go out to one side to get a little bunch of dry grass, and come back and take her place again as if she knew her duty. The other animals never tried to do this. The mule was evidently better versed in the art of getting a living than the horses.

"Above the rough bed of the cañon the bottom was gravelly and narrow, and the walls on each side nearly perpendicular. Our horses now poked slowly along and as we passed the steep wall of the cañon the white animal left the trail and walked with full force, head first, against the solid rock. She seemed to be blind, and though we went quickly to her and took off the load she carried, she had stopped breathing by the time we had it done. Not knowing how far it was to water, nor how soon some of our other horses might fall, we did not tarry, but pushed on as well as we could, finding no water. We reached the summit and turned down a ravine, following the trail, and about dark came to the water they had told us about, a faint running stream which came out of a rocky ravine and sank almost immediately in the dry sand. [Providence or Indian Joe's Spring, near the north end of Searles Lake valley]. There was water enough for us, but no grass. It seemed as if the horses were not strong enough to carry a load, and as we wanted them to get through if possible, we concluded to bury the wheat and get it on our return. We dug a hole and lined it with fine sticks, then put in the little bag and covered it with dry brush, and sand making the surface as smooth as if it had never been touched, then made our bed on it. The whole work was done after dark so the deposit could not be seen by the red men and we thought we had done it pretty carefully.

"Next morning the little mule carried all the remaining load, the horses bearing only their saddles, and seemed hardly strong enough for that. There was now seven or eight miles of clean loose sand to go over, across a little valley which came to an end about ten miles north of us, and extended south to the lake [Searles Lake] where we went for water on our outward journey and found it red alkali. Near the Eastern edge of the valley we turned aside to visit the grave of Mr. Isham, which they had told us of. They had covered his remains with their hands as best they could, piling up a little mound of sand over it. Our next camp was to be on the summit of the range just before us, and we passed the dead body of Mr. Fish, we had seen before, and go on a little to a level sandy spot in the ravine just large enough to sleep on. This whole range is a black mass rocky piece of earth, so barren that not a spear of grass can grow, and not a drop of water in any place. We tied our horses to rocks and there they staid all night, for if turned loose there was not a mouthful of food for them to eat.

"In the morning an important question was to be decided, and that was whether we should continue to follow the Jayhawker's trail which led far to the north [through Towne's Pass] or to cross the mountain, which stood before us, a mass of piled-up rocks so steep that it seemed as if a dog could hardly climb it [the Panamint Range]. Our wagons were nearly due east from this point over the range, and not more than fifty miles away, while to go around to the north was fully a hundred miles, and would take us four or five days to make. As we had already gone so long we expected to meet them any day trying to get out and if we went around we might miss them. They might have all been killed by Indians or they might have already gone. We had great fears on their account. If they had gone north they might have perished in the snow.

"The range was before us, and we must get to the other side in some way. We could see the range for a hundred miles to the north and along the base some lakes of water that must be salt. To the south it got some lower, but very barren and ending in black, dry buttes. The horses must have food and water by night or we must leave them to die, and all things considered it seemed to be the quickest way to camp to try and get up a rough looking cañon which was nearly opposite us on the other side. So we loaded the mule and made our way down the rocky road to the ridge, and then left the Jayhawker's trail, taking our course south so as to get around a salt lake [the Salt Lake in Panamint Valley] which lay directly before us. On our way we had to go close to a steep bluff, and cross a piece of ground that looked like a well dried mortar bed, hard and smooth as ice, and thus got around the head of a small stream of clear water, salt as brine. We now went directly to the mouth of the cañon we had decided to take, and traveled up its gravelly bed. [This probably was Pleasant Canyon.] The horses now had to be urged along constantly to keep them moving and they held their heads low down as they crept along seemingly so discouraged that they would much rather lie down and rest forever than take another step. We knew they would do this soon in spite of all our urging, if we could not get water for them. The cañon was rough enough where we entered it, and a heavy up grade too, and this grew more and more difficult as we advanced, and the rough, yellowish, rocky walls closed in nearer and nearer together as we ascended.

"A perpendicular wall, or rather rise, in the rocks was approached, and there was a great difficulty to pursuade the horses to take exertion to get up and over the small obstruction, but the little mule skipped over as nimbly as a well-fed goat, and rather seemed to enjoy a little variety in the proceedings. After some coaxing and urging the horses took courage to try the extra step and succeeded all right, when we all moved on again, over a path that grew more and more narrow, more and more rocky under foot at every moment. We wound around among and between the great rocks, and had not advanced very far before another obstruction, that would have been a fall of about three feet had water been flowing in the cañon, opposed our way. A small pile of lone rocks enabled the mule to go over all right, and she went on looking for every spear of grass, and smelling eagerly for water, but all our efforts were not enough to get the horses along another foot. It was getting nearly night and every minute without water seemed an age. We had to leave the horses and go on. We had deemed them indispensable to us, or rather to the extrication of the women and children, and yet the hope came to us that the oxen might help some of them out as a last resort. We were sure the wagons must be abandoned, and such a thing as women riding on the backs of oxen we had never seen, still it occurred to us as not impossible and although leaving the horses here was like deciding to abandon all for the feeble ones, we saw we must do it, and the new hope arose to sustain us for farther effort. We removed the saddles and placed them on a rock, and after a few moments hesitation, moments in which were crowded torrents of wild ideas, and desperate thoughts, that were enough to drive reason from its throne, we left the poor animals to their fate and moved along. Just as we were passing out of sight the poor creatures neighed pitifully after us, and one who has never heard the last despairing, pleading neigh of a horse left to die can form no idea of its human appeal. We both burst into tears, but it was no use, to try to save them we must run the danger of sacrificing ourselves, and the little party we were trying so hard to save.

"We found the little mule stopped by a still higher precipice or perpendicular rise of fully ten feet. Our hearts sank within us and we said that we should return to our friends as we went away, with our knapsacks on our backs, and the hope grew very small. The little mule was nipping some stray blades of grass and as we came in sight she looked around to us and then up the steep rocks before her with such knowing, intelligent look of confidence, that it gave us new courage. It was a strange wild place. The north wall of the cañon leaned far over the channel, overhanging considerably, while the south wall sloped back about the same, making the wall nearly parallel, and like a huge crevice descending into the mountain from above in a sloping direction.

"We decided to try to get the confident little mule over this obstruction. Gathering all the loose rocks we could we piled them up against the south wall, beginning some distance below, putting up all those in the bed of the stream and throwing down others from narrow shelves above we built a sort of inclined plane along the walls gradually rising till we were nearly as high as the crest of the fall. Here was a narrow shelf scarcely four inches wide and a space of from twelve to fifteen feet to cross to reach the level of the crest. It was all I could do to cross the space, and there was no foundation to enable us to widen it so as to make a path for an animal. It was forlorn hope but we made the most of it. We unpacked the mule and getting all our ropes together, make a leading line of it. Then we loosened and threw down all the projecting points of rocks we could above the narrow shelf, and every piece that was likely to come loose in the shelf itself. We fastened the leading line to her and with one above and one below we thought we could help her to keep her balance, and if she did not make a misstep on that narrow way she might get over safely. Without a moments hesitation she tried the pass. Carefully and steadily she went along, selecting a place before putting down a foot, and when she came to the narrow ledge leaned gently on the rope, never making a sudden start or jump, but cautiously as a cat moved slowly along. There was now no turning back for her. She must cross this narrow place over which I had to creep on hands and knees, or be dashed down fifty feet to a certain death. When the worst place was reached she stopped and hesitated, looking back as well as she could. I was ahead with the rope, and I called encouragingly to her and talked to her a little. Rogers wanted to get all ready and he said, 'holler' at her as loud as he could and frighten her across, but I thought the best way to talk to her gently and let her move steadily.

"I tell you, friends, it was a trying moment. It seemed to be weighed down with all the trials and hardships of many months. It seemed to be the time when helpless women and innocent children hung on the trembling balance between life and death. Our own lives we could save by going back, and sometimes it seemed as if we would perhaps save ourselves the additional sorrow of finding them all dead to do so once. I was so nearly in despair that I could not help bursting in tears, and I was not ashamed of the weakness. Finally Rogers said, 'Come Lewis' and I gently pulled the rope, calling the little animal, to make a trial. She smelled all around and looked over every inch of the strong ledge, then took one careful step, after another over the dangerous place. Looking back, I saw Rogers with a very large stone in his hand, ready to 'holler' and perhaps kill the poor beast if she stopped. But she crept along trusting to the rope to balance, till she was halfway across, then another step or two, when calculating the distance closely she made a spring and landed on a smooth bit of sloping rock below, that led up to the highest crest of the precipice, and safely climbed to the top, safe and sound above the falls. The mule had no shoes and it was wonderful how her little hoofs clung to the smooth rock. We felt relieved. We would push on and carry food to the people; we would get them through some way; there could be no more hopeless moment than the one just past, and we would save them all.

"It was the work of a little while to transfer the load up the precipice, and pack the mule again, when we proceeded. Around behind some rocks only a little distance beyond this place we found a small willow bush and enough good water for a camp. [This spring is still in existence.] This was a strange cañon. The sun never shown down to the bottom of the fearful place where the little mule climbed up, and the rocks had a peculiar yellow color. In getting our provisions up the precipice, Rogers went below and fastened the rope while I pulled them up. Rogers wished many times we had the horses up safely where the mule was, but a dog could hardly cross the narrow path and there was no hope. Poor brutes, they had been faithful servants, and we felt sorrowful enough at their terrible fate.

241

"We had walked two days without water, and we were wonderfully refreshed as we found it here. The way up this cañon was very rough and the bed full of sharp broken rocks in loose pieces which cut through the bottoms of our mocassins and left us with bare feet upon the acute points and edges. I took off one of my bucksin leggins, and gave it to Rogers, and with the other one for myself we fixed the mocassins with them as well as we could, which enabled us to go ahead, but I think if our feet had been shod with steel those sharp rocks would have cut through.

"Starting early we made the summit about noon, and from here we could see the place where we found a water hole and camped the first night after we left the wagons. Down the steep cañon we turned, the same one in which we had turned back with the wagons [Six Springs Canyon?] and over the sharp broken pieces of volcanic rock that formed our only footing we hobbled along with sore and tender feet. We had to watch for the smoothest place for every step, and then moved only with the greatest difficulty. The Indians could have caught us easily if they had been around for we must keep our eyes on the ground constantly and stop if we looked up and around. But we at last got down and camped on same spot where we had set out twenty-five days before to seek the settlements. Here was the same little water hole in the sand plain, and the same strong sulphur water which we had to drink the day we left. The mule was turned loose dragging the same piece of rawhide she had attached to her when we purchased her, and she ranged and searched faithfully for food finding little except the very scattering bunches of sage brush. She was industrious and walked around rapidly picking here and there, but at dark came into camp and lay down close to us to sleep.

"There was no sign that any one had been there during our absence, and if the people had gone to hunt a way out, they must either have followed the Jayhawker's trail or some other one. We were much afraid that they might have fallen victims to the Indians. Remaining in camp so long it was quite likely they had been discovered by them and it was quite likely they had been murdered for the sake of the oxen and camp equipage. It might be that we should find the

242

hostiles waiting for us when we reached the appointed camping place, and it was small show for two against a party. Our mule and her load would be a great capture for them. We talked a great deal and said a great many things at that camp fire for we knew we were in danger, and we had many doubts about the safety of our people, that would soon be decided, and whether for joy or sorrow we could not tell.

"From this place, as we walked along, we had a wagon road to follow, in soft sand, but not a sign of a human footstep could we see, as we marched toward this, the camp of the last hope. We had the greatest fears the people had given up our return and started out for themselves and that we should follow on, only to find them dead or dying. My pen fails me as I try to tell the feelings and thoughts of this trying hour I can never hope to do so, but if the reader can place himself in my place, his imagination cannot form a picture that shall go beyond reality.

"We were some seven or eight miles along the road when I stopped to fix my mocassin while Rogers went slowly along. The little mule went on ahead of both of us, searching all around for little bunches of dry grass, but always came back to the trail again and gave us no trouble. When I had started up again I saw Rogers ahead leaning on his gun and waiting for me, apparently looking at something on the ground. As I came near enough to speak I asked what he had found and he said—'Here is Capt. Culverwell, dead.' He did not look much like a dead man. He lay upon his back with arms extended wide, and his little canteen, made of two powder flasks, lying by his side. This looked indeed as if some of our saddest forbodings were coming true. How many more bodies should we find? Or should we find the camp deserted, and never find a trace of the former occupants.

"We marched toward camp like two Indians, silent and alert, looking out for dead bodies and live Indians, for really we more expected to find the camp devastated by those rascals than to find that it still contained our friends. To the east we could plainly see what seemed to be a large salt lake with a bed that looked as if of the finest, whitest sand, but really a wonder of salt crystal. We put the dreary steps steadily one forward of another, the little mule the only

243

unconcerned one of the party, ever looking for an odd blade of grass, dried in the hot dry wind, but yet retaining nourishment which she preferred.

"About noon, we came in sight of the wagons, still a long way off, but in the clear air we could make them out, and tell what they were, without being able to see anything more. Half a mile was the distance between us and the camp before we could see very plainly as they were in a little depression. We could see the covers had been taken off, and this was an ominous sort of circumstance to us, for we feared the depredations of the Indians in retaliation for the capture of their squashes. They had shot our oxen before we left and they have slain them this time and people too.

"We surely left seven wagons. Now we could see only four and nowhere the sign of an ox. They must have gone ahead with a small train, and left these four standing, after dismantling them.

"No signs of life were anywhere about, and the thought of our hard struggles between life and death to go out and return, with the fruitless results that now seemed apparent was almost more than human heart could bear. When should we know their fate? When should we find their remains, and how learn of their sad history if we ourselves should live to get back again to settlements and life? If ever two men were troubled, Rogers and I surely passed through the furnace.

"We kept as low and as much out of sight as possible, trusting very much to the little mule that was ahead, for we felt sure she would detect danger in the air sooner than we, and we watched her closely to see how she acted. She slowly walked along looking out for food, and we followed a little way behind, but still no decisive sign to settle the awful suspense in which we lived and suffered. We became more and more convinced that they had taken the trail of the Jayhawkers, and we had missed them on the road, or they had perished before reaching the place where we turned from their trail.

"One hundred yards now to the wagons, and still no sign of life, no positive sign of death, though we looked carefully for both. We fear that perhaps there are Indians in ambush, and with nervous irregular breathing we counsel what to do.

244

Finally Rogers suggested that he had two charges in his shot gun and I seven in the Colt's rifle, and that I fire one of the shots and await results before we ventured any nearer, and if there are any of the red devils there we can kill some of them before they get us. And now both closely watching the wagons I fired the shot. Still as death and not a move for a moment, and then as if by magic a man came out from under a wagon and stood up looking all around, for he did not see us. Then he threw up his arms high over his head and shouted—'The boys have come! The boys have come!' Then other bare heads appeared, and Mr. Bennett and wife and Mr. Arcane came toward us as fast as ever they could. The great suspense was over and our hearts were first in our mouths, and then the blood all went away and left us almost fainting as we stood and tried to step. Some were safe perhaps all of those nearest us, and the dark shadows of death that had hovered over us, and cast what seemed a pall upon every thought and action, was lifted and fell away a heavy oppression gone. Bennett and Arcane caught us in their arms and embraced us with all their strength, and Mrs. Bennett when she came fell down on her knees and clung to me like a maniac in the great emotion that came to her, and not a word was spoken. If they had been strong enough they would have carried us to camp on their shoulders. As it was they stopped two or three times, and turned as if to speak, but there was too much feeling for words, convulsive weeping would choke the voice.

"All were a little calmer soon, and Bennett soon found voice to say:—'I know you have found some place, for you have a mule,' and Mrs. Bennett through her tears, looked staringly at us as she could hardly believe our coming back was a reality, and then exclaimed:—'Good boys! O, you have saved us all! God bless you forever! Such boys should never die!' It was some time before they could talk without weeping. Hope almost died within them, and now when the first bright ray came it almost turned reason from its throne. A brighter happier look came to them than we had seen, and then they plied us with questions the first of which was:— 'Where were you?'

"We told them it must be 250 miles yet to any part of

California where we could live. Then came the question:—
'Can we take our wagons?' 'You will have to walk,' was our
answer, for no wagons could go over that unbroken road that
we had traveled. As rapidly and carefully as we could we told
them of our journey, and the long distance between the water
holes; that we had lost no time and yet had been twenty-six
days on the road; that for a long distance the country was
about as dry and desolate as the region we had crossed east of
this camp. We told them of the scarcity of grass, and all the
reasons that had kept us so long away from them."

CHAPTER FOURTEEN

"GOOD BYE DEATH VALLEY!"

One who never has suffered a terrible privation which has almost ended in death by starvation can appreciate the fearsome feeling of our little band of '49ers. As Manly and Rogers led the ragged party over the divide in the Panamints from the scenes of their sixty days of suffering they were moved almost beyond the power of speech. The memories of their recent trials were so fresh in their minds and the view over the vast Utah Desert, ending in the deep sink of Death Valley, so impressive that, almost as one they called out, "Good bye Death Valley!"

Several writers have tried to show that the name, Death Valley, was first given by government parties as late as 1860 and 1861 and that none of the Manly and Rogers party had anything to do with the naming. The facts are strong in favor of Manly's own account which in 1894 gave them as I have repeated them.

In Los Angeles Manly and Brier talked over their experiences, beginning only a few days after Manly and Rogers had led the group from Rancho San Francisquito to that village. There the name was used in the presence of many people, including all of the Manly-Rogers group and some of the Jay Hawks.

The years of 1859, 1860 and 1861 saw numerous groups prospecting and mining the Cerro Gordo, Coso and Death Valley regions. In these mining groups were Bennett, Manly and a number of other Death Valley '49ers. It was during this time that the use of the name, Death Valley, became widespread and that it was taken up and placed in print by government surveyors.

Adjectives failed Manly when he attempted to describe the feelings of that tattered band of men, women and children as they turned from Death Valley and began the dreary, grinding journey across three deserts and three mountain ranges to Rancho San Francisquito and the City of the Angels. But even with the failure of descriptive terms William Lewis Manly's account is the best that has been given of that heroic trek. Probably it is the most heart-gripping of any that ever will be written. I here give the stage from the summit of the Panamints to   247

Indian Wells, the place where all parties obtained their first good water and first vital relief from the effects of their struggle across the Utah desert and Death Valley:

"There was no end to the questions about the road we had to answer, for this was uppermost on their minds, and we tried to tell them and show them how we must get along on our return. We told them of the great snow mountains we had seen all to the north of our road, and how deep the snow appeared to be, and how far west it extended. We told them of the black and desolate ranges and buttes to the south, and of the great dry plains in the same direction. We told them of the Jayhawkers trail; of Fish's dead body; of the salt lake and slippery alkali water to which we walked, only to turn away in disappointment; of the little sheets of ice which saved our lives; of Doty's camp and what we knew of those gone before; of the discouraged ones who gave us their names to send back to friends; of the hawk and crow diet; of my lameness; of the final coming out into a beautiful valley, in the midst of fat cattle and green meadows, and the trouble to get the help arranged on account of not knowing the language to tell the people what we needed. They were deeply impressed that my lameness had been a blessing in disguise, or we would have gone on to the coast and consumed more time than we did in walking slowly to favor the cripple knee.

"Our sad adventures and loss of the horses in returning was sorrowfully told and we spoke of the provisions we had been able to bring on the little mule which had clambered over the rocks like a cat; that we had a little flour and beans, and some good dried meat with fat on it which we hoped would help to eke out the poorer fare and get them through at last. They were so full of compliments that we really began to think we had been brought into the world on purpose to assist some one, and the one who could forecast all things had directed us, and all our ways, so that we should save those people and bring them to a better part of God's footstool, where plenty might be enjoyed, and the sorrows of the desert forgotten. It was midnight before we could get them all satisfied with their knowledge of our experience.

"It was quite a treat to us to sleep again between good

blankets, arranged by a woman's hand, and it was much better resting than the curled up, cramped position we had slept in while away, with only the poor protection of the half blanket for both of us, in nights that were pretty chilly.

"We had plenty of water here, and there being no fear of the mule going astray we turned her loose. As the party had seen no Indians during our absence we did not concern ourselves much about them. At breakfast we cautioned them about eating too much bread, remembering our own experience in that way.

"They said they had about given up our coming back a week before, and had set about getting ready to try to move on themselves. Bennett said he was satisfied that they never could have got through alone after what we had told them of the route and its dangers. He said he knew it now that not one of them would have lived if they had undertaken the journey alone without knowledge of the way.

"They had taken off the covers of the wagons to make them into houses [housings or pack sacks] for the oxen, so they could be used as pack animals. The strong cloth had been cut into narrow strips and well made into breast straps and breeching, for the cattle were so poor and their hide so loose it was almost impossible to keep anything on their backs. They had emptied the feathers out of the beds to get the cloth to use, and had tried to do everything that seemed best to do to get along without wagons.

"The oxen came up for water, and the mule with them. They looked better than when we left, but were still poor. They had rested for some time and might feel able to go along willingly for a few days at least. I was handy with the needle, and helped them to complete the harness for the oxen, while Bennett and John went to the lake to get a supply of salt to take along, a most necessary article with our fresh meat. I looked around a little at our surroundings, and could see the snow still drifting over the peak of the snowy mountain as we had seen it farther east, where we were ourselves under the burning sun. This was now pretty near February first, or midwinter. The eastern side of this great mountain was too steep to be ascended, and no sign of a tree could be seen on the whole eastern slope. The range of moun-

249

tains on the east side of this narrow valley were nearly all volcanic, barren in the extreme, and the roughest of all the mountains we had ever seen. I had now looked pretty thoroughly, and found it to be pretty nearly a hundred miles long, and this was the only camp I had seen where water could be had.

"When Mrs. Bennett was ready to show me what to do on the cloth harness, we took a seat under the wagon, the only shady place and began work. The great mountain, I have spoken of as the snow mountain has since been known as Telescope Peak, reported to be 11,000 feet high. It is in the range running north and south and has no other peak so high. Mrs. Bennett questioned me closely about the trip, and particularly if I had left anything out which I did not want her to know. She said she saw her chance to ride was very slim, and she spoke particularly of the children, and that it was impossible for them to walk. She said little Martha had been very sick since we had been gone, and that for many days they had expected her to die. They had no medicine to relieve her and the best they could do was to select the best of the ox meat, and make a little soup of it and feed her, they had watched her carefully for many days and nights, expecting they would have to part with her any time and bury her little body in the sands. Sometimes it seemed as if her breath would stop, but they had never failed in their attentions, and were at last rewarded by seeing her improve slowly, and even to relish a little food, so that if no relapse set in they had hopes to bring her through. They brought the little one and showed her to me, and she seemed so different from what she was when we went away. Then she could run about camp, climb out and in the wagons, and move about so spry that she reminded one of a quail. Now she was strangely misshapen. Her limbs had lost all the flesh and seemed nothing but skin and bones, while her body had grown corpulent and distended, and her face had a starved pinched and suffering look, with no healthy color in it.

"She told me of their sufferings while we were gone, and said she often dreamed she saw us suffering fearfully for water, and lack of food and could only picture to herself as their own fate, that they must leave the children by the trail side, dead, and one by one drop out themselves in the same way. She said she dreamed often of her old home where bread was plenty, and then to awake to find her husband and children starving was a severe trial indeed, and the contrast terrible. She was anxious to get me to express an opinion as to whether I thought we could get the oxen down the falls where we had so much trouble.

"I talked to her as encouragingly as I could, but she did not cheer up much and sobbed and wept over her work most all the time. It was not possible to encourage her much, the outlook seemed so dark. Mrs. Arcane sat under another wagon and said nothing, but she probably heard all we had to say, and did not look as if her hopes were any brighter. Bennett and Rogers soon returned with a supply of salt and said the whole shore of the lake was a winrow of it, that could be shoveled up in enormous quantities.

"We now in a counsel of the whole, talked over the matter, and the way which seemed most promising. If we went by the Jayhawkers trail, there was a week of solid travel to get over the range and back south again as far as a point directly opposite our camp, and this had taken us only three days to come over as we had come. The only obstacle in the way was the falls, and when we explained that there was some sand at the bottom of them Bennett said he thought we could get them over without killing them, and that, as we knew exactly where the water was, this was the best trail to take. Arcane was quite of the same opinion, the saving of a week of hard and tiresome travel being in each case the deciding reason. They then explained to me what they had decided on doing if we had not come back. They had selected two oxen for the women to ride one to carry water and one to carry the four children. There were no saddles but blankets enough to make a soft seat, and they proposed to put a band or belt around the animals for them to hold on by, and the blankets would be retained in place by breast and breeching straps which we had made. They had found out that it was very difficult to keep a load of any kind upon an ox, and had devised all this harness to meet the trouble.

"Bennett had one old bridle ox called Old Crump, which had been selected to carry the children, because he was slow and steady. 'How in the world do you expect to keep the children on?'—said I. 'Well'—said Bennett, with a sort of comical air, about the first relief from the sad line of thought that had possessed us all—'We have taken two strong hickory shirts, turned the sleeves inside, sewed up the necks, then sewed the two shirts together by the tail, and when these are placed on the ox they will make two pockets for the youngest children, and we think the two others will be able to cling to his back with the help of a band around the body of the ox to which they can cling to, with their hands.' Now if Old Crump went steady and did not kick up and scatter things, he thought this plan would operate first rate. Now as to the mule they proposed as we knew how to pack the animal, that we should use her to pack our provisions so they would go safe.

"From a piece of hide yet remaining John and I made ourselves some new mocassins, and were all ready to try the trip over our old trail for now the third time, and the last, we hoped.

"Mrs. Bennett and Mrs. Arcane had taken our advice, and in cooking had not put too much of the flour or beans into the soup for the children and they had gotten along nicely, and even began to smile a little with satisfaction after a full meal. They got along better than John and I did when we got hold of the first nutritons after our arrival on the other side.

"We must leave everything here we can get along without. No clothing except that on our backs. Only a camp kettle in which to make soup, a tin cup for each one, and some knives, and spoons which each happen to have. Each one had some sort of a canteen for water, which we must fill up at every opportunity, and we decided to carry a shovel along, so we might bury the body of Capt. Culverwell, and shovel up a pile of sand at the falls to enable to get the oxen over. Every ox had a cloth halter on his head, so he might be led, or tied up at night when we had a dry camp, and they would most assuredly wander off if not secured. Old Crump was chose to lead the train, and Rogers was to lead him. We had made an extra halter for this old fellow, and quite a long strip of bed ticking sewed into a strap to lead him by.

"This packing business was a new idea, and a hard matter to get anything firmly fixed on their backs.

"We had made shoulder straps, hip straps, breast straps and breeching as the correct idea for a harness. The only way we could fasten the band around the animals was for one to get on each side and pull it as tight as possible then tie a knot, as we had no buckles or ring in our harness.

"The loads of the oxen consisted of blankets and bedding and a small, light tent of their sheeting about four by six feet in size. We rose early and worked hard till about the middle of the forenoon getting all things ready. They had been a state of masterly inactivity so long in this one camp that they were anxious to leave it now forever. Only in progress was there hope, and this was our last and only chance. We must succeed or perish. We loaded the animals from the wagons, and some of the oxen seemed quite afraid of this new way of carrying loads. Old Crump was pretty steady, and so was the one with the two water kegs one on each side but the other oxen did not seem to think they needed any blankets on these warm days.

"Mrs. Arcane was from a city, and had fondly conveyed thus far some articles of finery, of considerable value and much prized. She could not be persuaded to leave them here to deck the red man's wife, and have her go flirting over the mountains with, and as they had little weight she concluded she would wear them and this perhaps would preserve them. So she got out her best hat and trimmed it up with extra ribbon leaving some with quite long ends to stream out behind. Arcane brought up his old ox Old Brigham, for he had been purchased at Salt Lake and named in honor of the great Mormon Saint.

"Also, Mrs. Arcane dressed her little boy Charlie up in his best suit of clothes, for she thought they might as well wear them out as to throw them away. She made one think of a fairy in gay and flying apparel. In the same way all selected their best and most servicable garments, for it was not considered prudent to carry any load, and poor clothes were good enough to leave for Indians. We set it down as a principle that we must save ourselves all we could, for it would be a close contested struggle with us and death, at the very best, and we wanted to get all the advantage for ourselves we could. As we were making the preparations the women grew more hopeful, as it seemed as if something was really going to be accomplished.

"Bennett and Arcane were emphatic in their belief and expressions that we would succeed. 'I know it—Don't you Sally?' said Bennett very cheerfully, but after all Mrs. Bennett could not answer quite as positively, but said 'I hope so.' Mrs. Bennett's maiden name was Sarah Dilley, which I mention here as I may otherwise forget it afterward. She realized that hers was no easy place to ride, that they would have hard fare at best, and that it must be nearly or quite a month before they could reach a fertile spot on which to place her feet. One could easily see that the future looked quite a little dark to her, on account of her children, as a mother naturally would.

"High overhead was the sun, and very warm indeed on that day in the fore part of February 1850, when the two children were put on Old Crump to see if he would let them ride. The two small children were placed in the pockets on each side, face outward, and they could stand or sit as they should choose. George and Melissa were placed on top and given hold of the strap that was to steady them in their place. I now led up Mrs. Bennett's ox and Mr. Bennett helped his wife to mount the animal, on whose back as soft a seat as possible had been constructed. Mrs. Arcane in her ribbons was now helped to her seat on the back of Old Brigham and she carefully adjusted herself to position, and arranged her dress and ornaments to suit, then took hold of the strap that served to hold on by as there were no bridles on these two.

"Rogers led the march with his ox; Bennett and I started the others along, and Arcane followed with Old Crump and the children. Bennett and Arcane took off their hats and bade the old camp good bye. The whole procession moved, and we were once more going toward our journey's end we hoped. The road was sandy and soft, the grade practically level, and everything went well for about four miles, when the pack on one of the oxen near the lead got loose and turned over to one side, which he no sooner saw thus out of position, then he tried to get away from it by moving sidewise. Not getting clear of the objectionable load in this way he tried to kick it off, and thus really got his foot in it, making matter worse instead of better. Then he began a regular waltz and bawled at the top of his voice in terror. Rogers tried to catch him but his own animal was so frisky that he could not hold him and do much else, and the spirit of fear soon began to be communicated to the others and soon the whole train seemed to be taken crazy.

"They would jump up high and then come down, sticking their fore feet as far as possible into the sand after which, with elevated tails, and terrible plunges would kick and thrash and run till the packs came off, when they stopped apparently quite satisfied. Mrs. Bennett slipped off her ox as quick as she could, grabbed her baby from the pocket on Old Crump, and shouting to Melissa and George to jump, got her family into safe position in pretty short order. Arcane took his Charley from the other pocket and laid him on the ground, while he devoted his own attention to the animals. Mrs. Arcane's ox followed suit, and waltzed around in the sand, bawled at every turn, fully as bad as any of the others, but Mrs. Arcane proved to be a good rider, and hard to unseat, clinging desperately to her strap as she was tossed up and down, and whirled about at a rate enough to make any one dizzy. Her many fine ribbons flew out behind like the streamers from a mast-head, and the many fancy fixin's she had donned fluttered in the air in gayest mockery. Eventually she was thrown however, but without the least injury to herself, but somewhat disordered in raiment. When I saw Bennett he was standing half bent over laughing in almost hysterical convulsion at the entirely impromptu circus which had so suddenly performed an act not on the program. Arcane was much pleased and laughed heartily when he saw no one was hurt. We did not think the cattle had so much life and so little sense as to waste their energies so uselessly. The little mule stepped out one side and looked on in amazement, without disarranging any article of her load.

"Mrs. Bennett, carrying her baby and walking around to keep out of the way, got very much exhausted, and sat down on the sand, her face as red as if the blood were about to burst through the skin, and perspiring freely. We carried a blanket

255

and spread down for her while we gathered in the scattered baggage. Then the oxen were got together again, and submitted to being loaded up again as quietly as if nothing had happened. Myself and the women had to mend the harness considerably, and Arcane and his ox went back for some water, while Rogers and Bennett took the shovel and went ahead about a mile to cover up the body of Capt. Culverwell, for some of the party feared the cattle might be terrified at seeing it. All this took so much time that we had to make a camp of it right there.

"We put the camp kettle on two stones, built a fire, put in some beans and dried meat cut very fine, which cooked till Arcane came with more water, which was added, and thickened with a little of the unbolted flour, making a pretty good and nutritious soup which we all enjoyed. We had to secure the animals, for there was neither grass nor water for them, and we thought they might not be in so good spirits another day.

"We had little trouble in packing up again in the morning, and concluded to take a nearer route to the summit, so as to more quickly reach the water holes where Rogers and I camped on our first trip over the country. This would be a hard rocky road on its course leading up a small rocky cañon, hard on the feet of the oxen, so they had to be constantly urged on, as they seemed very tender footed. They showed no disposition to go on a spree again and so far as keeping the loads on, behaved very well indeed. The women did not attempt to ride but followed on, close after Old Crump and the children who required almost constant attention, for in their cramped position they made many cries and complaints. To think of it, two children cramped up in narrow pockets, in which they could not turn around, jolted and pitched around over the rough road, made them objects of great suffering to themselves and anxiety and labor on the part of the mothers.

"Mrs. Bennett said she would carry her baby if she could, but her own body was so heavy for her strength that she could not do it. Bennett, Rogers and myself hurried the oxen all we could, so that we could reach the water, and let Bennett go back with some to meet the rest and refresh them for the end of the day's march, and he could take poor little Martha from the pocket and carry her in his arms, which would be a great relief to her. Arcane also took his child when he met them, throwing away his double barrel gun, saying:—'I have no use for you.'

"When the women reached camp we had blankets already spread down for them, on which they cast themselves, so tired as to be nearly dead. They were so tired and discouraged they were ready to die, for they felt they could not endure many days like this.

"We told them this was the first day and they were not used to exercise therefore more easily tired than after they became a little used to it. We told them not to be discouraged, for we knew every water hole, and all the road over which we would pilot them safely. They would not consent to try riding again, after their circus experience, and Mrs. Arcane said her limbs ached so much she did not think she could even go on the next day. They had climbed over the rocks all day, and were lame and sore, and truely thought they could not endure such another day.

"The trail had been more like stairs than a road in its steep ascent, and our camp was at a narrow pass in the range. The sky was clear and cloudless, as it had been for so long for thus far upon this route no rain had fallen, and only once a little snow that came to us like manna in the desert. For many days we had been obliged to go without water both we and our cattle, and over the route we had come we had not seen any signs of a white man's presence older than our own. I have no doubt we were the first to cross the valley in this location, a visible sink hole in the desert.

"The women did not recover sufficient energy to remove their clothing, but slept as they were, and sat up and looked around with uncombed hair in the morning, perfect pictures of dejection. We let them rest as long as we could, for their swollen eyes and stiffened joints told how sadly unprepared they were to go forward at once. The sun came out early and made it comfortable, while a cool and tonic breeze, came down from the great snow mountain the very thing to brace them up after a thorough rest.

"The slope to the east was soon met by a high ridge and

Abigail Harriett (Ericsen) Arcan, who wore all of her finery rather than abandon it to the Panamint Indians. It has been said that she did this because of her French background and love of frills. But her descendants state that it was her Danish thrift that caused her to wear all of the fine clothes she had and even a linen tablecloth which she wrapped about her waist under her dress and carried afoot to Los Angeles.

She is buried in Evergreen Cemetery, Santa Cruz, California.

Photo courtesy of Mrs. Harder and now in Bear State Library.

between this and the main mountain was a gentle slope scattered over with sage brush, and a few little stools of bunch grass here and there between. This gave our oxen a little food and by dipping out the water from the holes and letting them fill up again we managed to get water for camp use and to give the animals nearly all they wanted. [Six Springs at the head of Six Springs Canyon? From here to Willow Springs they follow the same route over which Manly and Rogers returned to Death Valley.]

"While waiting for the women, Bennett and Arcane wanted to go out and get a good view of the great snowy mountain I had told them so much about. The best point of view was near our camp, perhaps three or four hundred yards away, and I went with them. This place where we now stood was lower than the mountains either north or south, but were difficult to climb, and gave a good view in almost every direction, and there, on the back bone of the ridge we had a grand outlook, but some parts of it brought back doleful recollections. They said they had travelled in sight of that mountain for months and seen many strange formations, but never one like this, as developed from this point. It looked to be seventy-five miles to its base, and to the north and west there was a succession of snowy peaks that seemed to have no end. Bennett and Arcane said they never before supposed America contained mountains so grand with peaks that so nearly seemed to pierce the sky. Nothing except a bird could ever cross such steep ranges as that one.

"West and south it seemed level, and low, dark and barren buttes rose from the plain, but never high enough to carry snow, even at this season of the year. I pointed out to them the route we were to follow, noting the prominent points, and it could be traced for fully one hundred and twenty-five miles from the point on which we stood. This plain, with its barren ranges and buttes is now known as the Mojave Desert. This part of the view they seemed to study over, as if to fix every point and water hole upon their memory. We turned to go to camp, but no one looked back on the country we had come over since we first made out the distant snow peak, now so near us, on November 4th, 1849. The only butte in this

Jean Baptiste Arcan, whose family in 1849-'50 was led by John Haney Rogers and William Lewis Manly from Tule Springs in Death Valley to Rancho San Francisquito near present Newhall and then to Los Angeles.

In Los Angeles Arcan traded his trusty telescope, the one Manly used to spy out the way from Division Springs, for a boat passage for his family as far toward San Francisco as the boat Captain would take him. That proved to be Santa Cruz. When the Arcans walked from the boat Mrs. Arcan was captivated with the beautiful San Lorenzo River and redwoods. She told Jean Baptiste, "You can go to the mines if you want to. I have seen all the God-forsaken country I am going to see, for I am going to stay right here as long as I live." She was a lady of her word.

Photo courtesy of Mrs. Harder, granddaughter of Arcan and now in Bear State Library.

direction that carried snow was the one where we captured the Indian and where the squashes were found.

"The range next east of us across the low valley was barren to look upon as a naked, single rock. There were peaks of various heights and colors, yellow, blue, firery red and nearly black. It looked as if it might sometime have been the center of a mammoth furnace. I believe this range is known as the Coffin's Mountains. [A portion of it is known as the Funeral Range.] It would be difficult to find earth enough in the whole of it to cover a coffin.

"Just as we were ready to leave and return to camp we took off our hats, and then overlooking the scene of so much trial, suffering and death spoke the thought uppermost saying:—'Good bye Death Valley!' then faced away and made our steps toward camp. Ever after this in speaking of this long and narrow valley over which we had crossed into its nearly central party, and on the edge of which the lone camp was made, for so many days, it was called Death Valley.

"Many accounts have been given to the world as to the origin of the name and by whom it was thus designated but ours were the first visible footsteps, and we the party which named it the saddest and most dreadful name that came to us first from its memories.

"Out of Death Valley we surely were. To Rogers and I, the case seemed hopeful, for we had confidence in the road and believed all would have power to weather difficulties, but the poor women—it is hard to say what complaints and sorrows were not theirs. They seemed to think they stood at death's door, and would about as soon enter, as to take up a farther march over the black, desolate mountains and dry plains before them, which they considered only a dreary vestibule to the dark door after all. They even had an idea that the road was longer than we told them, and they never could live to march so far over the sandy, rocky roads. The first day nearly satisfied them that it was no use to try, Rogers and I counted up the camps we ought to reach every day and in this way could pretty near convince them of time that would be consumed in the trip. We encouraged them in every way we could; told them we had better get along a little every day and make ourselves a little near the promised land, and the very exercise would soon make them stronger and able to make a full day's march.

"John and I told them we felt in much better spirits now than we did when we set out alone, and now that nothing but the arrows of an Indian could stop us. We said to them, 'We are not going to leave you two ladies out here to die for there is not a sign of a grave to put you in,—' and it was a pretty tough place to think of making one. We told them of the beautiful flowery hillsides over the other side and begged them to go over there to die, as it would be so much better and easier to perform the last sad rites there instead of here on the top of the dismal mountain. It seemed quite like a grim joke, but it produced a reaction that turned the tide of thoughts and brought more courage. We only laid out the march for this day as far as the falls and after a little prepared to move. The cattle seemed to have quit their foolishness, and they were loaded without trouble. The children fitted into the pockets better than usual, and the mothers with full canteens strapped across their shoulders picked out soft places on which to place their poor blistered feet at every step. They walked as if they were troubled with corns on every toe and on their heels into the bargain, and each foot was so badly affected, that they did not know on which one to limp. But still they moved, and we were once more on our way westward. They often stopped to rest, and Arcane waited for them with Old Crump, while they breathed and complained awhile and then passed on again.

"The route was first along the foot of the high peak, over bare rocks and we soon turned south somewhat so as to enter the cañon leading down to the falls. The bottom of this was thick with broken rock, and the oxen limped and picked out soft places about as bad as the women did. A pair of mocassins would not last long in such rocks and we hoped to get out of them very soon. Rogers and I hurried along, assisting Arcane and his party as much as we could, while Bennett staid behind and assisted the women as much as possible, taking their arms, and by this means they also reached camp an hour behind the rest.

"A kettle of hot steaming soup, and blankets all spread out on which to rest, was the work Rogers and I had done to prepare for them, and they sank down on the beds completely exhausted. The children cried some but were soon pacified and were contented to lie still. A good supper of hot soup made them feel much better all around.

"The first thing Bennett and Arcane did was to look round and see the situation at the falls, and see if the obstacle was enough to stop our progress, or if we must turn back and look for a better way. They were in some doubt about it, but concluded to try and get the animals over rather than to take the time to seek another pass, which might take a week of time. We men all went down to the foot of the fall, and threw out all the large rocks, then piled up all the sand we could scrape together with the shovel, till we had quite a pile of material that would tend to break a fall. We arranged everything possible for a forced passage in the morning, and the animals found a few willows to browse and a few bunches of grass here and there, which gave them a little food, while the spring supplied them with enough water to keep them from suffering with thirst.

"Early in the morning we took our soup hastily and with ropes lowered our luggage over the small precipice, then the children, and finally all the ropes were combined to make a single strong one about thirty feet long. They urged one of the oxen up to the edge of the falls, put the rope around his horns, and threw down the end to me, whom they had stationed below. I was told to pull hard when he started so that he might not light on his head and break his neck. We felt this was a desperate undertaking, and we fully expected to lose some of our animals, but our case was critical and we must take some chances. Bennett stood on one side of the ox, and Arcane on the other, while big Rogers was placed in the rear to give a regular Tennessee boost when the word was given.

" 'Now for it,' said Bennett, and as I braced out on the rope those above gave a push and the ox came over, sprawling, but landed safely, cut only a little by some angular stones in the sand pile. 'Good enough,' said some one and I threw the rope back for another ox. 'We'll get'em all over safely' said Arcane, 'if Lewis down there, will keep them from getting their necks broken.' Lewis pulled hard every time, and not a neck was broken. The sand pile was renewed every time and made as high and soft as possible, and very soon all our animals were below the falls. The little mule gave a jump when he pushed her and lighted squarely on her feet all right. With the exception of one or two slight cuts, which bled some, the oxen were all right and we began loading them at once.

"Bennett and Arcane assisted their wives down along the little narrow ledge which we used in getting up, keeping their faces toward the rocky wall, and feeling carefully for every footstep. Thus they worked along and landed safely by the time we had the animals ready for a march. We had passed without disaster, the obstacle we most feared, and started down the rough cañon, hope revived, and we felt we should get through. After winding around among the great boulders for a little while we came to the two horses we had left behind, both dear and near together. We pointed to the carcasses, and told them those were the horses we had brought for the women to ride, and that is the way they were cheated out of their passage. The bodies of the animals had not been touched by bird or beast. The cañon was too deep and dark for either wolves or buzzards to enter, and nothing alive had been seen by us in the shape of wild game of any sort. [This is undoubtedly present Pleasant Canyon.] Firearms were useless here except for defence against Indians, and we expected no real trouble from them.

"From what we could see, it was my opinion that no general rain ever fell in that region. There was some evidence that water had at times flowed down them freely after cloud bursts, or some sudden tempest, but the gravel was so little worn that it gave no evidence of much of a stream.

"We hurried on as rapidly as possible so as to get into the Jayhawker's beaten trail which would be a little easier to follow. When we reached the lowest part of the valley we had to turn south to get around a little, slow running stream of salt water, that moved north and emptied into a Salt Lake [Panamint Salt Lake]. No source of the stream could be seen from this point, but when we reached a point where we could cross, we had a smooth, hard clay bed to march over. It seemed to have been, some day, a bed of mortar, but now baked hard, and the hoofs of the oxen dented into it no more than half an inch. On our left hand was a perpendicular cliff, along which we travelled for quite a little way. The range of mountains now before us to cross black, nothing but rocks, and extremely barren, having no water in it that we knew of, so when we reached the summit we camped, tied all our animals to rocks, where they lay down and did not rise till morning. [They here skirted the edge of the Slate Range where the present Trona-Wildrose Highway crosses, and camped in the mouth of Water Canyon.] The women were so tired they were two hours late, and we had the fire built, the soup cooked and the bed made. As we did not stop at noon all were very hungry, and ate with a relish. The poor animals had to go without either grass or water. When Old Crump and the party came in the men were carrying the babies, and their wives were clinging to their arms, scarcely able to stand. When they reached the beds they fell at full length on them, saying their feet and limbs ached like the tooth ache. It seemed to be best for them to rest a little before eating. Mrs. Bennett said that the only consolation was that the road was getting shorter every day, but were it not for the children she would sooner die than follow the trail any farther. Their soup was carried to them in the bed, and they were covered up as they lay, and slept till morning. This day's walk was the hardest one yet, and probably the longest one of the whole journey, but there was no other place where we could find a place large enough to make a camp and free enough of rocks so that a bed could be made.

"Rogers and I had the kettle boiling early, and put in the last of the meat, and nearly all that was left of the flour. At the next camp an ox must be killed. Just as it was fairly light I went about 200 yards out wher the dead body of Mr. Fish lay, just as he died more than a month before. The body had not been disturbed and looked quite natural. He was from Oscaloosea, Iowa.

"The folks arose very reluctantly this morning, and appeared with swollen eyes and uncombed hair, for there was no means of making a toilet, without a drop of water, except what we had used in getting breakfast. We set the soup kettle near the foot of the bed so the women could feed the children and themselves. Now as we loaded the oxen, it was

Martha Bennett, who balanced Charlie Arcan in the hickory shirts from the Bennett Long Camp at Tule Spring, Death Valley, to Los Angeles.
Photo courtesy of Mrs. W. B. Hewett, daughter of Martha Bennett and now in Bear State Library.

agreed that Rogers and I should go ahead with all but Old Crump, and get in camp as soon as possible, and they were to follow on as best they could. There was a little water left in the canteens of Bennett and Arcane, to be given only to the children, who would cry when thirsty, the very thing to make them feel the worst.

"We were to kill an ox when we reached camp, and as each of the men had an equal number on the start each was to furnish one alternately and no disputing about whose were better or stronger, in any emergency.

"Our road now led down the western slope of the mountain, and loose, hard, broken rocks were harder on the feet of our animals than coming up, and our own mocassins were wearing through. The cattle needed shoes as well as we. Any one who has never tried it can imagine how hard it is to walk with tender feet over broken rock. It was very slow getting along at the best, and the oxen tumbled dreadfully in trying to protect their sore feet. At the foot of the mountain we had several miles of soft and sandy road. [This is the trough of the north end of Searles Lake Valley.] The sun shone very hot, and with no water we suffered fearfully. A short way out in the sandy valley we pass again the grave of Mr. Isham, where he had been buried by his friends. He was from Rochester, N.Y. He was a cheerful, pleasant man, and during the forepart of the journey used his fiddle at the evening camps to increase the merriment of his jolly companions. In those days we got no rain, see no living animals of any kind except these of our train, see not a bird nor insect, see nothing green except a very stunted sage, and some dwarf bushes. We now know that the winter of 1849-50 was one of the wettest ever seen in California, but for some reason or other none of the wet clouds ever came to this portion of the State to deposit the most scattering drops of moisture.

"Quite a long way from the expected camp the oxen snuffed the moisture, and began to hurry towards it with increased speed. A little while before it did not seem as if they had ambition enough left to make a quick move, but as we approached the water those which had no packs fairly trotted in their haste to get a drink. This stream was a very small one, seeping out from a great pile of rocks, and maintaining itself till it reached the sands, where it disappeared completely. A few tufts of grass grew along the banks, otherwise everything surrounding was desolate in the extreme. [This is Providence, or Indian Joe Spring, discovered by Jay Hawk Deacon Richards.]

"As soon as we could get the harness off the oxen, we went to look for our little buried sack of wheat, which we were compelled to leave and hide on our way out. We had hidden it so completely, that it took us quite a little while to strike its bed but after scratching with our hands awhile, we hit the spot, and found it untouched. Although the sand in which it was buried seemed quite dry, yet the grain had absorbed so much moisture from it, that the sack was nearly bursting. It was emptied on a blanket, and proved to be still sound and sweet.

"Our first work now was to kill an ox and get some meat to cook for those who were coming later. We got the kettle over boiling with some of the wheat in it, for the beans were all gone. We killed the ox saving the blood to cook. Cutting the meat all off the bones, we had it drying over a fire as soon as possible, except what we needed for this meal and the next. Then we made a smooth place in the soft sand on which to spread the blankets, the first good place we had found to sleep since leaving Death Valley.

"The next job was to make mocassins for ourselves and for the oxen for it was plain they could not go on another day barefooted. We kept busy indeed, attending the fires under the meat and under the kettle, besides our shoemaking, and were getting along nicely about sundown, when Old Christian Crump appeared in sight followed by the women and the rest of the party. The women were just as tired as ever and dropped down on the blankets the first thing. 'How many such days as this can we endure?'—they said. We had them count the days gone by, and look around to see the roughest part of the road was now behind them. They said that only five days had passed, and that two thirds of the distance still remained untraveled, and they knew they could never endure even another five day's work like the last. We told them to be brave, and be encouraged, for we had been over the road and knew what it was, and that we felt sure of being able to

268

do it nicely. They were fed in bed, as usual, and there they lay till morning. We men went to making mocassins from the green hide, and when we had cut out those for the men and women the balance of the hide was used in preparing some also for the oxen, particularly the worst ones, for if I remember correctly there was not enough to go round.

"The morning came, bright and pleasant, as all of them were, and just warm enough for comfort in the part of the day. The women were as usual, and their appearance would remind one quite strongly of half drowned hens which had not been long out of trouble. Hair snarled, eyes red, nose swollen, and out of fix generally. They did not sleep well so much fatigued, for they said they lived over their hard days in dreams at night, and when they would close their eyes and try to go to sleep, the visions would seem to come to them half waking and they could not rest.

"There was now before us a particularly bad stretch of the country as it would probably take us four or five days to get over it, and there was only one water hole in the entire distance. [the Argus Range and Indian Wells Valley]. This one was quite salt, so much so that on our return trip the horses refused to drink it, and the little white one died next day. Only water for one day's camp could be carried with us, and that was for ourselves alone and not for the animals.

"When the mocassins were finished in the morning we began to get our cattle together when it was discovered that Old Brigham was gone, and the general belief was that the Indians had made a quiet raid on us got away with the old fellow. We circled around till we found his track and then Arcane followed it while we made ready the others. Arcane came in with the stray namesake of the polygamous saint about this time shouting:—'I've got him—No Indians.' The ox had got into the wash ravine below camp and passed out of sight behind, in a short time. He had been as easily tracked as if he walked in snow. There was larger sage brush in the wash than elsewhere, and no doubt Brigham had thought this a good place to seek for some extra blades of grass.

"Immediately south of this camp now known as Providence Springs, is the salt lake [Searles Lake] to which Rogers and I

269

went on the first trip and were so sadly disappointed in finding the water unfit to use.

"As soon as ready we started up the cañon following the trail made by the Jayhawkers who had proceeded us, and by night had reached the summit, but passed beyond, a short distance down the western slope, where we camped in a valley that gave us good large sage brush for our fires, and quite a range for the oxen without their getting out of sight. This being at quite a high elevation we could see the foot as well as the top, of the great snow mountain and had a general good view of the country.

"This proved to be the easiest day's march we had experienced and the women complained less than on any other night since our departure. Their path had been comparatively smooth, and with the new mocassins their feet had been well protected, they had come through pretty nicely. We told them they looked better, and if they would only keep up good courage they would succeed and come out all right to the land where there was plenty of bread and water, and when safely out, they might make good resolutions never to get in such a trap again. Mrs. Bennett said such a trip could never be done over again, and but for the fact that Rogers and I had been over the road, and that she believed all we had said about it; she never would have had the courage to come thus far. Now, for the children's sake, she wished to live, and would put forth any effort to come through all right.

"The next day we had a long cañon to go down, and in it passed the dead body of the beautiful white mare Rogers had taken such a fancy to. The body had not decomposed, nor had it been disturbed by any bird or beast. Below this point the bed of the cañon was filled with great boulders, over which it was very difficult to get the oxen along. Some of them had lost their mocassins and had to suffer terribly over the rocks.

"Camp was made at the salt water hole, and our wheat and meat boiled in it did not soften and get tender as it did in fresh water. There was plenty of salt grass above; but the oxen did not eat it any more than the horses did and they wandered around cropping a bite of the bitter brush once in awhile, and looking very sorry. This was near the place where Rogers and I found the piece of ice which saved our

270

lives. [In a letter written many years after he had passed this place, Mr. Brier referred to this as the Sand Dune Spring. William Rice stated to this writer that the place was finally covered by the sand dune about 1895.] The women did not seriously complain when we reached this camp, but little Charley Arcane broke out with a bad looking rash all over his body and as he cried most of the time it no doubt smarted and pained him like a mild burn. Neither his mother nor anyone else could do anything for him to give him any relief. We had no medicines, and if he or any one should die, all we could do would be to roll the body in a blanket and cover it with a light covering of sand.

"From this camp to the next waterholes at the base of the great snow mountain, it was at last 30 miles [about twenty miles], level as to surface, and with a light ascending grade. The Jayhawkers had made a well marked trail, and it was quite good walking. The next camp was a dry one, both for ourselves and the oxen, nothing but dry brush for them, and a little dried meat for ourselves, but for all this the women did not complain so very much. They were getting used to the work and grew stronger with the exercise. They had followed Old Crump and the children every day with the canteens of water and a little dried meat to give them if they cried too much with hunger, and Arcane led his ox day after day with a patience that was remarkable, and there was no bad temper shown by any one. This was the way to do, for if there was any differences, there was no tribunal to settle them by.

"In all this desert travel I did not hear any discontent and serious complaint, except in one case, and that was at the Jayhawker's camp, where they burned their wagons at the end of the wagon road, in Death Valley. Some could not say words bad enough to express their contempt, and laid all the trouble of salt water to Lot's wife. Perhaps she was in a better position to stand the cursing than any of the party present.

"The next day we reached the water holes at the place where Rogers and I stole up to camp fire in the evening, supposing it to be Indians, but finding there Capt. Doty and his mess, a part of the Jayhawker's band. [These were present Indian Wells near Homestead Service Station on High-

271

way #6, seven miles north of Freeman Junction.] By dipping carefully from these holes they filled again, and thus, although there was no flow from them we gradually secured what water we needed for the camp, which was a small amount after so long a time without. There was some low brush here called greasewood, which grew about as high as currant bushes, and some distance up the mountain the oxen could find some scattery bunch grass, which, on the whole, made this cap a pretty good one. The women, however, were pretty nearly exhausted, and little Charles Arcane cried bitterly all day and almost all night.

"All began to talk more and more and feel more hopeful of getting through. The women began to say that every step brought them so much nearer to the house we had told them about on the other side and often said the work was not so very hard after all. Really it was not so bad travelling as we had at first. We were now nine days from the wagons. 'Are we half way?' was the question they began to ask. We had to answer them that more than one half the hard days were over, if one half the distance had not been traveled, and with the better walking and getting hardened to the work, they would get over the last half better than the first. One thing was a little hard. All of our beans and flour had been used up, and now the wheat was about gone also. We had cooked it, and it seemed best, trying to build up our strength, where it was most needed for the greatest trials, and now we thought they would be able to get along on the meat. We had reached the base of the great snow mountain. It seems strange with the mass of snow resting above, and which must be continually thawing more or less, no ravines or large streams of water were produced flowing down this side. It seemed dry all around its base, which is very singular, with the snow so near.

"We had now our barren cañon to go down, and right here was the big trail coming down from the north [the Joe Walker Trail], which we took and followed. We said all these good things about the road, and encouraged the people all we could to keep in good spirits and keep moving. We told them we thought we knew how to manage to get them safe over the road if they only fully endeavored to do it. We were all

272

quite young, and not in the decline of life as were most of them who had perished by the way.

"No reader can fully realize how much we had to say and do to keep up courage, and it is to this more than anything else that we did which kept up the lagging energies and inspired the best exertion. I don't know but we painted some things a little brighter than they were, and tried to hide some of the most disheartening points of the prospects ahead, for we found the mind had most to do with it all. We have no doubt that if we had not done all we could to keep up good courage, the women would have pined away and died before reaching this far. Whenever we stopped talking encouragingly, they seemed to get melancholy and blue.

"There was some pretty good management to be exercised still. The oxen were gradually growing weaker, and we had to kill the weakest one every time, for if the transportation of our food failed, we should yet be open to the danger of starvation. As it was, the meat on their frames was very scarce, and we had to use the greatest economy to make it last and waste nothing. We should now have to kill one of our oxen every few days, as our other means of subsistance had been so completely used up. The women contracted a strange dislike to this region and said they never wanted to see any part of it again.

"As the sun showed its face over the great sea of mountains away to the east of Death Valley, and it seemed to rise very early for winter season we packed up and started west [south] on the big trail. Rogers and I took the oxen and mule and went on, leaving the others to accompany Old Crump and his little charges. Arcane had found it best to carry Charley on his back, as it relieved the burning sensation, caused by the eruption on his skin, which was aggravated by the close quarters of the pockets. Thus leaving the pockets unbalanced, Bennett had to carry his baby also. This made it harder for them, but every one tried to be just as accommodating as they could and each one would put himself to trouble to accommodate or relieve others."

CHAPTER FIFTEEN

END OF THE TREK

By the time the north portion of Indian Wells Valley had been crossed and the weakening band of '49ers started south to El Paso Mountains and Last Chance Canyon, the beans were gone and they were almost entirely out of the unbolted wheat flour that Manly and Rogers had brought from Rancho San Francisquito. Instead of being out of all danger they again found themselves on a ration of coarse, stringy dry ox meat. But they were on the Joe Walker Trail at last and there was good water at the end of each two or three days' travel, so it was only a question of going slowly enough that the women and children would not fail.

Some who have written about these Death Valley '49ers have taken them over the route of Highway#6from Indian Wells through Red Rock Canyon to the clump of willows around the spring and the willow corral. There are several reasons why we are certain that few, if any of our '49ers, ever saw Red Rock Canyon.

First, neither Manly nor any of the Briers described Red Rock so that it can be recognized. Second, Manly mentions a very narrow canyon through which they passed in crossing El Paso Range, so narrow in places that a poor ox could just squeeze between the rocks. There could have been no such place in Red Rock Canyon, even with the changes which might have been brought about by repeated cloudbursts since January and February of 1850.

Also, Manly, and all others who mentioned distances and directions, here stated that when they came from the mouth of the canyon in El Paso Mountains they went about four miles across the plain south*west* to the spring with the clump of willows. If they had passed through Red Rock Canyon and followed the bottom of the wash, as they must certainly have done, they would have gone south*east* to the willow-surrounded spring. As Manly visited this place three times while rescuing the Bennett-Aŕcan families and also stayed there ten years later—and there was never any other with which it could be confused—there is no doubt about the spring he described. It looks the same today as it did 275

Indian Wells and the twenty-mile steeply sloping alluvial fan between that place and the Argus Range. It was here that on their famous trek from Death Valley to Los Angeles for help, Manly and Rogers overtook the Jay Hawks. In the far distance, at about the middle of the picture, dimly appears the dry, rocky pass over which our Death Valley '49ers struggled to see alkaline China Lake and another seemingly impassable desert ahead. The spring is below the brow of the hill in the extreme left foreground. A health resort is being developed among the nearby trees.

On July 9, 1950, there was dedicated to the memory of Death Valley and other pioneers a monument erected on California State Highway #6 in front of Indian Wells Resort. This marked the place as California Historic Landmark #457.

Photo by Frank F. Latta and now in Bear State Library.

John Burt Colton after his arrival in San Francisco and when he had regained only a portion of the one hundred pounds of weight he lost between Division Spring and Rancho San Francisquito. The photographer exhibited a duplicate of this old daguerreotype as that of a girl, the only girl miner and a '49er. In a year he sold many copies of the photo to curious miners. Later his fraud was discovered and exposed by Colton himself.

Photo courtesy of Huntington Library and now in Bear State Library.

in 1849 except that the corral is not of willows. It is of barbed wire. And, last of all, all pioneers interviewed by this writer have placed the old Joe Walker Trail and the Old Indian Horse Thief Trail in Last Chance, not Red Rock Canyon.

Across the Mojave Desert the route of Manly and Rogers and their little party is much the same as the present Mojave highway and then almost directly south across Antelope Valley to the head of Soledad Canyon in the north end of the San Gabriel Range of Mountains. But, again, William Lewis Manly furnished the best account of this brave plunge from Indian Wells to Rancho San Francisquito:

"Rogers and I made camp when we reached the proper place which was some distance from the mountain on a perfectly level plain where there was no water, no grass, nothing but sage brush would grow on the dry and worthless soil. We let the oxen go and eat as much of this as they chose, which was very little and only enough to keep them from absolute starvation. The great trail had a branch near here that turned northwest and went up a ravine that would seem to reach the snow in a little while. This was believed to be impassable at this time of year. This route is known as Walker's Pass, leading over a comparatively low ridge and coming out the south fork of the Kern River.

"We made our camp here because it was as long a march as the women could make, and, for a dry one, was good a location as we could find. The cool breeze came down from the snow to the north of us, not so very many miles away, and after a little it became uncomfortably cold. We gathered greasewood bushes and piled them up to make a wind-break for our heads. The oxen, even, would come and stand around the fire, seeming greatly to enjoy the warm smoke, which came from burning the greasewood brush, which by the way, burns about the best of any green wood. When we were ready to lie down we tied the animals to bunches of brush, and they lay contentedly till morning.

"To the north of us, a few miles away we could see some standing columns of rock, much reminding one of the great stone chimney of the boiler house at Stanford Jr., University; not quite so trim and regular in exterior appearance, but something in that order. We reckoned the only students in

278

the vicinity would be lizards. [This spectacular sandstone outcropping is known as Vasquez Rocks. From the summit of the tallest of these rocks the bandit, Tiburcio Vásquez, watched the travel on the old Joe Walker Trail and selected for his victims the most likely appearing travelers. Vasquez Rocks are about one mile due south of Coyote Holes.]

"From near this camp we have a low range of mountains to cross, a sort of spur or offshoot of the great snow mountain that reaches out twenty miles or more to the southeast and its extremity divides away into what seems from our point of view a level plain. We had attained quite an elevation without realizing it, so gradual had been the ascent, and our course was now down a steep hillside and into a deep cañon. In its very bottom we found a small stream of water only a few yards long, and then it sank into the sands. Not a spear of grass grew there, and if any had grown it had been eaten by the cattle which had gone before. This is the same place, where Rogers and I had overtaken the advance portion of the Jayhawkers when we were on our outward trip in search of relief, and where some of the older men were so discouraged that they gave us their home address in Illinois so that we could notify their friends of their precarious situation, and if they were never otherwise heard from they could be pretty sure they had perished from thirst and starvation when almost at their journey's end.

"The scenes of this camp on that occasion made so strong an impression on my memory that I can never forget it. There were poor dependent fellows without a morsel to eat except such bits of poor meat as they could beg from those who were fortunate enough to own oxen. Their tearful pleadings would soften a heart of stone. We shared with some of them even when we did not know the little store upon our backs would last us through. Our oxen here had water to drink, but nothing more. It might be a little more comfortable to drink and starve, than both choke and starve, but there are no very pleasant prospects in either one.

"Both ourselves and the oxen were getting barefoot and our feet very tender. The hill we had just come down was very rough and rocky and our progress very slow, every step made in a selected spot. We could not stop here to kill an ox

279

Coyote Holes as they appeared in 1949. This old watering place obtained its name from the fact that the water was in deep holes, or shallow wells, which resembled coyote holes and which might actually first have been dug by coyotes. This water was on the Walker's Pass branch trace only about two miles from the junction with the Joe Walker Trail. Those parties of Death Valley '49ers (Savage and Pinney, Martin, The Mississippi Boys, the Georgians, and others) who stayed with the original plan to go to the mines via Walker's Pass obtained water at Coyote Holes and at Soldier Well one mile west.

In fact, Manly and Rogers and the Bennett and Arcan families rescued from Death Valley by them probably watered at Coyote Holes. The old Joe Walker Trail must have led directly to it. In 1862, when Manly and Alvord were camped at Indian Wells, they knew of "the next water, about eight miles ahead." As they were headed south this could mean nothing but Coyote Holes or Soldier Well.

Photo by Frank F. Latta and now in Bear State Library.

and let the remainder of them starve, but must push on to where the living ones could get a little food. We fastened the oxen and the mule to keep them from wandering, and slept as best we could. The women and children looked worse than for some time, and could not help complaining. One of the women held up her foot and the sole was bare and blistered. She said they ached like toothache. The women had left their combes in the wagons and their hair was getting seriously tangled. Their dresses were getting worn off pretty nearly to their knees, and showed the contact with the ground that sometimes could not be avoided. They were in a sad condition so far as toilet and raiment were concerned. Life was in the balance however, and instead of talking over sad things, we talked of the time when we would reach the little babbling brook where Rogers and I took such long draughts of clear sweet water and the waiter at our dinner gave us the choice of *Crow, Hawk* or *Quail,* and where we took a little of all three.

"In the morning we were off again down the cañon, limping some as we trod its coarse gravelly bed with our tender feet and stiffened joints, but getting limbered up a little after a bit, and enduring it pretty well. We set out try to reach the bunch of willows out on the level plain where the cattle could get some water and grass, but night overtook us at the mouth of the cañon, and we were forced to go into camp. This cañon is now called Red Cañon. [Manly is here referring to Last Chance Canyon which contains extensive red formations.] This was on an elevated plain, with a lake near by, but as we had been so often deceived by going to the lake for water, and finding them salt in every instance, or poison on account of strong alkali, we did not take the trouble to go and try this one.

"Near us was some coarse grass and wet ground where we found water enough for our moderate use, and the oxen by perserverance could get something to eat and drink. After supper we were out of meat and we would have to kill an ox to get some food for our breakfast. In the night a storm came on, much to our surprise, for we had seen none since the night on the mountain east of Death Valley more than two months before. We tried to fix up a shelter to protect the

281

children and ourselves, but were not very successful. We tried to use our guns for tent poles, but could not keep them in place. We laid down as close as pigs in cold weather, and covered up as best we could, but did not keep dry, and morning found us wet to the skin, cold and shivering.

"We gathered big sage brush for a fire in the morning, and the tracks of our nearly bare feet could be plainly seen in the snow which lay like a blanket awhile over the ground, about two inches deep. Some lay in bed and we warmed blankets before the fire and put over them to keep comfortable till the sun should rise and warm the air. We selected an ox and brought him up before the fire where I shot him, and soon there was meat roasting over the fire and blood cooking in the camp kettle. We had nothing to season the blood pudding with but salt, and it was not very good, but answered to sustain life. We ate a hasty meal, then packed our animals and started for the willow patch about four miles away [Desert Spring]. The snow was about gone.

"I staid in camp to keep it till they could get through to the willows and some one to come back with the mule to carry forward the portion of meat that could not be taken at first. We intended to dry it at the willows, and then we could carry it along as daily food over the wide plain we had yet to cross. Having carried the meat forward, we made a rack of willows and dried it over the fire, making up a lot of mocassins for the barefooted ones while we waited. We were over most of the rocky road, we calculated that our shoemaking would last us through. This was a very pleasant camp. The tired ones were taking a rest. No one needed it more than our women and children, who were tired nearly out. They were in much better condition to endure their daily hardships than when they started out, and a little rest would make them feel quite fresh again. They understood that this was almost on the western edge of this desert country and this gave them good hope and courage.

"This wonderful spot in the level plain with a spring of pure water making an oasis of green willows and grass had been previously spoken of as:—'A spring of good water, and a little willow patch in a level desert away from any hill.' In all our wanderings we had never seen the like before. No mountaineer would ever dream of finding a lone spring away out in the desert, several miles from the mountain's base. [This is Desert Spring, just as strange and out of place today as in 1850.] Where the range we just came through leaves the mother mountain stands a peak, seemingly alone, and built up of many colored rocks, in belts, and the whole looks as if tipped with steel. [Manly here accurately places and describes the red outcropping south of Red Rock Canyon.]

"Arcane's boy Charley still suffered from his bogus measles or whatever else his disorder might be, and Bennett's little Martha grew more quiet and improved considerably in health, though still unable to walk, and still abdominally corpulent. The other two children George and Melissa seemed to bear up well and loved to get off and walk in places where the trail was smooth and level. Bennett, Arcane and Old Crump usually traveled with the same party as the women, and as each of them had a small canteen to carry water, they could attend to the wants of the children and keep them from worrying and getting sick from fretfulness. They often carried the two younger ones on their backs to relieve and rest them from their cramped position on the ox.

Arcane used to say he expected the boys—meaning Rogers and I—would try to surprise the party by letting them get very near the house before they knew how near they were. 'Be patient Mr. Arcane,' said we, 'we can tell you just how many camps there must be before we reach it, and we won't fool you or surprise you in any way.' 'Well,' said he. 'I was almost in hopes you would, for I like to be disappointed in that way.' 'What do you think the folks will say when we tell them that our little mule packed most of the meat of an ox four miles from one camp to another?' 'What will they say when we tell them that the oxen were so poor that there was no marrow in the great thigh bones?' Instead of marrow there was a thick dark liquid something like molasses in consistency, but streaked with different colors which made it look very unwholesome. Arcane said the whole story was so incredible, that he never would fight anyone, even if he should tell him he lied when he related the strange sad truth. He said he had no doubt many a one would doubt their story, it was so much beyond what people had ever seen or

Soldier Well, long a watering place on the old trail and stage road over Walker's Pass. It is about one mile west of Coyote Holes. Tunnels or wells have been dug at almost all of these old water holes or springs.
Photo by Frank F. Latta and now in Bear State Library.

Mrs. Fred Harder, granddaughter of Jean Baptiste Arcan. Mrs. Harder was born in Santa Cruz and passed away in Daly City, Calfornia, in 1951.
She furnished for this volume photographs of all three of the Arcan '49ers. Photo by Frank F. Latta and now in Bear State Library.

heard of before, and they might be accused of very strong romancing in the matter.

"They all felt more like talking; for we were thus far safe and sound, and though there was a desperate struggle of seventy-five miles or more, from this place to the next water in the foot-hills. [Here they are figuring on the spring where Robinson died, near the summit south of Antelope Valley. Manly and Rogers had missed Willow Springs on both of their crossings of Antelope Valley.] Possibly the snow storms had left a little in some of the pools, but we made no calculations on any. The promised land we had so steadily been approaching, and now comparatively so near, gave us great hope, which was better than food and drink to give us strength.

"There were surely two camps between this and the little pond John and I found, among the cabbage trees and not more than six by ten feet square. [This surface pool was probably east of Willow Springs, near present Rosamond.] As we worked away at our foot-wear we talked more in an hour than we had in a whole day before. We were slowly leaving Death Valley behind us all in our possession in that terrible spot, and simply with our lives we hoped to escape, and trust to Providence and humanity on the other side. Arcane now admitted that they could not have got along half as well, if we had not gone ahead and looked out the land. It was such a gain to know exactly where the next water hole was, so it could be steered for and struggled toward. He even went so far as to say they would have no chance alone, and that as he now saw the road, he was sure they would have all perished even before reaching as far as this. We had strong hopes of the morrow, when we would be all rested, all were shod, and would make every footstep count in our western progress.

"It seems quite a strange occurrence that the only two storms we had had since we turned westward on this route, Nov. 4th, were snow storms, and that both had come while we were asleep, so that all our days were cloudless. Sometimes the sun was uncomfortably warm even in the heart of the winter. One would have naturally expected that the great rainfall all over the California coast in the winter of 1849—50, and the deep snows that came in the Sierra

Charlie Aŕcan was about three years of age when he arrived at Rancho San Francisquito in March of 1850. He became a swimming instructor and life guard at Neptune Baths in Santa Cruz, California. He is buried in Evergreen Cemetery, Santa Cruz, beside his father and mother.

Photo courtesy of Mrs. Fred Harder, granddaughter of Jean Baptiste Aŕcan, and now in Bear State Library.

Nevada mountains the same winter, would have extended southerly the few hundred miles that separated the two places. Modern science has shown the tracks of the storms and partially explains the reasons for this dry and barren nature of this region. When rains do come they are so out of regular order, that they are called cloud-bursts or water-spouts, and the washes in the cañons and their mouths show how great has been the volume of water that sometimes rushed down the slope. If clouds at a warm or moderate temperature float against these snow peaks all the water they contain is suddenly precipitated. The country is an arid one and unless wealth should appear in the shape of mines, the country can never be inhabited. We considered ourselves very fortunate in finding the little pools and holes of water which kept us alive. It was not very good drinking water, but to us thirsty folks it was a blessing and we never passed it by on account of any little stagment bitter taste. Salt water we could not drink of course, though we sometimes used it to cook with.

"We were as well prepared next morning as possible for a move, and the long walk before us, the last one between us and the fertile land. They all talked of how delighted they would be to see once more a running brook, green grass and trees, and such signs of life as they had seen and been used to in the good land they had left behind. The women said they could endure the march of four or five days, if when all over, they could sleep off the terrible fatigue and for once drink all the pure sweet water they could desire. No more forced marches. No more grey road, stretching out its dusty miles as far as the eye could reach. The ladies thought the oxen would be as happy as themselves and the little mule, the most patient one of the whole train deserved a life of ease for her valuable services. This little black, one eyed lady wandered here and there at will seeking for grass; but never going astray or getting far enough from the track to alarm us in the least. She seldom drank much water, was always ready, never got footsore, and seemed made expressly for such a life and for such a desert.

288 "A good kettleful of soup for breakfast, dried meat fixed in

packages, kegs and canteens filled with water, and we were ready for an advance.

"There is one less ox to lead, and very little load for those we have, still the load is all such poor weak fellows ought to bear. Old Crump was not thus favored by a gradually lightened load. He bore the same four children every day, faithfully, carefully, with never a stumble nor fall, as though fully aware of the precious nature of his burden.

"In this new march John and I took the oxen and pushed on as usual, leaving the families to follow on, at a slower pace, the trail we made. The trail was slightly inclined. The bushes stunted at the best, getting smaller as we proceeded, and the horse bones, new and ancient are now thickly scattered along the way. The soil is different from that we have had. We can see the trail winding gently here and there, swept clean by the wind, and the surface is hard and good; but when the mule gets the least bit off of it she sinks six inches deep into the soft sand, and the labor of walking is immense. I stepped out to examine the peculiar soil, and found it finer than superfine flour. It was evident that a strong wind would lift it in vast clouds which might even darken the sky, but we were fortunate in this respect, for during all the time we were on this peculiar soil, there was no wind at all, and we escaped a sandstorm, a sort of storm as peculiar to this region as are blizzards to some of the states of the great west.

"Our first night's camp was out on the barren waterless plain, now known as the Mojave Desert. There were no shrubs large enough to make a fire of, and nothing to tie our cattle to, so we fastened all our animals together to keep them from scattering and getting lost. We ate a little dry meat and drank sparingly of the water, for our scanty stock was to last us another day, when we might reach prospective water holes. Starting early, John and I took all but Old Crump and the other travelers, and hurried on to try and find the water holes as early as possible. We, as well as the oxen were very dry, for we left all the water we had with the party, for the children, for they cannot endure the thirst as the older people can. We reached the camping place before night. Quite a time before we reached it, the cattle seemed to scent the water and quickened their pace, so we were confident it had not dried up. We got ahead of the oxen and kept there until we reached the little pond and then guarded it to keep them from wading into it, in their eagerness to reach some drink. They all satisfied their thirst, and then we removed the harness, built a fire of the dead cabbage trees which we found round about, laid down the beds and arranged them neatly, and had all nicely done before the rear guard came up, in charge of Captain Crump. The party was eager for water and all secured it. It was rain water and no doubt did not quench thirst as readily as water from some living spring or brook. There was evidence that there had been a recent shower or snow to fill this depression up for our benefit. The Jayhawkers had passed not more than a half mile north of this spot, but so sign appeared that they had found it, and it was left to sustain the lives of the women and children.

"It often occurs to me that many may read incredulously when I speak of our party eating the entire flesh of an ox in four or five days. To such I will say that one cannot form an idea how poor an ox will get when nearly starved so long. Months had passed since they had eaten a stomachful of good nutritous food. The animals walked slowly with heads down nearly tripping themselves up with their long, swinging legs. The skin loosly covered the bones, but all the flesh and muscles had shrunk down to the smallest space. The meat was tough and stringy as basswood bark, and tasted strongly of bitter sage brush the cattle had eaten at almost every camp. At a dry camp the oxen would lie down and grate their teeth, but they had no cud to chew. It looked almost merciless to shoot one down for food, but there was no alternative. We killed our poor brute servants to save ourselves. Our cattle found a few bunches out among the trees at this camp and looked some better in the morning. They had secured plenty of water and some grass.

"Young Charlie Arcane seemed to grow worse rather than better. His whole body was red as fire, and he screamed with the pain and torment of the severe itching. Nothing could be done to relieve him, and if his strength lasted til we could get

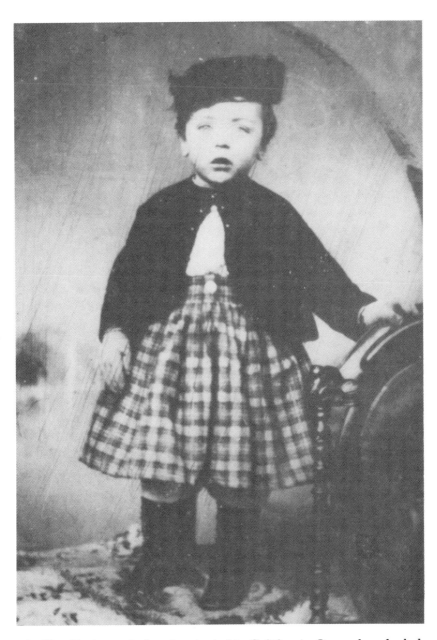

Little Charlie Arcan before he started to California. It was he who balanced Martha Bennett in the hickory shirts aboard the ox, Old Crump, from Tule Springs to Los Angeles.

Photo courtesy of Mrs. Harder and now in Bear State Library.

better air, water and food he might recover, but his chances were very poor.

"Not much rest at this camp for in the morning we aimed to start early and reach the water in the foothills. We thought we could do it if we started early, walked rapidly and took no resting spell at noon. Such a poor soil as this we were anxious to get away from, and walk once more on a soil that would grow something besides stunted sage brush. From all appearances the Jayhawkers were here in about the same predicament Rogers and I were when we lost the trail. By their tracks we could see they had scattered wide and there was no road left for us to follow, and they had evidently tried to follow our former tracks. Having no trail to follow we passed on as best we could and came to a wide piece of land on which were growing a great many cabbage trees.

"The soil was of the finest dust with no grit in it, and not long before a light shower had fallen, making it very soft and hard to get along in with the mocassins. The women had to stop to rest frequently, so our progress was very slow. Rogers and I had feet about as hard as those of the oxen, so we removed our mocassins and went barefoot, finding we could get along much easier in that way, but the others had such tender feet they could not endure the rough contact with the brush and mud. Only a few miles had been made before the women were so completely tired out that we had to stop and eat our little bit of dried meat and wait till morning. The little mule now carried all our stock of food, and the precious burden lightened every day. This delay was not expected, but we had to endure it and bear it patiently, for there was a limit to strength of the feeble ones of our party. We had therefore to make another barren camp. Relief seemed so near at hand we kept good courage and talked freely of the happy ending which would soon come. If we had any way to set a good table we would feast and be merry like the prodigal son, but at any rate we shall be safe if we can reach the fertile shore.

"When the sun went down we tied the mule and oxen to cabbage trees, and shortly after dusk lay down ourselves, for we had enjoyed a good fire made of the trunks of cabbage trees, the first really comfortable one in a long time. The air was cooler here for we were on higher ground, and there was some snow on the range of mountains before us, which sent these cool breezes down to us, a change of climate quite pleasing.

"For breakfast in the morning we had only dried meat roasted before the fire, without water, and when we started each one put a piece in his or her pocket to chew on during the day as we walked along. As we went ahead the ground grew dryer and the walking much improved. The morning overhead was perfectly lovely, as away east, across the desert the sun showed his face to us. Not a cloud anywhere, not even over the tops of the high peaks where great white masses sometimes cluster but dissolve as soon as they float away, and there was not wind enough to be perceptible. We remarked the same lack of animal life which we had noticed on our first passage over this section, seeing not a rabbit, bird, or living thing we could use for food. Bennett had the same load in his gun he put there when we left the wagons, and all the powder I had burned was that used in killing the oxen we had slain whenever it became necessary to provide for our barren kitchen.

"As we approached the low foot-hills the trail became better travelled and better to walk in, for the Jayhawkers who had scattered, every one for himself apparently in crossing the plain, seemed here to have drawn together and their path was quite a beaten one. [Here they have struck the branch trail which came in from Willow Springs and ran southeast.] We saw from this that they followed the tracks made by Rogers and myself as we made our first trip westward in search of bread. Quite a little before the sun went out of sight in the west we reached our camping place in the lower hills at the eastern slope of a range we must soon cross. [The present highway from Mojave and Lancaster to San Fernando enters the head of Soledad Canyon at this same place.] Here was some standing water in several large holes, that proved enough for our oxen, and they found some large sage brush and small bushes round about, on which they browsed and among which they found a few bunches of grass. Lying about were some old skulls of cattle which had sometime been killed, or died. These were the first signs of the

293

sort we had seen along this route. They might have been killed by Indians who doubtless used this trail.

"The next day in crossing the range before us, we reached the edge of the snow, which the sun had softened and we dare not attempt to cross. Early in the morning when it was frozen hard the cattle could travel it very well. The snow belt was five or six miles wide, and the snow two or three feet deep. This was a very good camping place except that we had to melt snow for all our water, but this being coarse and icy it was not a great job as we found enough dry juniper trees and twigs to make a very good fire. Here we also had to kill another ox. This one in its turn was Arcane's, and left him only two, and Bennett three, but we think that if we have no accident we shall get them along with us till we can get other food, as they have very light loads to pack. When the ox is killed and the meat prepared the mule has, for a time, a larger load than all the oxen have, but seems content and nips a bite of food whenever it can see a chance anywhere along the road, giving us no more trouble than a dog.

"And by the way, I think I have not mentioned our faithful camp dog, a worthy member of our party who stood watch always and gave us a sure alarm if anything unusual happened anywhere about. He was perhaps only one of a hundred that tried to cross the plains and had to be abandoned when they reached the upper Platte, where the alkali dust made their feet so sore they could not travel, and as they could not be hauled on wagons they were left behind. But this dog Cuff did not propose to be left behind to starve, and crippled along after us, we doing all we could for him, and proved as tough as the best of us. Bennett and I had trained him as a hunting dog in the East, and he was very knowing and handy in every particular.

"We were out of this camp at daylight. Very little rest for some of us, but we must make the best of the cool morning, while the snow is hard, and so move on as soon as we can see the way. As it got lighter and sun comes up red and hot out of the desert we have a grand view of the great spread of the country to south and of the great snow mountain to the north and east, the peak standing over the place where we left our wagons nineteen days before, on the edge of Death Valley.

The glare of the snow on the sun makes us nearly blind, but we hurry on to try to cross it before it becomes so soft as to slump under our feet. It is two or three feet in the deepest places, and probably has been three times as deep when freshly fallen, but it is now solid and icy. Our rawhide mocassins protect our feet from cold, and both we and the animals got along fairly well, the oxen breaking through occasionally as the snow softened up, but generally walking on the top as we did ourselves. The snow field reached much farther down the western slope than we had hoped, much father than on the eastern side. Before we got out of it, we saw the track of some animal which had crossed our route, but as it had been made some holes in the surface, we could not determine what sort of an animal it was.

"A mile or two down the hill we were at last out of the snow, and a little farther on we came to the little babbling brook Rogers and I had so long painted in the most refreshing colors to the tired women, with water, wood and grass on every hand, the three greatest blessings of a camper's life. Here was where Rogers and I had cooked and eaten our meal of crow, quail and hawk, pretty hard food, but then, the blessed water!

"There it danced and jumped over the rocks singing the merriest song one ever heard, as it said—Drink, drink ye thirsty ones your fill—the happiest sweetest music to the poor souls, wasted down almost to haggard skeletons. O! if some poet of wildest imagination could only place himself in the position of those poor tired travelers to whom water in thick muddy pools had been a blessing, who had eagerly drank the fluid even when so salt and bitter as to be repulsive, and now to see the clear, pure liquid distilled from the crystal snow, abundant, free, filled with life and health—and write it in words—the song of that joyous brook and set it to the music that it made as it echoed in gentle waves from the rocks and lofty walls, and with the gentle accompaniment of rustling trees—a soft singing hush, telling of rest and peace, and happiness.

"New life seemed to come to the dear women. 'O! What a beautiful stream!' say they, and they dip in a tin cup and drink, then watch in dreaming admiration the water as it

295

goes hurrying down; then dip and drink again, and again watch the jolly rollicking brook as if it were the most entertaining thing in the whole wide earth. 'Why can't such a stream as that run out of the great Snow Mountain in the dry Death Valley?' say they—'so we could get water on the way.'

"The men have felt as glad as any of them, but have gathered wood and made a fire, and now a camp kettle of cut up meat is boiling for our supper. It was not yet night, but we must camp in so beautiful a place as this, and though the food was poor, we were better off than we had been before.

"Bennett proposed that I take the mule and go back to where we saw the track of the animal in the snow and follow it in hope that we might get some game for we had an idea it might be an elk or bear or some large game, good to kill and give us better meat; so I saddled the mule and took the trail back till I came to the track, then followed it as best I could, for it was very dull and gave me no idea what it was. I traced out of the snow and then in a blind way through bushes as high as the mule's back—chaparral we called it now—among which I made my way with difficulty.

"I could now see that the track was made by an ox or cow—perhaps an elk—I could not tell for sure it was so faint. This chaparral covered a large piece of table land, and I made my way through it, following the track for a mile or two till I came to the top of a steep hill sloping down into a deep cañon and a creek, on the bank of which grew sycamore and alder trees, with large willows. I stopped here some minutes to see if I could see or hear the movement of anything. Across the creek I could see a small piece of perhaps half an acre of natural meadow, and in it some small bunches of sycamore trees. After a little I discovered some sort of a horned animal there, and I reckoned this was good enough game for me to try and capture, so led the mule out to one side and down the hill near the creek, then tied her, and crept along the bank, about four feet high, toward the little meadow. When about right, as I thought, I climbed up behind a bunch of sycamores, and when I slowly and cautiously raised up I was within fifty yards of a cow or steer of some sort which I could dimly see. I put a ball square in its forehead, and it fell without a struggle. I loaded again quick as possible and there saw two other smaller cattle stepping very high as though terrified, but not aware of the nature or location of the danger. I gave a low whistle and one of them looked toward me long enough for me to put a ball in it. The third one was now behind a clump of sycamores, and I soon saw its face through a little opening not more than three inches wide. I made a shot, and wounded it, and then rushed up and gave it a fatal shot.

"I examined my game and found the first one was a poor cow, but the others were yearlings, one of them very fat and nice, and I soon had the hind quarters skinned out, and all the fat I could find, which made a big load for the mule. It was now almost dark, and the next problem was to get back to camp again. The brushy hills would be terrible to cross with a load of meat, and by the way the ground lay I concluded our camp was on this same creek farther down.

"The only way that seemed at all feasible was to follow the course of the stream if possible, rather than return the course over which I had come. There were so many bushes and trees along the bank that I had to take to the bed and follow in the water, and as it was rocky and rough, and so dark I could not see well how to step, I stumbled into holes and pools up to my waist, wet as a rat. Coming to a small open place I decided I had better camp for the night and not attempt further progress in the darkness, and the decision was hastened by dark clouds, which began to gather and a few sprinkles of rain began to come.

"There was a good patch of grass for the mule, but all was uncomfortable for me, with the prospect for a rainy night, but as wood was plenty I decided to make a fire and take the chances. I looked for matches and scratched one. No go—they were damp, and scratch as careful and quickly as I could, there was no answering spark or flame, and darkness reigned supreme. A camp without a fire in this wet place was not to be thought of, so I concluded I might as well be slowly working my way down along the stream, through thick brush and cold water, as to sit here in the cold and wait.

"So the little mule and I started on, wading the creek in thick darkness, getting only the most dim reflected light from the sky through now and then an opening in the trees. I

297

did not know then how easy it was for a grizzly to capture myself, the mule and meat and have quite a variety for supper. But the grizzly stayed at home and we followed on through brambles and hard brush, through which it was almost impossible to force one's way. As it turned out, I was not in the track of the storm and did not suffer much from it. Soon the cañon grew wider, and I could make out on the right hand a piece of table land covered with brush that seemed easier to get through than the creek bed.

"The hill up to the table land was very steep, but not more than fifty yards high, and when the mule tried to get up she got along very well till near the top, when she slipped in the wet earth and never stopped till she reached the bottom and lay down. She was helped up to her feet again and we tried it in another place, I holding her from slipping when she stopped to rest, and at last we reached the top. The mule started on, seeming to follow a trail, but I could not see whether there was a trail or not, so thick was the darkness, but there was evidently something of the kind, for the brush was two or three feet high and very thick.

"After proceeding some distance the mule stopped and did not seem to wish to go any farther. I was pretty sure there was something in front of her that blocked the way, and so worked my way through the brush and carefully past her. I could partly see and partly hear something just ahead, and in a moment found it was our good faithful Cuff, and no frightful spook at all. The good fellow had discovered our approach and came out to meet us, and I am sure the mule was as glad as I was to see him. He crawled through the brush and smelled at the mule's load and then went forward in the trail, which we followed. It was a long time after midnight when we reached camp. There was a good fire burning, but all were asleep till I led the mule up to the fire and called out—'Wake Up,' when they were most of them on their feet in a minute without stopping to dress, for all had slept a long time without taking off their clothes.

"John took charge of the mule and unloaded it, telling me to get into his warm bed. I took off my wet clothes and told him to dry them, and then got between the dry, warm blankets in greatest comfort. Daylight came very quickly, it seemed to me, and before I finally rose, the sun had been up some hours before me. Before I fell asleep I could hear the women say, as they cut off the pieces of meat to roast—'See the fat! Only see how nice it is!' Quickly roasted on the coals they ate the delicate morsels with a relish and, most of all, praised the sweet fat. 'We like to have it all fat,' said they, showing how their system craved the nourishment the poor starved beef could not give. No one went to bed after I came, but all sat and roasted meat and ate till they were satisfied.

"This sporting trip was quite different from deer hunting in Wisconsin, and nothing like looking for game in Death Valley where nothing lived. It was the hardest night's work that ever came to me in many a day, and not the wild sport I generally looked for when on the chase. I felt pretty well when I got up and a chunk of my last night's prize which had been roasted for me was eaten with a relish, for it was the best of meat and I, of course, had a first class appetite. I had to tell them my last hunting story, and was much praised as a lucky boy.

"We would not be compelled to kill any more of our poor oxen in order to live. So far we had killed six of them, and there were five left. Our present situation was much appreciated, compared with that of a few days ago when we were crawling slowly over the desert, hungry, sore-footed and dry, when to lie was far easier than to take steps forward. We felt like rejoicing at our deliverance and there was no mourning now for us. The surrounding hills and higher mountains seemed more beautiful to us. They were covered with green trees and brush, not a desert place in sight. The clear little singing brook ran merrily on its way, the happiest, brightest stream in all my memory. Wild birds came near us without fear, and seemed very friendly. All was calm, and the bright sunshine exactly warm enough so that no one could complain of heat or cold.

"When ready to move it was announced that I had lost my saddle blanket in my adventure so they substituted another one and I took the back track to the place where the mule slipped down the bank, and there I found it. I soon overtook them again just as they were going to camp on Mrs. Bennett's account, as she had been suddenly taken sick with

299

Melissa Bennett, who was nine years of age in 1849 when her parents brought her to California, and who died in San Bernardino about 1866.

It was Melissa who with her brother George, rode on her father's ox, Old Crump, from Tule Springs in Death Valley over the Panamints to Los Angeles. At the age of twenty-two years she married Judge Rolfe of San Bernardino, and died only two years after her marriage. She had one child, later Mrs. Agnes Lindner of San Bernardino.

Photo courtesy of Mrs. Agnes Lindner and now in Bear State Library.

severe pain and vomiting, something as Rogers and I had been after eating our first California corn meal. The rich, fat meat was too strong for her weak stomach.

"Arcane all along had an idea that Rogers and I meant to surprise them by leading them to believe the house we had visited was quite a distance off, and then to so manage it that it should appear upon their sight suddenly. We assured them it would take two or more camps before we could get there, and if Mrs. Bennett did not soon recover, even more than that. Our camp here was under a great live oak, the ground deep covered with dry leaves, and near by a beautiful meadow where our cattle and mule ate, drank and rested, the oxen chewing their cud with such an air of comfort as had not come to them since leaving their far-off eastern pastures. They seemed as much pleased as any one. They would lie down and rest and eat at the same time in perfectly enjoyable laziness.

"Here we all rested and washed such clothes as we could do without waiting long enough to dry, and washed our faces and hands over and over again to remove the dirt which had been burned and sweated in so completely as not to come off readily. We sat on the bank of the brook with our feet dangling in the water, a most refreshing bath, and they too began to look clean again. We often saw tracks of the grizzly bear about, but in our ignorance had no fear of them, for we did not know they were a dangerous animal. An owl came and hooted in the night, but that was the only challenge any wild best or bird gave to our peaceful and restful camp. We were out of the dreadful sands and shadows of Death Valley, its exhausting phantoms, its salty columns, bitter lakes and wild, dreary sunken desolation.

"If the waves of the sea could flow in and cover its barren nakedness, as we now know they might if a few sandy barriers were swept away, it would be indeed, a blessing, for in it there is naught of good, comfort or satisfaction, but ever in the minds of those who braved its heat and sands, a thought of a horrid Charnel house, a corner of the earth so dreary that it requires an exercise of the strongest faith to believe that the great Creator ever smiled upon it as a portion of his work and pronounced it 'Very Good.' We had crossed the

301

In the foreground are the foremost cars of the long traffic jam leading back toward Death Valley Junction. To the upper right appear the first cars of the traffic jam which extended more than two cars wide to a point beyond Stovepipe Wells Hotel, more than twenty-seven miles away. To the left, where the bus is parked, is the road to Desolation Canyon.

Photo taken about 10:00 A.M., December 3, 1949, and courtesy of Death Valley National Monument Superintendent, T. R. Goodwin. Photo now in Bear State Library.

great North American Continent, from a land of plenty, over great barren hills and plains, to another mild and beautiful region, where, though still in winter months, we were basking in the warmth and luxuriance of early summer. We thought not of the gold we had come to win. We were dead, almost, and now we lived. We were starved so that we had looked at each other with maniac thoughts, and now we placed in our mouth the very fat of the land.

"We had seen our cattle almost perishing; seen them grow gaunt and tottering; seen them slowly plod along with hanging heads and only the supremacy of human will over animal instinct had kept them from lying down never to rise again. Now they were in pastures of sweet grass, chewing the cud of content and satisfaction. Life which had been a burden grew sweet to us, and though it may be that our words of praise to Him, whose will was to deliver us out of the jaws of death, were not set nor formal, yet His all-seeing eye saw the truth in our hearts, and saw there the fullest expression of our gratitude and thankfulness. Who shall say the thanks that arose were less acceptable, because not given on bended knees before gilded altars?

"Though across the desert and evidently in the long promised land our troubles and trials were not through by any means, but evidently we were out of danger. Our lives seemed to be secure, and we were soon to meet with settlerswho would no doubt extend to us the hand of human sympathy. Many long miles yet remained between us and the rivers in whose sands were hidden the tiny grains of gold we came to seek.

"The rest in the lovely camp had answered to cause Mrs. Bennett to feel quite well again by the next morning, and we made ready to proceed. We had the trail of the Jayhawkers to follow, so the vines, brambels and tangles which had perplexed Rogers and myself in our first passage were now somewhat broken down, and we could get along very well without further clearing of the road until the hills came down so close on both sides that there was no room except in the very bed of the stream. There was no other way, so we waded along after the oxen as best we could. Sometimes the women fell down, for a rawhide mocassin soaked soft in water was not a very comfortable or convenient shoe, however it might be adapted to hot, dry sands. The creek was shaded and the water quite cool. The trail, such as it was, crossed the creek often and generally was nothing else than the stream itself. The constant wading, and wet, cold clothing caused the women to give out soon and we selected the first dry suitable place which offered food for the oxen, as a place to camp.

"Wood was plenty and dry, so a good fire was soon burning, and the poor women, wet to the waist and even higher, were standing before it, turning round and round to get warm and dry. Someone remarked that they resembled geese hanging before the fire to roast, as they slowly revolved, and it was all owing to their fatigue that the suggestor did not receive merited punishment then and there at their hands. As they got a little dry and comfortable they remarked that even an excess of water like this was better than the desert where there was none at all, and as to their looks, there were no society people about to point their fingers at them, and when they reached a settled country they hoped to have a chance to change their clothes, and get two dresses a piece, and that these would be long enough to hide their knees which these poor tatters quite failed to do. One remarked that she was sure she had been down in the brook a dozen times and that she did not consider cold water baths so frequently repeated were good for the health.

"Young Charley Arcane had been getting better for some days. No medicine had been given him, and it was no doubt the change of air and water [and fresh, nutritious meat] that had begun to effect a cure. Arcane had a hard time of it to keep the brush from pulling George and Melissa off of Old Crump into the water. It was indeed one of the hardest day's work of the whole journey, but no one was low spirited, and all felt very well. The camping place was in a deep cañon, surrounded by thick brush, so that no wind came in to chill us.

"Everybody was cook and nobody was boss. Not a cent of money among us, nor any chance to use any if we had possessed it. We had nice, sweet, fat meat, cooked rare or well done as each one preferred, and no complaints about the

304

waiters. The conditions were so favorable, compared with the terrible Death Valley and its surroundings that every one remarked about it, and no one felt in the least like finding fault with the little inconveniences we were forced to put up with. It might cure an inveterate fault-finder to take a course of training in the desert.

"The next day we did not wade half as much, and after a few hours of travel we suddenly emerged from the brush into a creek bottom which was much wider, with not a tree to obstruct our way. The soil was sandy and covered more or less with sage brush, and the stream which has been strong and deep enough to make us very wet now sank entirely out of sight in the sandy bottom. The hills were thinly timbered on the left side but quite brushy on the right, and we could see the track of cattle in the sand. No signs of other animals, but some small birds came near, and meadow larks whistled their tune, quite familiar to us, but still sounding slightly different from the song of the same bird in the East. High in the air could be seen a large sailing hawk or buzzard.

"We stopped to rest at noon and noticed that the water ran a little in the creek bed; but, by the time we were ready to start we found none with which to fill our canteens. No doubt this water was poured into the cañon somewhere near the place where we killed the three cattle, and we had got out of it before the flood came down. It was astonishing to see how the thirsty sand drank up the quite abundant flow.

"The next day we came down to the point of hill that nearly crossed the valley, and we crossed the low ridge rather than make a longer trip to get around by way of the valley. As we reached the summit there appeared before us as beautiful a rural picture as one ever looked upon. A large green meadow of a thousand acres, more or less; its south-west side bounded by low mountains, at the base of which oak trees were plenty but no brush or undergrowth. It was like a grand old park, such as we read of in English tales. All over the meadow cattle of all sorts and sizes grazed, the 'Ring-streaked and speckled' of old Jacob's breed being very prominent. Some lazily cropped the grass; some still more lazily reclined and chewed their cuds while frisky calves exercised their muscles in swift races and then secured their dinner from anxious mothers. We camped at once and took the loads from all the animals that they might feed in comfort on the sweet grass that lay before them. [Later the town of Newhall was built here. San Francisquito Canyon comes into the valley near the old campsite.]

"We tarried here perhaps two hours, till the cattle stopped eating, and happily enjoyed the scene. Never again would any one of the party go back over that dreary desert, they said, and everyone wondered why all places could not be as green and beautiful as this one. I cannot half tell how we felt and acted, nor what we said in our delight over this picture of plenty. The strong contrasts created strong impressions, and the tongues so long silent in our dry and dreary trouble were loosened to say everything the heart inspired. Think as much as you can; you cannot think it all.

"We felt much better after our rest, and the oxen seemed stronger and better able, as well as more willing to carry their loads, so we soon prepared to move on down the valley, toward the house we had spoken of as the goal we were to reach. It was now the 7th day of March 1850, and this date, as well as the 4th of November 1849, will always remain an important one in memory. On the first named day we left the trail to take the unfortunate cut-off, and for four long months we had wandered and struggled in terrible hardship. Every point of that terrible journey is indelibly fixed upon my memory and though seventy-three years of age on April 6th, 1893 I can locate every camp, and if strong enough could follow that weary trail from Death Valley to Los Angeles with unerring accuracy. The brushy cañon we have just described is now occupied by the Southern Pacific Railroad, and the steep and narrow ridge pierced by a tunnel, through which the trains pass. The beautiful meadow we so much admired has now upon its border a railroad station, Newhall, and at the proper season some portion of it is covered with thousands of trays of golden apricots, grown in the luxuriant orchards just beyond the hills toward the coast, and here drying in the bright summer sun. The cattle in the parti-colored coats are gone, but one who knows the ground can see our picture.

"Loaded up again we start down the beautiful grassy val-

A portion of the grandstand at Desolation Canyon, December 3, 1949. At the extreme upper right appears a small portion of the long stream of cars trying to reach the site before the pageant started.

Photo courtesy Death Valley National Monument Superintendant, T. R. Goodwin, and now in Bear State Library.

ley, the women each with a staff in hand, and everything is new and strange to us. Rogers and I know that we will soon meet people who are strangers to us; who speak a strange language of which we know nothing, and how we, without a dollar, are to proceed to get our food and things we need, are questions we cannot answer nor devise any easy way to overcome. The mines are yet five hundred miles away, and we know not of any work for us to do nearer. Our lives have been given back to us, and now comes the problem of how to sustain them manfully and independently as soon as possible. If worse comes to worse we can walk to San Francisco, probably kill enough game on the way and possibly reach the gold mines at last, but the way was not clear. We must trust much to luck and fortune and the ever faithful Providence which rarely fails those who truly try to help themselves.

"We began to think some very independent thoughts. We had a mule to carry our blankets and odd loads, while Old Crump the christian could still carry the children; Bennett and I knew how to hunt, and had good rifles; so we could still proceed, and we determined that, come what may, we will be victorious.

"These were some of the plans we talked over at our camps and resting places, and as we walked along. If we could get the two families fixed in some way so they could do without Rogers and I, we could strike for the mines quite rapidly and no doubt soon get ourselves on good footing. We were younger than the rest and could endure more hardship. We decide to remain together till we get to Los Angeles, and then see what is best."

CHAPTER SIXTEEN

RANCHO SAN FRANCISQUITO
AND THE CITY OF THE ANGELS

The old del Valle home on Rancho San Francisquito was a place kept fresh in the memories of all Death Valley '49ers for they were there the recipients of old-time California hospitality long after the adobe walls of that old home had melted to earth.

Many readers of these pages have seen the site of that old home, although few have known the historic background of the old ruins.

Highway #99 crosses the Santa Clara River on a bridge, and the railroad on an overpass a few hundred yards north of its junction with the branch highway which leads to Newhall. It was down the very route of this Newhall branch road that Manly and Rogers came for help in January of 1850. In a few days they were followed by the Jay Hawks and the Briers. A month later Manly and Rogers led the Bennett and Arćan families over this route.

The present day student of California history who wants to visit the site of historic old del Valle home will continue the old Newhall route west across Highway #99 and follow a narrow concrete pavement along the south bank of the Santa Clara River. This is a former route of Highway #99, which once crossed the river one-third of a mile downstream from the present crossing. The pavement finally ends abruptly at the river bank where once there was the abutment of a bridge.

From the pavement a still narrower oiled road follows the south banks of Santa Clara River past some cattle corrals to an old frame ranchhouse. This is the fine "Yankee" home which del Valle family constructed after del Valle's widow married José Sálazar and the old adobe was not considered up to the "Yankee" standard. This building on the hill originally was constructed as an outpost storage warehouse when little water was needed at the site. It was abandoned because there was no water up there and Indian women at last became no longer available to carry water up from the river.

Drive through the ranch yard and past the corrals to an almost level bench high above the river and east of a hill which ends in a bluff at the 309 river. On this bench land once stood the old del Valle adobe home, the home with the red-tiled roof, the first sign of civilization seen by any of the Death Valley '49ers who came staggering down the Santa Clara River during those days in January, February and March of 1850. Dug partway into the hillside near the adobe stood a stone milk house. It was at this old tile-roofed adobe that all of our Death Valley '49ers were received with open arms by Sra. del Valle and her foreman, José Sálazar. It was from the old stone milk house that each of these same '49ers, except the Wades, received the first drink of milk and the first slice of cheese he had had since leaving Salt Lake. Years later those who remained of that little band of refugees of '49 held a reunion at this, to them, sacred site and picnicked under the trees beside the ruins of the old buildings. At this reunion Senator Antonio del Valle, grandson of Ignacio del Valle, founder of Rancho San Francisquito, made these aged '49ers and their descendants welcome.

It was a touching experience for all. The universal generosity of the pioneer *Californios* was symbolized in the del Valles who, in one year, without one cent of pay, were hosts to more than two thousand immigrants who were traveling to the gold mines of California.

The father of this writer was one of the vast horde which passed the del Valle home on the way to the mines, only a few months after our Death Valley parties had been rescued. He, with two of his brothers, undoubtedly were the recipients of the unbounded del Valle hospitality. In their case it was surely gratis. E. C. Latta landed at the Plaza in Los Angeles August 20 of 1850, fresh from a four and one-half month journey from Fort Smith, Arkansas, over the Old Spanish Trail via Socorro, New Mexico, with his whole store of worldly goods; a fine bay horse named Jocko, a good riding rig, a blanket, a rifle and a lone twenty dollar gold piece. He spent the gold piece in a Los Angeles hardware store for a pick, shovel and a gold pan, so had nothing with which to *pay* when he reached the del Valle adobe.

While the del Valle family are certainly entitled to all possible credit for their grand scale generosity toward the Death Valley and other '49ers, their generosity was only typical of all *Californios*. No person who knew those wholesouled, generous people ever had anything but unbounded praise for them. This writer has heard it from thousands of pioneers. But he has come across at least one written reference to those fine people and those old primeval days in California. It is a letter

310   written by Jay Hawk Tom Shannon, who, remember, was also a veteran

of the Mexican War, and could have been quite prejudiced against the old *Californios.*

In addressing his old Jay Hawk companions who had invited him to attend their reunion in 1896 at the home of Jay Hawk Mecum at Galesburg, Illinois, Shannon wrote:

> "I cannot be with you visibly, but my heart goes out to all of the brave old boys—. California is not the country it was when we came. Between Los Angeles and San Francisco along the coast the great herds of cattle and horses that there ranged are gone. Also the old adobe house has given place to buildings of more modern styles.
>
> "But the question remains, are the people any richer to day, or any better, or more honorable, or more charitable, or happier than those people who occupied the old adobes when we came? Draw your own conclusions.
>
> "We have many very rich people in California, but more very poor ones. When we came no man [was] so poor that he could not eat meat three times a day. Different now. The wild game that once abounded in our valleys, hills and mountains is almost extinct. The fish also—.
>
> "May God bless you,
> "Tom Shannon."

Again nothing can equal William Lewis Manly's account of the reception of his and John Haney Rogers' little band of tattered refugees at the del Valle home and of their experiences while they were recruiting in Los Angeles for their journey to the mines. I give it here as it was printed in Manly's *Death Valley in '49.*

> "We reached our camping place at the foot of the hill, about a hundred yards from the house we have so long striven to reach. Here we unloaded in the shade of a large willow tree, and scarcely had we removed the harness from the oxen when the good lady of the house and her little child came down to see us. She stood for a moment and looked around her and at the two small children on the blankets, and we could hear her murmur 'mucha pobre' (very poor). She could see our ragged clothes and dirty faces and everything told her of our extreme destitution.

311

"After seeing our oxen and mule which were so poor she said to herself, 'flaco, flaco' (so thin). She then turned to us, Rogers and I, whom she had seen before, and as her lively little youngster clung to her dress, as if in fear of such queer looking people as we were, she took an orange from her pocket and pointing to the children of our party, wanted to know if we had given them the four oranges she sent to them by us. We made signs that we had done as she requested, when she smiled and said 'Buenos Muchuchos' (good boys). In all this talk neither could say a word the other could understand, and the conversation was carried on by signs.

"Arcane said to her—'Me Catholic' which she seemed partly to comprehend and seemed more friendly. About this time two men rode up and took a ltok at us. Arcane, who was a mason, gave the masonic sign, as he told me afterward, but neither of them recognized it. We used such words of Spanish as I had taken down in my pass book and committed to memory and by motions in addition to these made them understand something of the state of affairs and that Mr. French who had assisted us before had told us we could get some meat (carne) from them. These men were finely mounted, wore long leggins made of hide, dressed with the hair on, which reached to their hips, stiff hats with a broad rim, and great spurs at their heels. Each had a coil of braided rawhide rope on the pommel of the saddle, and all these arrangements together made a very dashing outfit.

They seemed to understand what we had said to them, for they rode off with a rush and came back in a short time, leading a fine, fat two-year-old heifer. When near our camp the rider who was behind threw his riata and caught both hind feet of the animal when by a sudden movement of the horses the heifer was thrown. One of them dismounted, and at the command the horse backed up and kept the rope tight while the man went up to the prostrate beast and cut its throat. As soon as it had ceased struggling, they loosened their ropes and coiled them up: they came to us and pointed to the dead heifer in a way which said—'Help yourselves.'

"We were much gratified at the generosity of the people, and at once dressed the animal as it lay, cutting off some

312   good fat pieces which we roasted over the fire and ate with a

Scene in *Death Valley '49ers* when Harry Wade leaves the rest and starts to drive his ox team from the valley by the south exit. From a point behind the camera motion picture actor, James (Jimmy) Stewart read the script written by Hollywood script writer, Dr. N.B.C. Evans.

Photo courtesy Death Valley Monument Superintendent, T. R. Goodwin and now in Bear State Library.

relish. It seemed as if meat never tasted so good as that did,
sweet, fragrant, and juicy. If some French cook could only
cook a steak that would smell and taste to his customers as
that meal tasted to us, his art would be perfect. We separated
a hind quarter and hung it to a tree, and when the lady came
back we told her that the piece we had selected was enough
for our present use, so she caused the remainder with the
hide to be taken to the house.

"Toward night they drove up a lot of cows and calves and
other cattle into their cattle yard or corral, as it is called all
over California, a stockade of strong oak posts set deep in the
ground and close together, enclosing a space of about half an
acre. The horsemen now rode in and began to catch the
calves with their ropes. It seemed as if they were able to
throw a rope over a calf's head or around either leg they
desired, with better aim, and at as great a distance as one
could shoot a Colt's revolver, and we saw at once that a good
raw-hide rope, in the hands of an experienced man and
well-trained horse, was a weapon in many respects superior
to firearms of any kind. A man near the gate loosened the
ropes and pushed the calves into a separate corral till they
had as many as they desired.

"Rogers watched the circus till it was over and then returned to camp, meeting on the way Bennet and Arcane,
with their wives and children, carrying some blankets, for
the good lady had invited them to come up to the house and
sleep. They said we could go down and keep camp if old dog
Cuff was willing, for they had left him guarding the property. He was pleased enough to have us come and keep him
company, and we slept nicely, disturbed only a little by the
barking of the house dogs and the hooting of an owl that
came to visit our tree.

"The people came back to camp in the morning and had
their experience to relate. Their hosts first baked some kind
of slapjacks [tortillas] and divided them among their guests;
then gave them beans seasoned hot with pepper: also great
pieces of squash cooked before the fire, which they said was
delicious and sweet—more than good. Then came a dish of
dried meat pounded fine, mixed with green peppers and well
fried in beef tallow. This seemed to be the favorite dish of the

proprietors, but was a little too hot for our people. They called it chili cum carne—meat with pepper—and we soon found this to be one of the best dishes cooked by the Californians. The children were carefully waited on and given special attention to by these good people, and it was nearly ten o'clock before the feast was over: then the household had evening worship by meeting in silence, except a few set words repeated by some in turn, the ceremony lasting half an hour or more. Then they came and wished them buenos noches in the most polite manner and left them to arrange their blankets on the floor and go to sleep.

"The unaccustomed shelter of a good roof and the restless worrying of the children, who required much attention, for the change of diet had about the same effect on them as on Rogers and myself when we first partook of the California food, gave them little sleep, but still they rested and were truly grateful for the most perfect hospitality of these kind hearted people.

"In the morning the two horsemen and two Indians went to the corral, when the riders would catch a cow with their ropes and draw her head up to a post, binding it fast, while an Indian took a short piece of rope and closely tied the hind legs together above the gambrel joint, making the tail fast also. They had a large bucket and several gourds. The Indians then milked the cows they had made fast, getting from a pint to two quarts from each one, milking into a gourd and pouring into the bucket till they had all they desired. The calves were separated the night before so they could secure some milk.

"Cows were not trained to stand and be milked as they were at home. Setting down the bucket of milk before us, with some small gourds for dippers, we were invited to drink all we wished. This was a regular banquet to us, for our famished condition and good appetites made food relish wonderfully. When we made a sign of wishing to pay them for their great kindness they shook their heads and utterly refused. It was genuine sympathy and hospitality on their part, and none of us ever forgot it; the sight of a native Californian has always brought out thoughts of these good people, and respect and thankfulness to the race. This rancho, at which we were so kindly entertained was called San Francisquito, or Little San Francisco Rancho.

"This morning Mr. Arcane, with our assistance, made an arrangement with these people to give them his two oxen; they were to take him and his wife and child, to the sea-shore, at a place called San Pedro, from which place he hoped, in some way, to get passage to San Francisco in a sailing vessel. He had no money, and no property to sell, except perhaps his spy-glass, worth about ten dollars. [Arcan traded this telescope to a sea captain for passage from San Pedro to Santa Cruz.] With this poor prospect before him he started for the sea. He bade Bennett's folks good-bye, then came to me and put a light gold ring on my finger, saying that it and his interest in the little mule were mine. Then he gave his silver watch to Rogers and said it was all he had to give him, but if he had a million dollars, he would divide, and still think it a small compensation for the faithful services we had rendered him. 'I can never repay you,' said he, 'for I owe you a debt that is beyond compensation. You have saved our lives, and have done it when you knew you could get nothing for it. I hope we will meet again, and when we do you will be welcome. If you hear of me anywhere, come and see me, for I want to tell my friends who Manly and Rogers are, and how you helped us. Good Bye!' There were tears in his eyes, voice full of emotion, and the firm clasp of his hand told how earnest he was, and that he felt more than he could speak.

"He helped Mrs. Arcane on her horse, then gave Charlie to her, and, amid waving hands and many adios from our new-found friends, with repeated 'good byes' from the old ones, they rode away. Mrs. Arcane could hardly speak when she bade us farewell, she was so much affected. They had about sixty miles to ride to reach the sea, and as she rode on a man's saddle, and was unused to riding, I knew she would be sadly wearied before she reached the coast.

"Our little train now seemed much smaller. Three oxen and a mule were all our animals, and the adults must still walk, as they had done on our desert route. But we were comparatively happy, for we had plenty of good meat to eat, plenty of sweet water to drink, and our animals were contented and improving every day; grass and water seemed plenty everywhere. We put our luggage on the oxen and the mule, loaded the children on Old Crump as we had done before, and were ready to move again. Our good friends stood around and smiled good-naturedly at our queer arrangements, and we, not knowing how to say what our hearts would prompt us to, shook their hands and said good bye in answer to their 'adios amigos' as we moved away, waving hands to each other.

"The men then detained me a little while to ask me more about the road we had come over, how far it was, and how bad the Indians were, and other particulars. I told him by signs that we had been twenty-two days on the road, and the Indianos, as they called them, had not bothered us, but that there was very little grass or water in all that land. He made a sort of map on the ground and made me understand that he would like to go back and try to bring the wagons we had left behind out, and he wanted me to go back with him and help him. I explained to him by the map he had made, and one which I made myself, that I considered it impossible to bring them over. He seemed much disappointed, and with a shrug of his shoulders said 'mucho malo' (very bad) and seemed to abandon the idea of getting a Yankee wagon. They very much admired an American wagon, for their own vehicles were rude affairs, as I shall bye-and-bye describe. We bade each other many adios, and I went on my way, soon catching up with the little party. We had been informed that it was ten leagues, or thirty miles to Los Angeles, whither we were now headed.

"We had now been a whole year on the road between Wisconsin and California, much of the time with the ground for a bed, and though our meals had been sometimes scanty and long between, very few of us had missed one on account of sickness. Some, less strong than we, had lain down to perish, and had been left behind, without coffin or grave; but we were here, and so far had found food to nourish us in some degree with prospects now of game in the future if nothing better offered. We still talked of going to the gold mines on foot, for with food and rest our courage had returned, and we wanted to succeed.

317

The Epilogue to the pageant, *Death Valley '49ers*, December 3, 1949, show-
ing the marching units and the Twenty Mule Borax Team (center) in action.
Photo courtesy Death Valley National Monument Superintendent, T. R.
Goodwin and now in Bear State Library.

"Our camp this night was in a nice watering place, where dry oak wood was plenty and grass abundant. It was at the foot of the San Fernando Mountain, not rocky, as we had found our road some time before, but smooth and covered with grass. It was rather steep to climb, but an infant compared with the great mountains so rough and barren, we had climbed on our way from Death Valley. Our present condition and state of mind was an anomalous one. We were happy, encouraged, grateful and quite contented in the plenty which surrounded us, and still there was a sort of puzzling uncertainty as to our future, the way to which seemed very obscure. In the past we had pushed on our very best and a kind Providence had kept us. This we did now, but still revolved the best plans and the most fortunate possibilities in our minds. We talked of the time when we should be able to show hospitality to our friends, and to strangers who might need our open hand as we had needed the favors which strangers had shown us in the last few days.

"We ate our supper of good meat, with a dessert of good beans our kind friends had given us, and enjoyed it greatly. As we sat in silence a flock of the prettiest, most graceful birds came marching along, and halted as if to get a better view of our party. We admired them so much that we made not a move, but waited, and they fearlessly walked on again. We could see that there were two which were larger than the rest, and from twelve to twenty smaller ones. The little top-knot on the head and their symmetrical forms made them specially attractive, and Mrs. Bennett and the children were much pleased. The beauty of the California quail is especially striking to one who sees them for the first time.

"In the morning we began to climb the hill, getting along very well indeed, for our raw-hide mocassins were now dry and hard and fitted the foot perfectly. We did not try to make great speed, but kept steadily on, and as we were used to climbing, we reached the summit easily. From this elevation we could get a fine view of the big grassy plain that seemed to extend as far as the eye could reach, and, not far from us the buildings and gardens of the San Fernando Mission. If we could shut out the mountains, the landscape would remind us of a great Western prairie. We never could get over

319

comparing this country with the desolate Death Valley, for it seemed as if such strange and striking opposites could hardly exist.

"We rested here a little while and then wound our way down the hill to the level land. A few miles brought us to the mission houses and the church of San Fernando. There was not much life about them, in fact they seemed comparatively deserted, for we saw only one man and a few Indians. The man brought some oranges and gave the children one each. After a little rest we moved on over our road which was now quite smooth and gently descending. Night overtook us in a place where there was no water, but we camped and suffered no inconvenience. A stream was passed next day, and a house near by unoccupied. The road now began to enter gently rolling hills covered with big grass and clover, which indicated rich soil, and we never got tired of talking about it.

"At the top of these hills we had another beautiful view as far south and west as the eye could reach. Small objects, probably horses and cattle, were scattered about the plain, grazing in the midst of plenty. Our own animals were given frequent opportunities to eat, and again and again we rejoiced over the beauty. Of course it was not such a surprise and wonder as it was when such a view first burst upon our sight, but it pleased and delighted us ever. On the east was a snow-capped peak, and here we were in the midst of green fields of grass and wild flowers, in the softest climate of an early spring. These strong contrasts beat anything we had ever seen. Perhaps the contrast between the great snow mountain and the hot Death Valley was greater in point of temperature, but there the heat brought only barrenness, and of the two the snow seemed more cheerful.

"Here the vegetation of all sorts was in full balance with the balmy air, and in comparison the snow seemed a strange neighbor. It was quite a contrast to our cold, windy March in Wisconsin, and we wonder if it is always summer here. We were satisfied that even if we could get no further we could live in such a land as this. The broad prairie doubtless belonged to the United States, and we could have our share and own a little piece of it on very easy terms, and raise our own cattle and corn. If the people were all as kind as those we had met we were sure at least of neighborly treatment. I have endeavored to write this just as it seemed to us then and not clothe the impressions with the cover of later experience. The impressions we then daily received and the sights we saw were stranger than the wildest fiction, and if it so strikes you, my friendly reader, do not wonder.

"As we came over the hills we could see a village near the southern base and it seemed quite near us. it was a new and strange sight to us as we approached. The houses were only one story high and seemed built of mud of a gray color, the roofs flat, and the streets almost deserted. Occasionally a man could be seen, sometimes a dog, and now and then an Indian, sitting with his back to the house. The whole view indicated a thinly populated place, and the entire absence of wagons or animals was a rather strange circumstance to us. It occurred to us at first that if all the emigrants were gone our reception might be a cool one in this city of the mud. One thing was in its favor and that was its buildings were about fire proof for they had earthen floors and flat roofs.

"We rested half an hour or so just outside, and then ventured down the hill into the street. We met an American almost the first man, and when we asked about a suitable camping place, he pointed out the way and we marched on. Our strange appearance attracted the attention of children and they kept coming out of the houses to see the curious little train with Old Crump carrying the children and our poor selves following along, dirty and ragged. Mrs. Bennett's dress hardly reached below her knees, and although her skirts were fringed about the bottom it was of a kind that had not been adopted as yet in general circle of either Spanish-American or good United States society. The shortness of the dress made the curious raw-hide mocassins only the more prominent, and the whole makeup of the party was a curious sight.

We went down the hill a little further to the lower bottom to camp, while the barefooted, bareheaded urchins followed after to get a further look at the strangers. [They were camping on the low flat below the present Plaza in front of the old Los Angeles Mission Church.] Before we selected a suitable place, we saw two tents and some wagons which looked like those of overland travelers, and we went toward them. When within fifty yards two men suddenly came to their feet and looked at our little party approaching as if in wonder, but at twenty steps they recognized Bennett and came rushing forward. 'My God! It's Bennett' said they, and they clasped hands in silence while one greeted Mrs. Bennett warmly. The meeting was so unexpected they shed tears and quietly led the way back to camp.

"This was the camp of R. G. Moody and H. C. Skinner, with their families. They had traveled together on the Platte and became well acquainted, the warmest of friends, and knowing that Bennett had taken the cut off, they more than suspected he and his party had been lost, as no sight of them had come to their eyes. They had been waiting here six weeks in order to get some reliable news, and now Mr. Bennett answered for himself. Rogers and I, belonging to another party, were of course strangers.

"Leaving them to compare notes, Rogers and I took charge of Old Crump, the oxen, and the mule, unpacked them, and arranged camp under a monstrous willow tree. Bennett and his wife were taken into Mrs. Moody's tent, and an hour or so later when Mrs. Bennett appeared again, she had her face washed clean, her hair combed, and a new clean dress. It was the first time we had found soap, and the improvement of her looks and feelings was surprising. Bennett looked considerably cleaned up too, and appeared bright and fresh. The children had also been taken in hand and appeared in new clothes selected from the wardrobe of the other children, and the old dirty clothes were put in process of washing as soon as possible.

"Supper came, and it was so inviting. There was real bread and it looked so nice we smiled when it was offered to us. Mrs. Bennett broke pieces for the children and cautioned them not to eat too much. It did seem so good to be among friends we could talk with and be understood. After supper was over and the things cleared away we all sat down in a circle and Bennett told the story of where he had been these many days on the cut off that was to shorten the trail. Mr. Moody said he had about given the party up and intended to start up the coast tomorrow. The story was so long that they talked till they were sleepy and then began again after breakfast, keeping it up till they had a good outline of all our travels and tribulations.

"Rogers and I now took the pack-saddle we had borrowed from Mr. French to use on our trip to Death Valley and return, and carried it to the saloon on the east side of the plaza, where we were to place it when we got back safely, and delivered it to the man in charge, with many thanks to Mr. French for his favors to us, and sent him word that we would always remember him and be ready to do him a similar favor if ever we were able. We considered him a good benevolent man, and such he proved to be when he offered us fat oxen, good beans, and any other thing we needed. He told the people in the house who we were, which no doubt influenced them kindly in our favor when we arrived.

"At the saloon there was a large room with tables in it and gambling going on actively. Money changed hands very rapidly, drinks at the bar were frequent, and the whole affair moved forward with the same regularity as any mercantile business. The door stood wide open and any one could come and go at his pleasure. Quite a number of black-eyed, fair looking women circulated among the crowd, and this, to us, seemed quite out of place, for we had never seen women in saloons before. We watched the game awhile to see some losing and some gaining, the result being quite exciting; but as neither of us had any money, we could not have joined in the game had we been so disposed; so we looked on awhile and then took a seat on the ground outside of the house.

"Here we talked over our chances of getting to the mines. All the clothes we had were on our backs and feet and those were the poorest of the poor. We had no money. I had the little black-eyed mule, and Rogers had the watch Arcane had given him. Mr. Moody had said it was 500 miles to San Francisco, and 150 miles further to the mines, so that after the hard travel of a year we were still a long way off from the place we started for.

"We could not see any way to make a living here. There was no land cultivated, not a fence, nothing to require labor of any kind. The valley was rich enough and produced great crops of grass, and the cattle and horses we had seen grazing

The Twenty Mule Borax Team in Death Valley, December 1, 1949.
Photo courtesy Death Valley National Monument Superintendent, T. R.
Goodwin and now in Bear State Library.

seemed to be about all the use they put it to. It looked as if the people must live principally on meat. I thought if we could manage to get a little provision together, such as flour and beans, that I could pack there on the mule, and I was pretty sure I could find game that would be better meat than we had lived on during the last two months on the desert.

"We looked around to see if we could find something to do to earn a little for a start, but were not successful. In our walk about this city of mud we saw many things that seemed strange to us. There were more women than men, and more children than grown-up people, while the dogs were plenty. At the edge of the town, near the river were some grape vines fenced in with living willows, interlaced in some places with dry vines. The Indians moved very moderately around and no doubt had plenty of beef to eat, with very few wants to provide for. We noticed some few people paying for small things at the stores with small money. The women all dressed much alike. The dress was of some cheap material, sandals on feet, and a kind of long shawl worn over the head and thrown over the shoulder. There seemed to be neither hoops nor corsets in their fashions. The men wore trousers of white cotton or linen, with a calico shirt, sandals, and a broad rimmed snuff colored hat. The Indians and their wives went bareheaded.

"Near the end of the street we came to a boarding house and went in and sat down in the empty room. Soon a man came in, better dressed than ourselves, and much to our surprise it was one of the old Death Valley travelers, the Rev. J. W. Brier whom I last saw in his lone camp in the desert, discoursing to his young sons on the benefits of an early education. I know the situation struck me very strangely, with death staring them in the face and he preaching!

"We had a long talk about the hard journey we had each experienced. As his party had not waited they had come through ahead of us. He said himself and Mr. Granger had started a boarding house when they arrived, and had been doing a good business. He said that as long as the emigrants continued to come he could get along very well. We asked him if there was any chance for us to work and get money to get some provisions to help us on the way to the mines. He said he could give work to one of us hauling water for the house with oxen and cart, and the one who could manage oxen was the man. I was an ox driver and so told him I would take his team and cart and set out with the work. He said he could pay fifty dollars a month, and I accepted the offer quickly as I saw it was a good chance to build up my exhausted strength and flesh.

"I turned the little mule out in the hills near by, and began my work. It was not hard, for the boarders were thinning out. The natives did not patronize this hotel very much, but grub disappeared pretty fast at my corner of the table, for my appetite began to be ravenous. There was not much variety to the food and very few luxuries or delicacies, which were hard to obtain on such a bare market, but all seemed satisfied with the food, and to me it tasted extra good.

"Rogers went back to the old camp and helped them there, and I often went over after dark, when my work was done. Moody and Skinner had been active in trying to get Mr. Bennett ready to go up the coast with them. Bennett had sold his repeating rifle and with the proceeds and the help of his friends and had got another ox, making two yoke for him. They fixed up a wagon for him, and yokes enough could be found where people had traded off their oxen for horses. Provisions enough had been gathered by Moody and Skinner for them all, and Rogers would go along with the party to help them with the teams.

"I was left alone after they started, and it was my idea to quit when I had worked a month, if my mule staid with me, and to start for the mines even if I went alone. The majority of the male inhabitants of this town had gone to the mines, and this accounted for the unusual proportion of women. We learned that they would return in November, and then the gambling houses would start up in full blast for these native Californians seemed to have a great natural desire to indulge in games of chance, and while playing their favorite game of monte would lay down their last reale (12½ cents) in the hope of winning the money in sight before them on the table.

"As the boarding house business got dull I was taken over

to a vineyard and set to work, in place of hauling water. The entire patch was as green as a meadow with weeds, and I was expected to clean them out. I inquired of Brier how he came to get hold of this nice property, and he said that during the war the soldiers had taken possession of this piece of ground, and had their camp there, so he considered it was government land, and therefore had squatted on it and was going to hold it, and pay for it as regular government land, and that he already considered it his own, for said he, 'I am an American, and this is a part of the public domain.' 'All right,' said I, 'I will kill weeds for you, if you wish, when I have time to spare, and you don't want the oxen worked at any other work'.

"I could see every day that I was improving in health and weight and would soon become myself again, able to take the road to the mines. When about two weeks of my time had expired two oldish men came to the house to stop for a few days and reported themselves as from Sacramento, buying up some horses for that market. Thus far they had purchased only six or eight, as they had found the price too high to buy and then drive so far to a market to sell again. They had about decided to go back with what they had and undertake some other kind of business. I thought this would be a pretty good chance for me to go, as I would have company, and so went to Brier and Granger and told them what I would like to do, and that with their permission I would quit and go on with them. They readily consented, for their money was coming in rather slow, and they paid me twenty-five dollars for half a month's work. This made me feel pretty rich and I thought this would give me food enough to reach the mines.

"Having two or three days to get ready in, I began doing the best I could. I found an old saddle tree which had been thrown away, and managed to fix it up so I could use it. I also found an old gun some traveler had left, and with a little work I fitted the breech of that to my own gun which was broken, and had been roughly tied together with strips of raw-hide. I now had a good sound gun if it was not very handsome. I bought a Spanish blanket, not so wide as ours, but coarse and strong, and having a hole in the center through which to put the head and wear it as a garment in

327

case of storm, or at night. I went to a native store and bought a supply of carne seca (dried beef) and some crackers, put some salt in my pocket and was now provisioned for another trip. I found my mule in the hills back of town, not far from where I left her, and the rest and good feed had made her look better and feel better, as well as myself.

"The drivers had found two other men who wanted to go with them and help drive the horses for their board. I put my blanket on under the saddle, packed my little sack of meat and crackers on behind, and when I was in the saddle with my gun before me I considered I was pretty well fixed and able to make my way against almost anything. I said to myself that the only way now to keep me from getting to the gold mines was to kill me. I felt that there was not a mountain so high I could not climb it, and no desert so wide and dry that I could not cross it. I had walked and starved and choked and lived through it, and now I felt so strong and brave I could do it again—any way to reach the gold mines and get some of the 'dust.'

"I had not much idea how the gold from the mines looked. Everybody called it gold dust, and that conveyed an idea to me that it was as fine as flour, but how to catch it I did not know. I knew other people found a way to get it, and I knew I could learn if anybody could. It was a great longing that came to me to see some of the yellow dust in its native state, before it had been through the mint.

"At the last meal I took at the house there were only a few at the table. Among them was a well dressed Californian who evidently did not greatly fancy American cooking, but got along very well till Mrs. Brier brought around the dessert, a sort of duff. This the Californian tasted a few times, and then laid down his spoon saying it was no bueno, and some other words I did not then understand, but afterward learned that they meant 'too much grease.' The fellow left the table not well pleased with what we generally consider the best end of a Yankee dinner, the last course.

"While here I had slept in a small store room, where I made a pallet out of old rags and blankets. While I was looking round for material to make my bed I came across a bag partly full of sugar, brought from Chili. It was in very

The Twenty Mule Borax Team in front of Furnace Creek Inn, December 1, 1949.
Photo courtesy Twenty Mule Team Borax Company and now in Bear State Library.

coarse crystals, some as large as corn. There were some other treasures and luxuries there that perhaps I was expected to guard. I however had a sweet tooth and a handful or so of the sweet crystals found their way into my pocket.

"I bade Mr. Brier and the rest good bye and rode away to join my company."

Too much cannot be written in recognition of the generosity and hospitality of the old *Californios*. Probably no people in the world ever excelled them in those characteristics. In fact, it honestly can be said that those two most admirable characteristics became grievous faults in the pioneer Spanish of California, for almost without exception they gave away what would now be equal to the holdings of many kings.

While the father of this writer was ever warm in his praise of the pioneer Californios he was never a booster for the City of the Angels. In August of 1850 he joined the bands of immigrants who thronged the old Plaza and found his way about the narrow, crooked streets for a week while outfitting for the journey northward by way of Santa Barbara. That was his only visit to Los Angeles. But, to the day of his death in 1909, he always referred to Los Angeles as "a sleepy little Mexican village of mud huts with flat-topped, tar-covered roofs. Everytime you went in or out of a house the tar which strung from the eaves dripped down your neck."

It is of interest to readers of these pages to know that the tar in question was taken from the tar pits on Wilshire Boulevard where La Brea now is located. Thousands of specimens of prehistoric animals' bones have been taken from the old asphaltum traps there. The tar for the roofs of old Los Angeles was hauled from the pits by ox-freighter López of San Fernando. When bones began to appear in the asphaltum, López claimed they were those of a cow of his which had fallen into the tar bog. When elephant bones appeared López changed the subject, but he never failed to snort in disgust when it was stated that they were prehistoric.

Such was the village into which our Death Valley '49ers, including the Briers, Wades, Bennetts, Arcans, Manly, Rogers and many of the Jay Hawks straggled in January, February and March of 1850. The old plaza was in those days the camping ground for all out-of-town people. Not just the present plaza, which represents only a portion of the forty acre town common, but the area on the lower ground toward the Los 330 Angeles River. There the Indians lived while the mission was being built and there the old *paisanos* staked their horses while they attended church after the mission was completed.

Until '49 and the arrival of the immigrants from Santa Fe and Salt Lake the most exciting moments about the old Plaza had been the exhibition of horsemanship when the worshipers left church and began to mount their spirited horses. *Cinchos* were tightened, *tapaojos* were lifted from the eyes of the trembling steeds and away went a dozen or more *paisanos,* straddling their plunging *caballos* as gracefully as any circus rider of today.

When the *Yankees* began to pour in there was no more room on the old Plaza for the tethered horses and there never has been since. In December of '49 John Zumwalt was a young immigrant camped on the old Plaza. In 1929 John had never seen Los Angeles in eighty years. At the urge of this writer, on a Sunday in December of '29 John persuaded his son to drive him from Bakersfield to Los Angeles for a last visit to the scenes of '49.

On the way to Los Angeles John repeated a dozen times, "It was just a little Spanish pueblo when I was there, just a little pueblo." In three hours they covered the distance which had taken John three days on his last journey over the route. John could not recognize a single place on the road after he left Gorman Station. Before he knew where he was and as he was repeating, "just a little pueblo," they drove by the front of the old Los Angeles mission church. "But," said John, "we weren't camped here. We were down toward the river."

Down toward the river they went. The entire forty acre flat was covered with streets and buildings. There was not a single thing John could recognize. "Take me back to that mission church and let me look around," said John; "maybe I can locate myself." Back they went. But there was no place to park within blocks, and John was ninety-odd years of age and too shaky to walk a mile from a parking lot.

So they drove around the block several times. John got a glimpse of the front of the old mission church when, in desperation, his son stopped traffic and pointed it out. A threatening traffic officer whistled and started toward them. John began to swear: "Take me back to Bakersfield. I don't care if I *never* see any more of this place. This is *too damned much pueolo now.*" And they returned to Bakersfield without John having set foot on his stamping grounds of eighty years before.

Next of the Death Valley '49ers to leave a description of the del Valle adobe and the City of the Angels in '50 was John Welsh Brier who wrote   331 an extremely interesting account for the 1880 report of the California State Mineralogist. It is the only detailed account recorded telling of the journey of the Briers from the del Valle home to Los Angeles and of the simple village life which was then being smothered out of existence. I reproduce it in full:

"When the time had come for our departure, we experienced a feeling of sharp regret. I cannot express my own sense of the wonderful beauty and opulence of the valley and its surroundings. The green earth and the blue sky; the level plain and the oval hills; the lowing of cattle and the neighing of horses; the busy life of the pastoral people whose language was so sweet, and whose hospitality was so simple, gracious and sufficient. I shall never forget their sympathy, such quality was not strained, and was in strong contrast with that selfishness which is arrogant in prosperity and petulant in adversity. I shall never fail to be moved when I recall the womanly virtue that caused the wife of our host to meet my mother, at the brow of the hill, and embrace her with loud cries and the demonstration of sisterly affection. [Note here how the old California life has broken down the narrow religious prejudices of that day. When he wrote these lines his father, Rev. J. W. Brier, was one of the most prominent, enthusiastic Protestant Ministers in California.]

"From San Francisquito to the Mission of San Fernando was barely three leagues. But we started late in the afternoon, and camped within a stone's throw of the den of a grizzly bear—for which luxury we paid with a mule. The next morning vaqueros overtook us and carried my brother and myself on horseback to the mission.

"It was a perfect day—the air full of the odor of spring flowers and the song of birds, sweet beyond measure to us, fresh from months of the terrible trail across the desert. And most perfect was the courteous kindliness with which we were received.

"We were entertained at the table of the Father Superior, and were instructed by the Doctor to taste every dish, but to 'put the knife to our throats,' as, at the time, we were peculiarly 'given to appetite.' Our sleeping apartment was a large room whose high windows were heavily barred, and whose strong door we were requested to secure against the murderous intrusion of the Mission Indians, who, aware of the transfer of California to United States, were under an impression that Americans had come to drive them from their homes. The old gardner was loud in the expression of his jealousy, but Dr. Irving assured him of our kind intentions, and managed to quiet his suspicions.

"We were permitted to sample the oranges and pomegranates, and the ripe olives which lay under the trees were so tempting to sight, that we filled our mouths with them. Never were appearances more deceiving. My mother asked Dr. Irving what they were, and he exclaimed in reply, 'Where in God Almighty's world have you lived that you don't know what olives are!' To be sure! A Vermont woman, educated in a Vermont Seminary, and not to know olives by the double proof of sight and taste!

"The morning after our arrival, the Indians were ordered to drive up a band of horses and mules, that animals might be selected for our journey to Los Angeles. A quiet bay pony was chosen for my mother, two pillows served for a saddle; and when she was placed in position, I was lifted to a seat behind her. My younger brother was secured at the back of Dr. Irving, by the use of a silk handkerchief. I cannot recall other dispositions for the day. An amusing incident, however, is still fresh in my memory. Young Lummis St. John had taken a fancy to a handsome gray mule, and it was promptly caught and delivered to him. There was no saddle at hand, and a hackamore was used in lieu of a bridle. Nothing daunted, however, the novice vaulted lightly to its back, but he did not stay there. The level spine rose to an arch, the long, alert ears dropped upon the close-roached neck, the clean head was thrown between the stiffened forelegs, and after a few lunges, St. John measured his length on the ground. He arose, brushed his soiled garments, recovered his hat, and deliberately inquired 'what might be the name of so peculiar and agitating a gait?'

"Twenty miles to Los Angeles; we had walked twice as far within twenty hours, over waterless wastes of sand and stony mesa. This was a pleasure trip; and every rod of the way was enchanting.

333

Photo of an original Twenty Mule Borax Team.

Shown left to right are Jim Wolf, Skinner, and Claude Bohanan, Swamper.

The saddle mule, tied to the rear of the trail wagon, was used in scouting road, as was the mare, Pet, led behind the Wade covered wagon.

Photo courtesy Mrs. A. Wefferling, whose husband sometimes drove this team. Phow in Bear State Library.

"We passed great herds of broad-horned cattle, graceful, swift and spirited; other herds of sleek mares, with their foals; adobe haciendas with their outlying huts of domesticated Indians; vaqueros breaking refractory broncos or rounding up the scattered cattle; occasionally a cart with great wheels of solid wood, drawn by oxen whose yokes were bound to their heads by rawhide thongs.

"About half way, we halted before a small hacienda, and were saluted by a Señora, who invited us to enter for rest and refreshment. We were glad to accept her hospitality; and she served us with tortillas, milk and cheese. The former were sandwiched with beans and chile colorado, and the latter was made of sweet curd, much better, I think, than the smeercase of the Germans.

"During our repast an Indian entered through a back door, shouting, 'Mucho malo Americanos.' He charged towards my mother, but was promptly met by Patrick's fist and fell like a log, only to be dragged out and imprisoned under a cartbed. He made his escape, however, and was in the act of renewing the assault, when he yielded to another blow and was locked away until our departure. 'El Indio muy borracho [The Indian is very drunk.] exclaimed our hostess, with a disgusted and apologetic air.

"The remainder of our journey was without incident, and we halted in the evening on a hill overlooking Los Angeles.

"The vesper chimes were calling to prayer: a violent use of the word chimes, I admit, as the old copper bells were out of time, and the boys who wagged their clappers were out of time. Yet, somehow, all was harmony, whose secret we did not know, but whose power we felt.

"My mother asked Dr. Irving if the pueblo market contained a variety. 'Yes,' he replied, 'Everything in God Almighty's world.' Our first stay was at the home of this generous-hearted man. His Spanish wife not only supplied our wants, but taught us to use the familiar words of her own language.

"At the southwest corner of the Plaza there was a hotel in which my father obtained a half interest. This he was enabled to do by disposing of seven choice oxen, reserved out of a score, to illustrate 'the survival of the fittest'. The region was

The entire Brier family of Death Valley '49ers, from a daguerreotype made in Marysville, California in 1852. They followed the Jay Hawks from Division Spring to Los Angeles. Mrs. Brier saved the lives of many Jay Hawks by giving them soup and other nourishing things and forcing them to take new courage, get on their feet and continue.

Back row, left to right, Mrs. Juliette Brier, C. Columbus Brier, Rev. J. W. Brier and John Wells Brier. Seated, Kirk White Brier.

overflowing with oxen, but trained animals were in demand for freighting to the mines.

"Our boarders were Americans; and they were always craving something to remind them of home. Some one discovered that the leaf stem of the yellow dock was a fair substitute for rhubarb, and my elder brother and I were sent in quest of the plant. As we found it in quantity along the stream that partly engirdled the town, our occupation soon ceased to be a diversion. These excursions brought us into frequent contact with Indians who seemed to have a peculiar delight in the terror they inspired.

"The house was equipped with a bakery, a barber shop and a blacksmith shop. My father also had a personal charge of a fine old vineyard; and when I afterwards saw Mission grapes discharged at Long Wharf, San Francisco, and sold at an enormous figure, I heartily wished that we had retained our interest long enough to market at least one crop.

"There was a private school in the house of Mr. Wolfskill, where I learned how much I had forgotten. Our proximity to a large gambling house was a source of positive misery. Indeed there was always something to remind us that we were in a town whose normal conditions were not improved by the new influx. True there was no conflict between the people and the Americans, but the latter seemed to have left the best that was in them at home; their immoral example could not fail of its effect upon simple-minded people of strong passions.

"Shortly after our arrival a number of Southern bloods decided to assert authority upon the negroes employed by our house. One of them was staked down on his back, sorely beaten and left, undiscovered, and without food or drink during four days and nights. Our steward—a tall and powerful black man—escaped from his enemies by leaping over a wall eight feet high, while the bullets whistled about him. A mulatto was brutally flogged, and the most trifling negro I ever saw was so tremendously aroused by fear that he distanced pursuit and did not rest till he was safe in Northern California.

"I recall a tragedy of a another kind, enacted in the center of the Plaza. An Indian had unyoked two large oxen whose

gigantic horns spread like the antlers of an elk. They had
always gone from their pasture to their work and from their
work to their pasture, willingly and obediently; but, on this
occasion, they halted, midway the Plaza, evincing signs of
aggressive hostility. An application of the goad only enraged
them, and the driver was fortunate in escaping instant destruction. There the great creatures stood, pawing the
ground, roaring and foaming at the mouth. Soon the arena
was crowded with footmen and cavaliers, and the sidewalks
with men, women and children. Barefooted Indians taunted
the furious animals, and pricked them on to the encounter.
Young Dons were there, mounted on superb horses, whose
trappings were most elegant and expensive—housings of
stamped leather decorated with floral designs in silk, and
round, polished argents, finished in the perfection of the
engraver's art.

"Here was an occasion; and nothing could exceed the skill
and courage of those who addressed themselves to it. The
Indians were fearless; and I saw several of them tossed from
the long, curving horns, fortunately blunted at their tips.
Four of the reckless creatures were reported killed. One
horse was lifted but sustained no injury. The wild sport was
indulged amid laughter, whoops and 'carambas;' and when it
had exhausted itself, reatas were thrown—rattling like
hail-stones—over the horns of the bellowing monsters and
they were hustled away, ignominiously, to their enclosure.

"To describe the Los Angeles of an early date, would be to
describe a town of Mexico. As to the ranch life, it was not
widely different from life in town. The adobe house was
everywhere, practically, the same—a low structure with
thick walls and roof of tiles. At its best, it was two stories
high, with a ground floor that was generally the ground. The
windows and doors were in recession, and the building was
proof against heat and cold, though not against 'temblors.'
Outdoor ovens were in use, but the simple cooking was done
by an open fire.

"The women were kind-hearted and sometimes beautiful.
As a child, even, I could not help remarking the red lips and
the 'splendor of the dark eye.'

338   "The men lived on horse-back and were peerless riders.

The best horses were carefully bred; and the approved type was of matchless beauty, action and endurance. The people who love horses do not always love work. They are bold, daring, fond of adventures, fandangos and fiestas. Life in the metropolis was very picturesque, and seemed to be free from care and anxiety.

"The most vivid impression I retain of it, is the long and gaudily attired procession, winding like a serpent, and led by a mounted crier whose words were, to me, unintelligible.

"Altogether it was a wonder-world to me, and I have witnessed, with sorrow, the passing of it as of a dream. The extinction of Mexican titles; of long horns, mustangs and burros; the dilapidation or ruin of the old missions and the old time haciendas; the poverty and decay of the old families; the expulsion or extermination of coyotes, vultures, eagles and the sacred buzzards; the division and subdivision of the great ranges! Orchards, vineyards, and grain fields, now, and frame houses; schools, colleges, railroads and commercial towns full of hum and bustle; the ancient glory departed forever!"

In bringing our story of Death Valley '49ers to a close it is necessary to remember that John Haney Rogers has been the forgotten hero of the Death Valley tragedy. Until this manuscript was being prepared little was known of what happened to Rogers after William Lewis Manly parted from him in 1854. Manly wrote that they waved good-bye to each other as they left Benecia on separate steamboats.

In April of 1894, before Manly's book was published, Rogers dictated to a *Merced Star* reporter a brief account of his part in the rescue of the Bennett-Arcan party. Although he added little to what Manly wrote, I have at the proper places on these pages reproduced a portion of his story.

Of his arrival and stay in Los Angeles Rogers stated:

"We put the babies on the oxen and started for Los Angeles. Arrived there March 7, 1850, dead broke. I went to work in a blacksmith shop at $1.00 per day, and after earning a few dollars all hands started for the mines. We struck the mines at Sonora. I then drifted down to Mariposa County. And here I am, a cripple for life. John H. Rodgers."

In 1895, soon after Manly published his book, *Death Valley in '49,* he learned that John Rogers was living near Merced. Manly took the train from San Jose to Merced and then hired a liveryman to drive him to Rogers' home. In his accounts of this visit to Rogers, Manly stated that Rogers was living fourteen miles from Merced with a man named Ellis, who had known him from birth.

Rogers had stated in his own account that he had come to Mariposa County about 1851 and had been there ever since. Because Mariposa County was east of Merced, I naturally supposed that would mean east of Merced. It will later appear how wrong I was.

Manly also wrote several letters about Rogers. They were addressed to his old companions of '49. They finally have come to rest among the "Jayhawker" Papers in the Huntington Library at San Marino, California. From all of these I have selected the following items of interest concerning the forgotten hero, Big John Rogers. I have deleted the unrelated portions of Manly's letters.

On January 15, 1895, Manly wrote to his Jay Hawk friends.:

"John H. Rogers is found, the man who went with me from Death Valley to hunt a settlement and returned to their [the Bennetts' and Arćans'] relief in '49.—The last time we saw each other was on the steamboats at Benecia where we bade each other goodbye the last time.

"Yesterday a man called on me by Rogers' request. He [Rogers] has lived at Merced ever since we parted. He is now an old boy, a cripple, a pauper and is dependent on charity. He is sheltered under a friend's roof and is still happy and content and is known well in Merced County as Big John Rogers. He has a heart as big as the oxen we picked the bones of on the desert. Now John is leaning on his staff and wandering along slowly on the beach of the Dark River and will soon, like many of us Jayhawkers, pass over, never to return. So the little historical monument I have erected to our memory [Manly is referring to his book.] may be compared among the early histories to a picket pin standing alone on a large uninhabited prairie."

In another letter, undated, but probably written at about the same time as the above, Manly wrote:

"The next man that has come to life is John Rogers of Tennessee, who crossed the plains in '49. I was his daily companion. We left Death Valley on foot in hunt for a settlement and we were 26 days without a blanket. We came awful near choking to death, 60 hours without water. Before I commenced to write upon our trip, which occupied more than a whole year, I tried to find Rogers, but was unsuccessful. He could help me very much I well knew. But after the book was published I found him at Merced. I had not seen or heard from him for 41 years. When on the plains he was a beardless youth. He lives with a man by the name of Ellis, a man he has known from birth. When I visited him a short time ago, he, like myself, was an old man with a hair-covered face and walked with a cane. He had in retorting gold inhaled so much quicksilver that it had settled and came out at his toes and now both his feet are off at the instep. With the aid of a cane, he hobbles around. I received his picture a few days ago. It took me some time to study over those early times and try and make the face of 41 years ago and now conform. He writes me he thinks he is better looking than the picture."

But the most detailed account of Manly's visit to his old pal of '49 appeared in the *San Jose Pioneer*, July 15, 1895. I reproduce it in full:

"Visit to a Pioneer.

"I left the cars at Merced June 3, 1895, on a visit to my old friend, John H. Rogers, who crossed the plains with me in 1849. I hired a man, with horses and buggy, to take me the fourteen miles to Rogers' home. My escort knew John, and inquired how long since we had met each other. When I told him it had been forty-one years, he said 'You two won't know each other.' On reaching the house, an old man hobbled out, supported by a heavy cane, and saluted the driver, who asked him, 'Do you know this man?' The answer was, 'I think not.' Said the driver: 'I will introduce you. Mr. Rogers, this is Mr. Manly.' Rogers replied: 'I used to know Lewis Manly, a long time ago.' John looked me over, and after a short pause said, 'Lewis, is this really you?' and I replied 'Yes, if you are John.' He then declared that he was the genuine John H.

Rogers, a Death Valley man of 1849. As he spoke the words, I knew that he was the man I crossed the plains with in '49. His eyes ran over as he grasped my hand, the big tears rolling dow his cheeks, for the lost was found. My own optics were not experiencing a drouth.

"For two days and nights, Rogers and I rehearsed the story of our journey to California, from the time we left the Missouri river to our arrival in the land of gold. We called to mind the tortuous trail, the trip up the Platte River and down Green River canyon, across Salt Lake Valley, and into Death Valley, where many of our party died of thirst and hunger, and where John and I came near losing our own lives, in an effort to save the women and children, which we accomplished, and for our determination to rescue them have received the congratulations of those saved from a terrible fate in that awful country. Our reminiscences included a thousand and one incidents of the journey, many of them pathetic, others romantic and some laughable. We remembered how we had danced with some of Utah's native daughters, beautiful aboriginees, a little off-color; that through the influence of these dusky denizens of the wilderness we had been saved from going into the Colorado Canyon, to encounter obstacles in Death Valley of equal magnitude to those which might have befallen us by another route.

"We dwelt upon the narrow escapes we had from dying of thirst, drowning, starvation, and Indians, told of the strange characteristics of our companions—many noble, others not altogether so, but in that respect more than an average. Sad indeed were the recollections of our disaster in Death Valley, with women and children, and weak men, suffering for food and water, our wagons abandoned, and cattle perishing, with but little hope or prospect of obtaining relief. The final rescue of the survivors through our united efforts was revived. In the sad rehearsal of our varied experiences on the memorable trip, we were often reminded of some amusing occurrence far out on the wild desert waste, which would cause a shout of laughter from the pioneers of whom we are writing. Two days and nights were all too short for recalling all the interesting events of our eventful journey across the plains, through Death Valley, to California, in 1849, but the visit was thoroughly enjoyed, and served to remind us that we are passing and the scenes of our youth will soon be known only in story.

"John H. Rogers, like many other Pioneers, has not received the smiles of Dame Fortune, and says that he 'will not need any pocket in his shroud, as he will take nothing with him,' when he goes over the divide. He was one of California's pioneers, who assisted to develop the country, and it will matter little if he has failed to acquire wealth. Already he leans heavily upon his staff and moves about with difficulty. We are old men now."

While the manuscript for this volume was being prepared, Mrs. Latta and I set out to locate descendants of the Ellis family with whom Rogers had lived and to learn what had become of him. It was in June of 1949, more than one hundred years after Rogers had started to California and fifty-four years after Manly had visited him. It seemed an easy undertaking to talk to some of the ancients in Merced and learn where the Ellis descendants were living. But it was *not* easy.

I stated that it was a day in June, but I did not state the kind of a day it was, 111° in the shade. And our investigations for the most part were carried on in the sun. But it was an extremely interesting experience and we really didn't mind the perspiration that poured from us as the heat-saturated pavements and roads reflected upon us, and when we parked, our closed, locked car became as hot as a baker's oven.

To the southeast of Merced about fourteen miles is the old village of Plainsburg. Settled in 1853 among the oaks along the banks of Mariposa Creek, it was one of the first valley settlements south of Stockton, being probably antedated only by Hills Ferry and Visalia. The oldest settler we could find was Warren Morley. His father had operated a stationary thresher at old Plainsburg in 1856 and had settled in Plainsburg in 1869. Warren had been born there in 1871. We inquired of Warren about John H. Rogers. Yes, Warren had known an old crippled, pioneer Rogers. He had been connected in some way with a famous trek across the plains in '49. Perhaps he was our man.

At Plainsburg we spent the entire day and some of the night running down information about this Rogers who appeared to answer the description of our John H. Rogers. When it was 10:00 P.M. we found that we had probably been on the trail of the wrong Rogers.   343

We drove to the home of Mr. Bert Waller and found that neither Bert nor Mrs. Waller had gone to bed. Bert was born in Plainsburg and for many years had been sexton of the Plainsburg cemetery. Bert should know all about our man Rogers and probably could tell us where he was buried. Bert did know. He soon blew our pioneer Rogers completely out of the picture. He was certainly not the man we wanted.

We wanted *"Big John"* Rogers who used to work for "Old Man" Givens and who had lived with an Ellis family fourteen miles south*west* from Merced. I had simply got Rogers' directions reversed. In 1851 when Rogers came to the locality where he was living in 1894, it was then in Mariposa County. Merced County was not formed until 1855. It was my fault that we spent an entire torrid day searching in the wrong portion of Merced County looking for *Big* John Rogers. It was then 11:00 P.M. and cool enough to go to bed. We found a vacant cabin on Highway 99, seven miles south of Merced and turned in.

Next morning we were up at 6:30. Both of us forgot about breakfast—forgot until 12:30 P.M.—and located the old Givens' homestead. Tom Givens was an early riser. He was in the field, mending fence. As soon as I stated our mission and mentioned "Big John" Rogers, he put down his hammer and said, "I remember him. Let's go to the house. Maybe my wife will know more about him."

On the way to the house Tom told me that the only thing he could remember about Rogers was that he was a very large man and that he rode a mule when he worked for Givens, Sr., about 1885. "I was only seven years old then, but I can remember Rogers and that mule. Father called her Jimble Jaw. She had a parrot mouth. Her upper teeth overhung and never wore down, so they grew out to great length. Once a blacksmith cut them off with a hacksaw.

"Well, that old mule was a good saddle animal, but she had a rawhide mouth and and an iron neck. Rogers was helping Father gather hogs in the mountains on Mariposa Creek. He was chasing a hog. The mule wanted to go on one side of a chapparal and Rogers wanted to go on the other side. The mule had an iron neck all right, but Big John had iron arms. He heaved on the reins and they compromised by piling up in the middle of that chapparal so tight that father had to put his reata on them and pull them out."

Mrs. Givens had not known Rogers; so Tom told us to go over and see "Virg" (Virgil), his brother, who was two years older than Tom and might know more about Rogers. So we drove a mile or two over to Virg's. And Virg did know more.

344

" 'Big John' Rogers was a bigger man than you are [later proved to be six feet two inches and two hundred ten pounds] and a fine old fellow when I knew him, as late as 1895. He had a long beard and was badly stooped from long years of work in the mines and on the ranches about Merced and Mariposa. He was crippled. He had been salivated by using mercury in the mines and had lost the fore part of both of his feet. These feet bothered him as long as he lived." [This was the first positive identification we had heard of our John H. Rogers and in spite of the heat, which had already reached 100°, we were surely thrilled to hear it.]

"Rogers worked for my father for many years, the last time about 1889 or 1890. He was a good worker and a most reliable man. He did not drink. At least he was never a drunkard, as I remember nothing about his ever drinking.

"Rogers hurt one of his feet the last time he worked for Father. He was cutting a limb off a tree and was depending on jumping to the ground when it fell. As he jumped, his foot slipped and he landed on the stump of another tree. This badly injured one of his crippled feet and it was never strong again.

"When Rogers left Father the last time, he went back to Ellis and stayed there a long time, doing chores. The last time I saw him he came to Father's and was still limping on the injured foot. He was on his way to a hospital; I believe it was the county hospital in Merced. I do not know what became of him."

But "Virg" knew of another man who would be able to tell us all about "Big John" Rogers. It was not one of the Ellis family, for they were all dead. It was John Flanagan. John had lived in the "Sandy Mush" country more than seventy-five years. He had known Rogers as long as he was in the country. Flanagan was the man to see. He was eighty-four years of age, and he lived in the Lone Tree District a mile west of El Nido. So we climbed in the car and drove over the rough, narrow roads southwest to El Nido.

John Flanagan was at home, very bright and glad to see us. But when I began to question him about John Rogers, he developed a bad memory and began to ask the questions himself. After I had explained my interest in John Rogers and told Flanagan that Rogers was the forgotten hero of the 1849 Death Valley expedition, Flanagan soon remembered everything. Flanagan wasn't going to have the memory of his old friend Rogers disturbed by an unsympathetic historian.

"Yes, I knew Big John Rogers for many years. He was as fine an old   345 pioneer as ever lived. He was a lonely old fellow, an old bachelor as long as I knew him, and I am certain that he had never been married. He was a '49er and had been connected with the Death Valley party, but I never knew him to more than mention it in speaking of the early days. He is the man you have been looking for.

"I was about fourteen or fifteen years of age when Rogers first came here to the Sandy Mush Country. That would be about 1880. The Ellis ranch was four and one-half miles west of El Nido and a little north. The Ellis family has passed out of existence.

"Rogers had been salivated in the mines by breathing mercury fumes while retorting amalgam. Both of his feet were cut off at the instep. [Maybe we weren't thrilled again at this second identification!] But that did not keep him from making a living. He was an excellent separator man. He tended separator on stationary threshing machines all over this country until they were replaced by combines and then he tended separator on the combines. Between harvest seasons he worked at carpentering or at any kind of mechanical work. He was a good mechanic. He always earned his way. He never sponged off anyone and he never accepted charity. He was a good butcher and used to slaughter for the Ellis family.

"John Rogers lived with the Ellis family for a number of years. Once their old homestead shack burned. Old man Ellis had about a dozen children and had no money with which to rebuild. Well, Rogers helped Ellis get together some material and he built Ellis another house, one with a stick and mud chimney.

"He was a big, powerful man, John Rogers, as tall as six feet two or three inches, and he weighed more than two hundred pounds when I knew him. In spite of his crippled feet he would do a long day of hard, heavy work as well as anyone. He had never abused himself. I never knew of him to drink at all. He was a kind, generous old fellow and a square shooter if there ever was one."

When we finished our interview with John Flanagan Mrs. Latta and I drove to Merced, located an air conditioned restaurant and enjoyed a long-delayed breakfast. Then we drove to the County Court House.

Billy White, County Recorder, was a West sider seventy-five years ago, before I was born. It was hard to stop reminiscing with Billy and to begin thinking of such things as searching records, but we finally did search. No record was found showing that John H. Rogers ever had died.

346   The newspaper files contained no item regarding the death of Rogers;

neither did the mortuary records or any of the cemeteries. Except for the fact that he would then be more than one hundred and twenty-four years of age, it seemed that Big John had not died or that we would never learn more than William Lewis Manly had written about him.

Finally one of us thought of looking in the old register of voters. So we went up to see County Clerk Cothran and to engage in another hour of reminiscences, for the County Clerk was another old-time West Sider. But, again, we were finally able to get down to the business of the day. Almost the first volume opened had the following entry:

> John Haney Rogers, Laborer
> Age 71, height 6 feet 2½ inches
> Dark complexion, eyes brown
> Hair grey
> Both feet cut off at the instep
>   [The third positive identification
>   of our John H. Rogers.]
> Native of Tennessee
> Registered in Lone Tree District,
>   July 28, 1896.

So, with the mercury at 106° at four o'clock P.M., we wearily climbed in our car and began the one hundred and sixty mile journey to Bakersfield.

While "Big" John Rogers surely is entitled to first place as the forgotten hero of the Death Valley '49ers, there is another. In 1893 Manly wrote about this "Faithful Pioneer" in the *San Jose Pioneer* newspaper. I have reproduced below most of this article. It will be of great interest to every reader of these pages:

> "Born in Iowa County, Wisconsin, more than forty-five years ago, and coming across the plains with a company of gold seekers in '49, the subject of our sketch had a most eventful career—both in his early days in his native State and on his journey to the land of gold. On the trip across the plains, he walked the entire distance, standing guard every night. When the company arrived at Salt Lake and took what was supposed to be a better route than that traveled by a majority of the other emigrants, he remained with them, journeying without road or trail, and enduring the sufferings

347

incident to the Death Valley disaster without a murmur. Eating only the poorest food, usually that which had been rejected by other members of the company, he continued in good health. He saw strong men lie down and die for want of proper nourishment; women and children cried for bread, and he uttered not a word of complaint when he got nothing. No party ever had a more faithful and reliable friend on the plains or elsewhere than Asabel Bennett's dog 'Cuff.' A redskin never approached without warning from the intelligent brute. He seemed willing to die for his friends. Arriving at Georgetown, El Dorado county, Cal., his intelligence and usefulness excited the cupidity of some rascally fellow, and 'Cuff' was feloniously abstracted—stolen—and never again heard of by his owner. The many endearing references to his former history and exploits, by his friends, were pathetic, and would make a volume. He had been a mighty hunter before coming to California. Many a 'bar' had succumbed to his fierce attacks. His mother was a greyhound; his father a mastiff. He was nearly white, weight about 80 pounds, and had inherited all the good qualities of his ancestors.

"The pioneers who crossed the plains often became much attached to their horses and cattle, and especially to the dogs that accompanied them on their long journey; tenderly caring for them in their old age, and burying them, with tears, when they died. Every train had its dogs, and faithful and true they ever proved. Truly, the dog is man's best friend. Kindred may desert him; poverty and misery be his lot in life, but his dog remains true to him. No matter if the master be debased and cruel, dying, his dog mourns for him and will not be comforted. It has been said that the dog is the only animal that will leave its kind to live with a man from choice."

It was not only the dogs that had crossed the plains that were so dearly loved by all pioneers. Through the slender thread of the memory of John Frémont Bonham this writer in 1933 learned that his father had pensioned off the old saddle animal that had carried him from Vineyard, Arkansas, over the Old Santa Fe Trail to the Diggings in the Mother Lode of California. In 1861 "Jocko" was left to his memories of '49 and '50 in a pasture in Green Valley, Sonoma County, California.

The old Wade home in Alviso. Harry Wade and his family moved into this house in 1851 when they left Saratoga. They lived in it until both Harry and Mary passed away. Mary Wade kept the Alviso Post Office in the left end of this building during the last sixteen years of her life. It was one of the first buildings constructed in Alviso. The tracks of the railroad appear close to the left post supporting the porch roof. The mail bags were hung from a peg on this post by the baggage clerk without stopping the train. Sometimes Mary handed him the outgoing mailbag and the baggage clerk handed her the incoming bag without stopping the cars. one of Dow Stevens' earliest windmills for pumping water peeks over the roof.

Photo courtesy of Margaret (Wade) Higgins and now in Bear State Library.

Young Bonham used to ride him occasionally when driving home the family milk cow.

Until "Old Pet", the mare that had crossed the deserts of Utah and California with the Wades, died at the age of thirty years, Harry and Mary Wade cared for her. Pet became the mother of a famous California race-horse named Ab Dallah. The Wade family "milch" cow that was tied to the tail gate of the only wagon to come to California through Death Valley in the winter of '49-'50 was also cared for until she died of old age. Wade descendants still proudly display the bell that she carried across the plains and about the tidal swamps of Coyote and Guadalupe Creeks at Alviso.

Last, but not least of all of these four footed pioneers was Asabel Bennett's ox, Old Crump. He carried the four small children of Bennett and Arcan from the Bennett Long Camp near Tule Springs over the Panamint, and Indian Wells Valleys and Mojave Desert to the City of the Angels. He then helped to draw the Bennett wagon from Los Angeles to San Jose and to Georgetown in the northern mines. When Bennett left that part of California, Old Crump was left behind. But William Lewis Manly found him about 1856. As a fitting end to our story of California Argonauts, I quote what Manly wrote about this faithful, old, forgotten four-footed hero of Death Valley in '49:

> "Near French Camp, on the east side of the San Joaquin Valley, many cattle were feeding on the plains, and among them, much to my surprise, I found 'Old Crump', the ox that brought Bennett's and Arcane's children safe through from Death Valley in February 1850. He was now fat and sleek and as kind and gentle as he was when so poor upon the terrible journey. I got off my horse and went up to him, and patted my old friend. I was glad to find him so contented and happy, and I doubt not that he too was glad. I met a man nearby and asked him about the ox, and he said the owner would not sell him nor allow him to be worked, for he knew of the faithful part he had performed in the world, and respected him for it."

INDEX

INDEX

Each town, place and area is located in its present-day State.

Italicized numerals indicate photograph pages and captions.

INDEX

359

INDEX

AUTHOR'S PROFILE

Frank F. Latta was born near the mouth of Orestimba Creek in Stanislaus County, September 18, 1892, son of Cumberland Presbyterian minister, Eli C. Latta, and schoolteacher Harmonia (Campbell) Latta. In 1919 while in the U.S. Army he married Jeanette M. Allen born in Oakland, September 3, 1897. Frank and Jean with their four children have shared equally in the efforts and sacrifices made to gather, prepare and publish these data.

In 1906 Occidental Elementary teacher, Edith V. Hollingsworth, encouraged him to gather the history of the school district by interviewing the original settlers, many of whom then were still living. Latta started with James Hitchcock who came to California before the discovery of gold by James Marshall. He came with the first wagons to cross the Sierra Nevada, lead by Captain Elijah Stevens, and was scalped by the Indians on the way.

To date, Latta has gathered more than 17,000 stories of San Joaquin Valley pioneers. His combined books, newspaper and magazine articles total more than 3000 publications, some of which are listed at the beginning of this article.

DALTON GANG DAYS, SAGA OF RANCHO EL TEJON and TAILHOLT TALES were published by the Latta family press, Bear State Books, in 1976 honoring that year with the Bear States Books Bicentennial seal. The second edition of HANDBOOK OF YOKUTS INDIANS, first edition issued in 1949, was published in 1978.

ARTIST'S PROFILE

Monna S. Olson was born in Gustine, California, in 1921 and is the eldest member of Jean and Frank Latta's family. She is a fifth generation Californian.

After elementary school in Tulare and high school in Shafter she attended the University of California at Berkeley graduating in 1942 as a history major and a decorative arts minor.

That same year she married Carl A. Olson, now a Vice President of Kaiser Engineers.

Monna worked for two years as a draftsman at the Lawrence Laboratory in Berkeley, designed little girls' dresses during part of the Olsons' eight year stay in Detroit with the Kaiser automotive division, and taught the first grade for nine years in bilingual schools in Córdoba and Buenos Aires, Argentina. They and their two children, Chris and Carol, lived for thirteen years in Argentina as part of Kaiser's automotive operation in that country.

The Olsons returned to the States in 1968 and made their home in Danville, California.

Since 1976 Monna has been Managing Editor of Bear State Books. She also is Co-Editor of the Diablo Country Club monthly newspaper. In the little time left for hobbies she enjoys golf and working in media such as clay, glass and felt.